CORNELL STUDIES IN ENGLISH

XII

MILTON ON EDUCATION

THE TRACTATE *OF EDUCATION*

WITH SUPPLEMENTARY EXTRACTS FROM

OTHER WRITINGS OF MILTON

EDITED WITH AN INTRODUCTION AND NOTES BY

OLIVER MORLEY AINSWORTH

ASSOCIATE PROFESSOR OF ENGLISH IN BELOIT COLLEGE

NEW HAVEN: YALE UNIVERSITY PRESS

LONDON: HUMPHREY MILFORD

OXFORD UNIVERSITY PRESS

MDCCCCXXVIII

CORNELL STUDIES IN ENGLISH
XII

MILTON ON EDUCATION

THE TRACTATE *OF EDUCATION*

WITH SUPPLEMENTARY EXTRACTS FROM
OTHER WRITINGS OF MILTON

EDITED WITH AN INTRODUCTION AND NOTES BY
OLIVER MORLEY AINSWORTH
ASSOCIATE PROFESSOR OF ENGLISH IN BELOIT COLLEGE

NEW HAVEN: YALE UNIVERSITY PRESS
LONDON: HUMPHREY MILFORD
OXFORD UNIVERSITY PRESS
MDCCCCXXVIII

CORNELL STUDIES IN ENGLISH

VOLUME XII

EDITED BY

LANE COOPER

TO

LANE COOPER

PROFESSOR OF THE ENGLISH LANGUAGE
AND LITERATURE IN CORNELL UNIVERSITY

MILTON ON EDUCATION

PREFACE

For Milton's Tractate *Of Education*, my text is based upon a rotograph facsimile of a copy of the first edition in the British Museum, supplemented by a copy of the second edition in the Cornell University Library. I have normalized the punctuation, and in general made the orthography conform to present usage. My essential departures from the first edition in favor of the second are recorded in the Notes.

A distinctive feature, I hope, of the present volume is the body of Supplementary Extracts. As compared with the brief Tractate, this appendix may seem to be disproportionately large; yet so frequently do the writings of Milton reveal his interest in the growth and training of the human spirit that many of those who know him best may wish for passages which I have not included. Of the passages that have here been listed, an arrangement by topics has been adopted; nevertheless certain excerpts, though their content falls under more than one topic, have, on account of their narrative interest, been kept intact. The topical divisions, therefore, are not quite mutually exclusive.

My indebtedness to publishers of copyright material is elsewhere acknowledged in detail. In addition, I wish to express a sincere gratitude to my colleagues, Professor Robert K. Richardson and Professor Floyd McGranahan, of Beloit College, for their kindness in reading portions of the manuscript; to Dr. Walter MacKellar, Instructor in English in New York University, for permission to quote from his forthcoming translation of Milton's Latin poems; and to my teachers, Professor Lane Cooper and Professor Joseph Q. Adams, of Cornell University, for their encouragement and assistance throughout.

This work was begun about twelve years ago at the suggestion of Professor Cooper, and was submitted in the year 1920 as a doctoral dissertation. Since then, the manuscript has been thoroughly revised; and the volume is now published in the hope that Milton's little treatise, freed from various misconceptions, partly traditional, that often attend the reading of it, and reinforced by other utterances of his, may help to solve the educational problems of to-day.

BELOIT, WISCONSIN
DECEMBER 31, 1927

CONTENTS

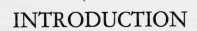

INTRODUCTION

INTRODUCTION

I

THE PLACE OF THE TRACTATE IN MILTON'S
LIFE AND WORK

Of Education is one of Milton's earlier pamphlets on reform in Church and State. It belongs, therefore, to the second great epoch in his life, which extended from the day in 1638 when his Continental tour was interrupted by the news of civil disturbance in England to his retirement from public service at the Restoration. During these years the poet was obliged by his sense of patriotic duty mostly to defer his chosen work of epic or dramatic composition, and to expend his talents in the defence of liberty, both religious and civil.

The bulk of Milton's writings throughout this period is in prose. Some critics have lamented that he so long devoted himself to a species of composition in which, as he says, he had but the use of his left hand;[1] but Verity not long since maintained that Milton improved as a poet by the experience of public life.[2] The prose works alone, although at times they have suffered detraction, nevertheless contain so much of idealism and eloquence as to give to their author a very high place among English writers.

Of all Milton's pamphlets, the Tractate *Of Education* perhaps least owes its occasion to the urgency of political events, and most spontaneously grows out of his natural tastes and pursuits. In the *Second Defence*, to be sure, he enumerates it among his earlier writings as if it had been a part of a systematic plan. After speaking of his tracts on episcopacy, he says:

When the bishops could no longer resist the multitude of their assailants, I had leisure to turn my thoughts to other subjects:

[1] See below, p. 176.
[2] Milton, *Paradise Lost*, ed. by Verity, p. xxi.

I

to the promotion of real and substantial liberty, which is rather to be sought from within than from without, and whose existence depends, not so much on the terror of the sword, as on sobriety of conduct and integrity of life. When, therefore, I perceived that there were three species of liberty which are essential to the happiness of social life—religious, domestic, and civil; and as I had already written concerning the first, and the magistrates were strenuously active in obtaining the third; I determined to turn my attention to the second or the domestic species. As this seemed to involve three material questions—the conditions of the conjugal tie, the education of the children, and the free publication of the thoughts—I made them objects of distinct consideration. I explained my sentiments, not only concerning the solemnization of the marriage, but the dissolution, if circumstances rendered it necessary. . . . I then discussed the principles of education in a summary manner, but sufficiently copious for those who attend seriously to the subject; than which nothing can be more necessary to principle the minds of men in virtue—the only genuine source of political and individual liberty, the only true safeguard of states, the bulwark of their prosperity and renown.[1]

This account, however, does not necessarily imply that Milton composed his pamphlets in a fixed and definite order. If he had done so, the Tractate, of course, would occupy the position of a chapter in a treatise on personal liberty. But nowhere else does he mention a definite plan; and the list that he gives is not chronologically exact. We probably may assume that Milton classified his works as he did, in order the better to defend himself against calumny by making clear the public spirit of all his writings.

The Tractate, then, is not a minor part of a formal treatise, but an individual structure, brief though it be. Nor was it directly instigated, like *The Tenure of Kings and Magistrates*, by 'the tumults of those unhappy days'; nor yet, like the first treatise on divorce, as some suppose, by domestic affliction. It is the 'voluntary idea of a better education' that had 'long, in silence, presented itself' to the poet and scholar; the 'few observations'

[1] *The Second Defence of the People of England, Prose Works* 1. 258. See below, p. 102–3.

2

that had 'flowered off'—'the burnishing of many studious and contemplative years, altogether spent in the search of religious and civil knowledge.' It therefore, no doubt, more fully than some other of Milton's prose works, reflects the deeper elements of his nature.

Some plan of educational reform he probably had intended to publish in the course of his writing on practical affairs. The need of it seems to have been deeply impressed upon his mind, for in two of his last political treatises there are included educational projects, less detailed than the plan of the Tractate, but more definitely related to his two ideal systems of government, ecclesiastical and civil.[1] These two schemes were in fact called forth by political exigency. Both look to immediate practical ends—one, indeed, seems frankly vocational; and to either, therefore, the Tractate *Of Education*, in breadth of outlook and clarity of ideal, is far superior.

Milton's chief account of his views on education was published at the earnest solicitation of a friend. Samuel Hartlib, to whom the Tractate is addressed, singularly merits our esteem. So much engrossed was he in bringing to notice the hidden talents of other men, and so little did he seek fame or honor for himself, that his own true worth has sometimes been lost to view.

Hartlib was born in Prussia, of Polish-English parentage, and came to London probably about 1628. He was ostensibly a merchant, but his real interest lay in the promotion of human welfare, both physical and intellectual. In his active encouragement of every scheme for the public good, he reminds one of Benjamin Franklin; but in Hartlib's character the sagacity of 'Poor Richard' was tempered with the more spiritual outlook of the seventeenth century. His varied interests embraced not only the reform of education, and the improvement of agriculture and the mechanic arts, but also the uniting of the Protestant churches throughout all Europe. His sincerity in these projects was attested by

---

[1] See below, pp. 222-3; 273-4.

3

pecuniary generosity as well as by personal effort. His biographer, Henry Dircks, says of him:

We are constrained to consider Samuel Hartlib's prevailing pious disposition as governing, guiding, and outweighing all other obligations. He advocated the acquirement of knowledge and the means of improving its attainment, and strenuously labored to extend every useful art and trade favoring industry and tending to strengthen the arms of the State; but these were accessories to brighter hopes—they were to be employed but as the means to a far nobler end, and were not esteemed by him as man's *summum bonum* in this life. That he was, therefore, rather out of his sphere, while occupied in the mercenary operations of ordinary business, we may surmise from the absence of all allusion to commercial gains in his correspondence; while his letters, on the contrary, are replete with learned allusions, theological matters, references to men of letters, and to subjects of a literary or philosophical bearing. . . .

Samuel Hartlib's life throughout excites our admiration. His piety and enthusiasm, his varied tastes and plastic genius, are conspicuous in all his multifarious labors. In whatever he was engaged, we observe the same earnestness, ardor, and sobriety of conduct. He is always solid and sincere, and begets in us, at a glance, a predisposition in his favor; we see in him the meek true Christian and the gentleman. His amiability is without affectation; he is obliging without sycophancy, and religious without intolerance. He never assumes mental superiority, or knowledge beyond his information, and, while directing oppressed talent into channels of enlarged usefulness, his judgment and experience rather suggest than dictate. Had it been his lot to be differently situated, and blessed with a superior education, he would have proved himself a sublime genius; for under great personal disadvantages, together with the adverse influence of distracted and dissolute times, he worked wonders to ameliorate the condition of society, with little other encouragement than the approval of his own conscience.[1]

The details of Hartlib's acquaintance with Milton, and the reason why he so earnestly besought him to write on education,[2]

---

[1] Dircks, *Memoir of Samuel Hartlib*, pp. 47–9.
[2] See below, pp. 51–2.

are matters of conjecture. For some years, however, before the Tractate was published, Hartlib had been endeavoring to assist the renowned Moravian educator, John Amos Comenius. He had twice published translations from Comenius' writings, and was instrumental in bringing the great reformer to England in 1641.[1] But, much to Hartlib's disappointment, Comenius left England within a year, not having found opportunity there to put his theories into practice. Despairing, possibly, of Comenius' return, and unwilling to give up the hope of educational reform, Hartlib nearly two years later applied to Milton as the Englishman of whom he expected most—a man of eminent attainments, and already known as a writer on current affairs, and one, moreover, whose views on education were quite as definite and emphatic as those of Comenius himself. At all events, Hartlib's urgent solicitations finally induced Milton to postpone for a time his meditations upon marriage and divorce, and upon the freedom of the press, and somewhat prematurely,[2] as Milton felt, to publish his views on education.

[1] Laurie, *John Amos Comenius*, p. 74.
[2] See below, p. 51.

II

EDITIONS

The first edition of the Tractate *Of Education* is a quarto of eight pages, and is simply headed: 'Of Education, To Master *Samuel Hartlib.*' It was published without date or signature, or even a title-page. Our first information on these details is from George Thomason, a famous London bookseller and collector of pamphlets in Milton's time.[1] Says Masson: 'The date of the publication is fixed, and the fact that the authorship was known at the time is proved, by this manuscript note of Thomason on the copy among the King's Pamphlets in the British Museum: "By Mr. John Milton: 5 June, 1644." '[2]

The second edition was published in 1673, at the end (pp. 95–117) of a volume of the Minor Poems. In this volume the wording of the title-page is as follows: 'Poems, &c. upon Several Occasions. By Mr. John Milton: Both English and Latin, &c. Composed at several times. With a small Tractate of Education to Mr. Hartlib. London, Printed for Tho. Dring at the White Lion next Chancery Lane End, in Fleetstreet, 1673.'[3]

Milton's nephew and biographer, Edward Philips, speaks of the Tractate as 'one sheet *Of Education* which he dedicated to Mr. Samuel Hartlib, he that wrote so much of husbandry (this sheet is printed at the end of the second edition of his *Poems*).'[4]

Milton's inclusion of the Tractate in a volume of his poems may have no special significance; but so far as I am aware, it is the only one of his prose works to have been thus distinguished.

[1] Masson, *Life of Milton* 3. 45, note.
[2] *Ibid.* 3. 233, note.
[3] 'In some copies the imprint gives "for Tho. Dring at the Blew Anchor next Mitre Court over against Fetter Lane in Fleet-street, 1673," as if Dring had changed his premises in the course of the year.' Masson, *Life of Milton* 6. 687.
[4] Milton, *Of Education, Areopagitica, The Commonwealth,* ed. by Lockwood, p. lxvii.

EDITIONS

Of Education has probably been reprinted the most frequently of all Milton's prose works, except possibly the *Areopagitica*. The most recent editions are:

Milton's *Tractate on Education;* a Facsimile Reprint from the Edition of 1673. Edited by Oscar Browning, Cambridge, 1905. (Pp. xxv+43.)

Tractate of Education, by John Milton. Edited with an Introduction and Notes by Edward E. Morris. London, 1905. (Pp. xlv + 50.)

Of Education, Areopagitica, the Commonwealth, by John Milton, with Early Biographies of Milton, Introduction, and Notes. Edited by Laura E. Lockwood. The Riverside Press, Boston, 1911. (Pp. lxxxvi+205.)

III

THE TRACTATE AS A HUMANISTIC DOCUMENT

In substance, Milton's Tractate generally agrees with the
humanistic theory of education that grew up in Western Europe
during the fifteenth and sixteenth centuries, under the impulse of
the Revival of Learning. This theory is marked by two or three
outstanding characteristics, all of which are prominent in
Milton's treatise. One of these is a clearer consciousness, among
teachers and students, of education as a discipline for active life.[1]
A second is an insistence upon the more extensive reading of
ancient writers, both classical and Christian, as the principal
means of securing this discipline.[2] A third characteristic is an
attitude of severe and often hostile criticism toward mediæval
education and culture.[3] Of these characteristics, the first two
proceed from the whole nature of the movement that is called the
Renaissance, and especially from the greater interest that people
in general during the fifteenth century began to take in the present
life; they also proceed from the activity of scholars and men of
wealth in the discovery and study of the records of the past. The
third feature, that of hostility toward the Middle Ages, probably
grew out of the opposition that the new learning often encountered, especially in the universities.

Of the humanistic theory in practice, the best illustration for
the present purpose is offered by the school established at Mantua
by Vittorino da Feltre. A disciple of the new learning,[4] Vittorino
came to Mantua in 1423, and there remained until his death in
1446.[5] 'During these two-and-twenty years,' says W. H. Wood-

---

[1] See below, p. 55.
[2] See below, pp. 52-3.
[3] See below, p. 54.
[4] Woodward, *Vittorino da Feltre*, p. 25.
[5] *Ibid.*, p. 24.

ward, 'he established and perfected the first great school of the Renaissance—a school whose spirit, curriculum, and method justify us in regarding it as a landmark of critical importance in the history of classical education. It was indeed the great typical school of the Humanities.'[1]

The system of education conceived and carried out at Mantua by Vittorino was framed on the ideal of combining 'the spirit of the Christian life with the educational apparatus of classical literature, whilst uniting with both something of the Greek passion for bodily culture and for dignity of the outer life.'[2] This ideal reminds one of the end of education proposed by Milton, and of the religious studies that he combines with a preparation for life, both active and contemplative. In Vittorino's school, moreover, one may observe a remarkable similarity to the ideal Academy later described by Milton. The 'spacious house and ground about it'[3] are represented by the palace called 'La Gioiosa' (the Pleasure-house), which the Marquis Gonzaga devoted to the purpose of the school, and the name of which Vittorino modified to 'La Giocosa' (the Pleasant House). Its situation was healthful and attractive, and in this house and the adjoining buildings Vittorino and his pupils made their home. The intercourse between teacher and student was intimate and cordial, and the greatest precautions were used to protect the pupils, especially the younger ones, from influences that were vicious or distracting. The number of students, it is true, was only about one-half that mentioned by Milton. 'Their studies, their exercise, and their diet' were supervised by Vittorino himself with the solicitude of a father.

The curriculum was, of course, humanistic. The outlines of the mediæval Trivium and Quadrivium were to some extent observed, but the spirit and method of the study were such as to make it far different from the earlier instruction of the schools and universities.

[1] *Ibid.*, p. 24.
[2] *Ibid.*, p. 27.
[3] See below, p. 55.

For example, the figment of the four senses of a passage—the literal, the metaphorical, the allegorical, the anagogical—which Grammar and Dialectic jointly endeavored to exhibit, gave way to a desire to find out what the author's words meant to a plain intelligence. To Vittorino, Grammar and Rhetoric, combined, implied the critical scholarship of Greek and Latin, a facility in composition in either language, and a power of entering into and absorbing the spirit of the literature, history, and thought of the ancient world. Dialectic, instead of dominating all other subjects, . . . sank into a comparatively insignificant place. All was rational, objective, in method; the aim was erudition, and not speculation, as a means of adorning and moralizing life. The essential foundation of education was Letters.[1]

Daily physical exercise was required of all. In this, Vittorino 'aimed rather at strengthening the frame, inducing habits of hardiness, and power of bearing fatigue, than at any special athletic skill.'[2] Although he placed less emphasis upon martial exercises than did Milton, his ideal of bodily culture was in part derived from that of the Greeks and the Romans.[3]

As the whole aim of Vittorino's teaching was the complete and harmonious development of life, so with him as with Milton the secular part of education was throughout accompanied by the inculcation of Christian principle.

Reverence, piety, and religious observance formed the dominant note of Vittorino's personal life. The dignity of human life was with him based upon its relation to the Divine. Hence the transparent sincerity of his religious teaching; the insistence upon attendance at the ordinances of the Church; the inculcation of forgiveness and humility. . . . Part of the religious instruction he himself took every day. Apart from the light that is thus thrown upon his personality, what is of chief interest in this aspect of Vittorino is its relation to his Humanism. This was with him no nominal reconciliation between the new and the old. Christianity and Humanism were the two co-ordinate factors necessary to the development of complete manhood. There is no

[1] Woodward, *Vittorino da Feltre*, p. 38.
[2] *Ibid.*, p. 66.
[3] *Ibid.*, p. 65.

reason to suppose that Vittorino was embarrassed by a sense of contradiction between the classical and the Christian ideals of life. To him, and to men of his temper since, the thought and morals of the ancient world were identified with the ethical precepts of the Stoics and the idealism of Plato; and it was easy for them to point to the consistency of this teaching with the broader aspects of the Christian life.[1]

On the whole, Vittorino's school, as 'the great typical school of the humanities,' was the first modern prototype of Milton's Academy. The likeness, to be sure, consists more in organization, general aim, and underlying spirit than in the details of curriculum and method.

Of early humanistic treatises on education, the *De Tradendis Disciplinis*, by the Spanish courtier and scholar, Juan Luis Vives (1492–1540), is undoubtedly for us the most important. In this work, Vives, more fully perhaps than any previous writer, interprets and adapts for the Renaissance the doctrines of Quintilian—the main classical authority on humanistic education—and with them combines the principles of Christianity. He also assumes a critical attitude toward mediæval education, and especially toward the scholastic philosophy—the attitude that is so prominent in Milton's Tractate, of which, indeed, Vives' work has been plausibly suggested as the immediate source.[2]

As a representative of humanism Vives is the more convincing because he occupies the position of a convert. His utterances may be taken as evincing serious and reasoned judgments rather than opinions merely acquired from other persons. His earlier education, obtained at the Academy or University in his native city of Valencia, was not such as to dispose him favorably toward the new learning, which at this time (1507–8) had but recently found an advocate in that part of Spain, and met with much opposition from several scholars, among them Vives' own teachers. In 1509, at the age of seventeen, Vives entered the University of Paris.

[1] *Ibid.*, p. 67.
[2] See below, p. 14.

Here in the course of his studies took place his conversion to humanism. The controversy between its advocates and those of dialectic—a dispute that was especially vigorous at Paris—turned upon the value of reading the classics, as opposed to the settling of all questions by the method of debate. The warmth of Vives' championship of reading, and his relentless exposure of the obscurities and barbarisms of the dialecticians, seem well-nigh prophetic of Milton in the Tractate.[1] Probably in 1514 Vives settled at Bruges, where he became the pupil of Erasmus. The cordial friendship which sprang up between them lasted with but one interruption until Erasmus' death. It was at Erasmus' suggestion that Vives undertook his most important piece of editorial work (on St. Augustine's *De Civitate Dei*). Vives differed from Erasmus, however, in his attitude toward scholarship. Erasmus' outlook was cosmopolitan, and his devotion to learning never was threatened by the promptings of immediate and local civic duty. Vives, on the other hand, from a period rather early in his residence at Bruges, was more clearly conscious of the important part that the new learning had to play in social and civic reform. He wrote a treatise on the question of poor-relief in his adopted city, and in other ways manifested the conviction that scholarship should immediately lead to practical results. That this phase of devotion to learning is also to be found in Milton the Tractate itself offers evidence enough.

In 1522 Vives made his first visit to England. He found a hearty welcome at the Court of Henry the Eighth, and on a second visit became the tutor of the Princess Mary, for whose benefit he composed a plan of studies. Thus he shared with Ascham, among others, the work of teaching in the royal household. During his residence in England Vives was a frequent and intimate guest at the house of Sir Thomas More, where he met a number of distinguished scholars. He also visited Oxford, where rooms were set apart for him, and where for a time he held a lectureship.

[1] Watson, *Vives on Education*, p. lvii.

Until 1528 Vives annually spent several months in England. In that year, by reason of his avowed sympathy with Queen Catharine on the question of the divorce, he was compelled to leave the country for good and all.

Until recently the importance of Vives in the history of education doubtless has been generally underestimated. Of two of our standard text-books on the subject, one dismisses Vives with a brief paragraph;[1] the other barely mentions him.[2] And yet, as we have seen, Vives for some time was a distinguished member of the group that contained such men as Erasmus, More, Linacre, Elyot, and Tunstall.[3] Moreover, in his writings one can trace educational ideas that are more commonly associated with the name of Ascham, Mulcaster,[4] Bacon, or Comenius.[5] Watson says:

In the early part of the 19th century [Vives] almost dropped out of notice. The explanation probably is to be found in the educational influences connected with the French Revolution. The world entered into a new economic and educational order, not less than into a revolution of political ideas. Without doubt, the old educational thinkers who had survived to the second half of the 18th century—let us say, John Milton or John Locke, in England, or Rabelais and Montaigne, in France—were absolutely submerged in the whirlpool of change.[6]

One term in which Vives' contemporaries expressed their esteem of him is especially significant.

Vives was often called the second Quintilian. In an age in which the return to antiquity was the only way to recapture the intellectual enthusiasm which could make further progress possible, there could be no higher compliment paid to an educationist than to compare him on equal terms with the greatest of the Roman thinkers and critics on education. Nor must it be forgotten that it was only in 1416 that Poggio discovered in the Abbey of St. Gall

---

[1] Graves, *A History of Education*, p. 166.
[2] Monroe, *A Text-book in the History of Education*, pp. 350, 470.
[3] Watson, *Vives on Education*, p. lxxvi.
[4] *Ibid.*, pp. xxxiv–xxxv.
[5] *Ibid.*, p. cliv.
[6] *Ibid.*, p. xxv.

MSS. of Quintilian's *Oratorical Institutions*, lost, in a complete form, for so many centuries. When the printing-press multiplied copies of this precious complete work, it became 'the code' of the best educationists of the age. But if the term 'second Quintilian' were to be taken in the sense of reproducing the views of Quintilian or of authors of antiquity solely, a sense in which it was certainly not meant by the 16th century, it would be an inadequate description of Vives, and we should lose part of its complimentary import. For Vives was to the Europe of his time what Quintilian had been in the first century [of the Christian era] to Rome. He was the modern Quintilian, prepared to incorporate what was best and permanent in humanity from the ancients, but to use the ancient writers as a starting-place, and not as a goal, in education and in all other 'arts' and branches of knowledge. [1]

De Tradendis Disciplinis, Vives' chief educational work, was first published at Antwerp in 1531, the only English edition appearing at Oxford in 1612. In this work Watson has traced some interesting parallels to Milton's Tractate.[2] The more notable ones may be summarized as follows:

Both writers declare that the end of learning is the knowledge of God.[3] They also agree that this knowledge is best attained through the study of the visible creation,[4] and that language is but a means or instrument of knowledge, not an end in itself.[5] Both writers criticize the scholastic method, that of disputation, although Vives would use it with caution;[6] and both give a prominent place to reading. Each writer sketches a curriculum that is encyclopædic in extent; the two curricula coincide in many details—notably in the study of nature.[7] Each describes in outline an ideal academy, and the two plans are similar in most

[1] Watson, *Vives on Education*, p. ci.
[2] Watson, 'A Suggested Source of Milton's Tractate *Of Education*,' *The Nineteenth Century* 66 (1909). 607.
[3] See below, p. 52; Watson, *Vives on Education*, p. 28.
[4] See below, p. 52; *Vives on Education*, p. 168.
[5] See below, p. 53; *Vives on Education*, pp. 90, 163.
[6] See below, p. 54; *Vives on Education*, p. 177.
[7] See below, pp. 57–8; *Vives on Education*, pp. 166 ff.

of the essential features. Both writers would place a number of such institutions in different parts of the country.[1]

In conclusion Watson submits 'that Milton's idea of his Academy is a reminiscence from his reading of Vives' proposed academies—that Milton's extensive curriculum is founded on the encyclopædic curriculum of Vives, and that the magnificence of conception of education and the exacting expectation from students are shared and suggested by Vives.'[2]

In his translation of Vives' *Dialogues*, Watson says: 'Vives' conception of a school was afterward followed by Milton';[3] and in his translation of the *De Tradendis Disciplinis*: 'We can hardly help thinking that Milton had Vives' Academy before his mind, when he suggests the "spacious house and ground" to be "at once a school and university, not needing a remove," but to be "absolute" for all studies.'[4]

These parallels throw light upon certain points in the Tractate that are likely to be misunderstood. For example, some persons have been confused by Milton's twofold definition of education, supposing its two parts to be unrelated or even inconsistent. Milton, it is true, first says that the end of learning is mental and moral regeneration,[5] and later that education ought to prepare one for the duties of life.[6] But these aims, combining as they do the classical spirit with the Christian, are of the essence of humanistic educational doctrine. They look, indeed, respectively to the inner and the outer aspects of the same individual, normally developed. Milton, like other genuine humanists, cared little for virtue apart from practice, or for talent without principle.

Others have too hastily censured Milton's curriculum for its variety and extent.[7] But here again the poet is in general accord

[1] See below, p. 55; *Vives on Education*, p. 72.
[2] *Nineteenth Century* 66. 617.
[3] Watson, *Tudor School-boy Life*, p. xxvii.
[4] Watson, *Vives on Education*, p. cli.
[5] See below, p. 52.
[6] See below, p. 55.
[7] See Lamb, *The Old and the New Schoolmaster*, in *Works*, ed. by Macdonald, 1. 103; and see below, pp. 18-9.

with other humanistic educators. Milton's encyclopædic principle, and a number of the texts that he mentions, are to be found also in Vives.[1] The encyclopædic aim of 'erudition, and not speculation,' characterizes the teaching of Vittorino da Feltre.[2] Quintilian, moreover, declares that oratory needs the assistance of many arts,[3] and would thoroughly train his pupils in the course of study 'which the Greeks call ἐγκύκλιος παιδεία.'[4]

Again, Milton's plan has been classified as utilitarian in purpose. A recent text-book in the history of education lists the Tractate under the head of 'Humanist-Realistic' schemes.[5] An interesting American edition of the Tractate is bound in the same volume with Locke's *Thoughts Concerning Education*—a work which, whether deservedly or not, has become a main source of utilitarian doctrine.[6] As a reason for associating the two treatises in this manner, the editor says that the Tractate 'seemed more in harmony with the topics discussed by Mr. Locke than with the contents of any other volume in the intended series.'[7]

However close the relation of the 'Humanist-Realists' with the 'Sense-Realists' of the seventeenth century,[8] or of these in turn with Locke, Milton's aim is probably not to be confused with modern utilitarianism in education. Two facts, indeed, in Milton's writings may lead to such a confusion; but neither fully justifies it.

First, in the Tractate, after mentioning the writers on agriculture, Milton says: 'And here will be an occasion of inciting and enabling them hereafter to improve the tillage of their country, to recover the bad soil, and to remedy the waste that is made of good.'[9] Secondly, in his later plan for the education of ministers,

---

[1] See above, p. 14. Watson, *Vives on Education*, pp. 48–9, 209.
[2] See above, p. 10.
[3] Quintilian, *Institutio Oratoria* I. 10. 7.
[4] *Ibid.* I. 10. I.
[5] Monroe, *A Text-book in the History of Education*, pp. 448–51.
[6] Newman, *The Idea of a University*, pp. 158-63.
[7] *Library of Education* I. vii.
[8] Monroe, *A Text-book in the History of Education*, p. 461.
[9] See below, p. 57.

he suggests that, in the schools of clerical training, the pupils learn some handicraft by which to maintain themselves, instead of depending upon salaries or contributions.

The mention of agriculture has led some persons to look upon Milton's proposed Academy as an agricultural school. Yet agriculture is much less prominent in its curriculum than are medicine and law; and no one has supposed that Milton intended his Academy to vie with the special institutions of training in those studies. In fact, he expressly refers to such institutions as special colleges to which his pupils must 'remove,' if they mean to become practitioners.[1] He unmistakably shows his intention by definitely limiting the range of his curriculum to 'general studies.'[2] The reference to the improvement of agriculture, therefore, is probably little more than a courteous recognition of Hartlib's interest in that laudable design.

The educational project that is offered in *Considerations Touching the Likeliest Means to Remove Hirelings out of the Church* (1659) must be frankly recognized as vocational. The public schools that Milton proposes, 'where languages and arts may be taught free together,' are specially intended for educating the clergy. In order that the ministers, without aid from the State, may be safeguarded against want, the 'foundations are to be so instituted as the youth therein may be at once brought up to a competence of learning, and to an honest trade.'[3]

At first glance this scheme resembles that of the earlier 'Academy,' with a new and not very attractive feature. But Milton's aim and outlook in the whole treatise on *Hirelings* are far different from what they were in the Tractate *Of Education*. The Puritan regime had nearly run its course. No longer ardently confiding in 'the vigor of the Parliament,' and 'the courage of the people,'[4]

[1] See below, p. 55.
[2] See below, p. 55.
[3] See below, p. 223.
[4] *Prose Works* I. 257.

but disillusioned by the ambition of the sectarian preachers,[1] Milton offers them a plan of education that, unlike his generous and liberal design of fifteen years earlier, is at the opposite extreme from the elaborate and aristocratic training of the universities. It is possible that he did not expect the proposal to be seriously entertained;[2] and the whole scheme may well have been suggested in a mood of bitter irony. So different is its spirit from that of the Tractate that the two plans can hardly be compared, much less considered the same. One might almost believe that, in losing faith in popular government,[3] Milton had for the time lost faith in higher education.[4]

Though not utilitarian, then, in the narrower sense of directly teaching industrial arts, the plan of studies outlined in the Tractate has encountered another objection, which is stated by Dr. Johnson as follows:

The purpose of Milton, as it seems, was to teach something more solid than the common literature of schools, by reading those authors that treat of physical subjects, such as the Georgick, and astronomical treatises of the ancients. . . .

But the truth is that the knowledge of external nature, and the sciences which that knowledge requires or includes, are not the great or the frequent business of the human mind. Whether we provide for action or conversation, whether we wish to be useful or pleasing, the first requisite is the religious and moral knowledge of right and wrong; the next is an acquaintance with the history of mankind, and with those examples which may be said to embody truth, and prove by events the reasonableness of opinions. Prudence and Justice are virtues, and excellences, of all times and of all places; we are perpetually moralists, but we are geometricians only by chance. Our intercourse with intellectual nature is necessary; our speculations upon matter are voluntary, and at leisure. Physiological learning is of such rare emergence that one man may know another half his life without being able to esti-

[1] Compare the sonnets, *On the New Forcers of Conscience*, and *To the Lord General Cromwell*.

[2] See Masson, *Life of Milton* 5. 615-6.

[3] See below, pp. 274-6; but see also *Prose Works* 2. 125.

[4] See below, pp. 224-226.

mate his skill in hydrostatics or astronomy; but his moral and prudential character immediately appears.

Those authors, therefore, are to be read at schools that supply most axioms of prudence, most principles of moral truth, and most materials for conversation; and these purposes are best served by poets, orators, and historians.[1]

Dr. Johnson, we must note, objects to physical science, not because it is useful, but because it is not useful enough. According to his view, Milton, in quite properly attempting to select practical studies—that is, studies that prepare one for living in the world—simply made a wrong choice, and selected those that were less practical than the ones already in use.

No better statement of the genuinely humanistic spirit in education could be desired than these remarks of Dr. Johnson. The very term 'humanities' signifies the pursuits, the activities, proper to mankind, and it was so understood by educators early in the Renaissance.[2] The answer to Johnson's criticism lies in the history of the classical curriculum. Some of those who most fully represent the humanistic ideal, by keeping education in contact with life, approve of studying mathematics and the natural sciences. Erasmus recommends cosmography.[3] Vives, 'the second Quintilian,' gives a prominent place to the study of nature;[4] and Quintilian himself insists upon including geometry,[5] which Dr. Johnson declared could be useful 'only by chance.' Hemsterhuys, the illustrious contemporary of Johnson, 'often regretted that mathematics and philosophy were no longer included among the *studia humanitatis.*'[6]

Though recommended by the earlier humanists, mathematics and natural science were definitely subordinated to the general aim of a liberal education. They were not to be pursued in the

---

[1] Johnson, *Lives of the English Poets*, ed. by Hill, 1. 99–100.
[2] Monroe, *A Text-book in the History of Education*, p. 370.
[3] Woodward, *Erasmus Concerning Education*, pp. 144–5.
[4] Watson, *Vives on Education*, pp. cxi, 163 ff.
[5] Quintilian, *Institutio Oratoria* 1. 10. 34–49.
[6] Sandys, *A History of Classical Scholarship* 2. 452.

indulgence of curiosity,[1] and their direct applicability to the affairs of life was not expected to compare with that of the humanities in the more restricted sense. Contrary to the view of Dr. Johnson and of certain modern educators, Milton, too, subordinated his 'real' studies to a purpose that was strictly humanistic. This fact is shown by the order of his curriculum, as will later appear.[2] With regard, indeed, to the relative importance of 'real' and 'ideal' studies, Milton in *Paradise Lost* had expressly stated the opinion that is advanced by Johnson.[3] It is also worth note that Milton concludes his survey of the natural sciences with a reading of the poets who treat of nature and add to it what Wordsworth calls 'the breath and finer spirit of all knowledge'—'the impassioned expression which is in the countenance of all Science.'[4]

Milton's humanism also explains his attitude toward the writings of Comenius. The disparaging allusion to 'many modern *Januas* and *Didactics*'[5] probably indicates that Hartlib had brought the works of Comenius to Milton's notice. The English poet and the Moravian bishop had thus much in common—they both desired to simplify and to expedite the teaching of Latin; both insisted upon the study of things rather than words; both upheld the encyclopædic ideal. But Milton, though at one with Comenius in making all knowledge the province of his student, chiefly emphasized an educational medium for which Comenius appears to have had less regard. Milton, as a humanist, would instruct through literature—preferably the best literature. Comenius, as a rationalist, would codify all knowledge into systems, for memorization. With implicit faith in the importance attached by Bacon to the natural sciences—perhaps even overemphasizing that importance—Comenius would make the study

[1] Watson, *Vives on Education*, p. 166.
[2] See below, pp. 43–7.
[3] See below, pp. 298, 301, and 320.
[4] Wordsworth, *Poetical Works*, ed. by Hutchinson, p. 938.
[5] See below, p. 52.

of external nature the chief part of secular education.[1] The knowledge of things is, indeed, as with Milton, to lead to the knowledge of God.[2] Comenius to some extent even follows the 'scale of nature'[3]—proceeding in the order of his curriculum from the material to the intellectual, and finally to the moral.[4] Practical piety and religion he would also teach from the first. But with Milton's study of human nature through the noblest achievements of the human spirit, as recorded in history and literature, one finds in the system of Comenius nothing worthy of comparison. Rather did he look upon the classics with disfavor, as studies inappropriate to a Christian school.[5]

Had Milton glanced through a copy of the *Janua Linguae Latinae Reserata*, which, one may fancy, Hartlib had sent him, he would have found what purported to be '*The Gate of Languages Unlocked, or the Seminary of all Languages and Sciences*: that is, a compendious method of learning Latin or any other tongue, along with the elements of all the Sciences and Arts, comprehended under a hundred chapter-headings and in a thousand sentences.'[6] Scarcely a hint is there, either in the *Janua* or in the *Didactic*, of that effectually refining influence of art and literature—scarcely a trace of that humane love of the noble and the beautiful, in man and nature—of that intellectual idealism, through which alone, in the Middle Ages, Virgil attained to the esteem of a divine prophet, and which gives to Milton's educational structure its very spirit and form! After observing how the genius of the English poet animates his educational doctrine and practice, one little wonders that his inclination should have led him to read no further in the projects of Comenius.

[1] Laurie, *John Amos Comenius*, pp. 251-2.
[2] *Ibid.*, pp. 104-5.
[3] See below, pp. 44-5; 295-6.
[4] Keatinge, *The Great Didactic*, pp. 140-6.
[5] Laurie, *John Amos Comenius*, p. 162.; Keatinge, *The Great Didactic*, pp. 383-400.
[6] Laurie, *John Amos Comenius*, p. 213.

IV

SOME IMPORTANT RESULTS OF HUMANISM
IN ENGLAND

One of the principal censures that Milton brings against
English education in his day reflects the common attitude among
humanist scholars toward the Middle Ages as compared with
classical antiquity. Woodward says of Erasmus, whom he accepts as 'a representative personality of the age of Revival in
Teutonic Europe':

Antiquity laid its spell upon him not less stringently than upon
Bruni or Poliziano. To him, as to them, it stood for a Golden Age.
Humanist scholarship did not, as yet, admit of a critical judgment of the actual conditions, moral, social, or economic, of the
great age of Athens, or of the Augustan empire. The Roman
world was, it is not unfair to say, presented as the ideal, once
realized, of a universal state ruling in peace and justice the entire
human race, adorned with arts, letters, and achievements of
practical skill, which mankind had lost through barbarism, and
was then struggling to recover. Hence, to Erasmus, antiquity was
not a subject of liberal study alone, but partook of the nature of a
working ideal of social order, to be adjusted to modern conditions, chief among which was the supremacy of the Christian
faith. Hence the passionate note discernible in all that he has to
say concerning the function of ancient literature in the education
of the new generation. To deny the claims of antique learning was
to take stand against human progress; for the illumination that
the age craved for in every department of life lay there. Progress
meant, therefore, to hark back to an ideal once perfectly realized
in a historic past.[1]

That Milton agreed with this view is indicated by his remark
upon the universities, which, he says, are 'not yet well recovered
from the scholastic grossness of barbarous ages.' Many other

[1] Woodward, *Education during the Renaissance*, pp. 111-2.

passages in his writings express the same opinion; for instance, what he says, in *Of Reformation in England*, on the Revival of Learning;[1] and, in the *History of Britain*, on the decline of culture in Britain after the final departure of the Romans.[2] Such, indeed, was the prevalent view among scholars—especially Protestant scholars—during the Renaissance.[3] Even to-day, or until very recently, many persons seem to believe that the Middle Ages were an era of moral and spiritual darkness, lightened by hardly a single ray of intelligence or piety; and that the Revival of Learning in the fifteenth century took place with a suddenness but little short of miraculous. Before we can fully appreciate the importance of Milton's educational doctrine, we must briefly examine the justice of this attitude toward the Middle Ages, and inquire whether humanistic learning was totally in abeyance during that period.

The revival of antiquity, of course, was one of the earliest and most conspicuous features of the Renaissance. But it was not unheralded by previous attempts at reasserting the classical ideal;[4] nor is it certain that the tradition of classical learning in Western Europe was ever completely broken. The familiar metaphor that Macaulay applied to mediæval Italy[5] may possibly be extended to Gaul and Britain as well. The Roman educational system, which under the Empire was fundamentally the system of Quintilian, dominated the schools of Gaul until a period well into the fifth century.[6] The encyclopædic programme of the great teacher was not fully carried out, but so little was its essential character changed that the paganism of the ethical training included in Quintilian's scheme became obnoxious to the stricter

[1] See below, p. 287.
[2] See below, p. 278.
[3] See below, pp. 329–30.
[4] Rashdall, *The Universities of Europe in the Middle Ages* 1. 30 ff.
[5] 'The night which descended upon her was the night of an Arctic summer.' *Machiavelli*, in *Essays* 2. 4.
[6] Roger, *L'Enseignement des Lettres Classiques d'Ausone à Alcuin*, pp. 7, 87.

churchmen of the period.[1] At the beginning of the sixth century, classical learning among the Gallic people, and classical education in their schools, seem to have been almost entirely obscured by the grossness and materialism of barbarian invaders.[2] But before the close of the same century the Irish monks had begun the study of ancient letters,[3] and in the ninth century it was an Irishman, Joannes Scotus, who helped to re-establish sound learning in Gaul.[4]

To England the classics were probably brought from three sources: directly from Rome, while Britain was still under the imperial rule; in later times from Ireland by the ministry of Irish monks in the north and the south-west of England; but most of all by the Archbishop Theodore and the Abbot Hadrian, following the mission of St. Augustine in 597. Almost from the beginning of the conversion of the English people, schools were opened in connection with the cathedrals, as the different dioceses were organized. The first English grammar-school was established at Canterbury, in 598.[5] The primary purpose of such foundations was the instruction of candidates for the clergy in Latin, the language of the Church. The schools were constituted, however, on the Roman model, as prescribed by Quintilian.[6] Their larger aim, therefore, was to prepare men for citizenship or for public service, by imparting a general knowledge of arts and affairs, supplemented by a training in expression. That this ideal was eventually realized with considerable success is shown by Alcuin's account of the school at York in the eighth century.[7] The learning, too, of men like Alcuin, and, before him, Bede and Aldhelm, was in essence humanistic. The cathedral schools in England, and the monastic schools and palace-schools on the Con-

---

[1] Roger *ibid.*, p. 17.
[2] *Ibid.*, p. 89.
[3] *Ibid.*, p. 229.
[4] Sandys, *A History of Classical Scholarship* 1. 491.
[5] Leach, *The Schools of Mediæval England*, p. 3.
[6] *Ibid.*, pp. 13, 15.
[7] Leach, *Educational Charters and Documents*, pp. 10–7.

tinent, carried on the tradition of classical studies until the rise of the universities in the twelfth century.[1] By that time it is probable that the grammar-schools in England were sufficiently numerous and well-distributed to enable promising students, at least those from families of moderate fortune, to prepare for the university at almost any considerable town.[2] In earlier times, notably at York in the eighth century, some of the cathedral grammar-schools united the functions of school and university.[3] Some of them even conferred the Bachelor's degree.[4] This fact is noteworthy in connection with Milton's plan of making his school independent of the university.[5]

It was against the university, indeed, with its scholastic philosophy, that Milton and other humanists directed their most severe attacks, and probably with best reason. Whereas the mediæval grammar-schools adhered to a literary programme,[6] the study of logic dominated the university curriculum from the twelfth century until the close of the fifteenth, and even in Milton's time still held a prominent place.[7] Its pre-eminence over humanistic studies was probably occasioned less by the force of authority than by the fascination of logic for the mediæval student, until the interest finally worked itself out, and logic declined in popular favor.[8] The shortcomings of the Schoolmen in the matters of historical criticism and natural science have, without doubt, since the Reformation, enjoyed their due share of notice. It is only just also to recognize the educational virtues of mediæval dialectic, which was a most rigorous exercise of the analytical faculty,[9] and which in the field of speculative thought not only prepared the way for certain of the conclusions of mod-

[1] Leach, *The Schools of Mediæval England*, p. 129.
[2] *Ibid.*, p. 131.
[3] *Ibid.*, p. 59.
[4] *Ibid.*, p. 186.
[5] See below, pp. 55, 223.
[6] Leach, *The Schools of Mediæval England*, p. 248.
[7] Masson, *Life of Milton* 1. 259–66.
[8] Rashdall, *The Universities of Europe in the Middle Ages* 1. 67.
[9] Bacon, *Essays*, No. 50, *Of Studies*.

ern philosophy, but also in some degree anticipated them.[1] Moreover, in the universities, the study of Quintilian, though his works were but imperfectly known to the Schoolmen, at least kept humanism alive; for grammar and rhetoric, as distinct from logic and dialectic, 'stood for the critical reading and study of authors.' 'It is hardly an exaggeration to say that the subjects and the methods of education remained the same from the days of Quintilian to the days of Arnold, from the first century to the mid-nineteenth century of the Christian era.'[2]

The Revival of Learning in the fifteenth century, which gave so strong an impulse to thought and experiment in education all over Western Europe, had by Milton's time produced some of its characteristic effects in the English schools and universities. In England, as in Italy, one must observe, intellectual acceleration coincided with a more extensive study of ancient letters, and especially with the renewal of interest in the Greek language and literature—the interest that is always so intimately associated with scholarly taste and enterprise.[3] The study of Greek flourished in Western Europe during a portion of the Middle Ages, but eventually fell into neglect. Among the newly Christianized English, in the seventh century, under Theodore and Hadrian, 'the introduction of Greek in addition to Latin gave an impetus to English learning which made English scholars the first in the world, and conduced to the production of Bede, himself the sanest of historians for eight hundred years.'[4] Greek was also known to Alcuin.[5]

From the eighth century, however, until the fifteenth, we hear but little of Greek in England. Careful historians do not assert that it was entirely lost to Western Europe at any time; but for various reasons it almost disappeared from the general education. Like other human attainments of supreme worth, the taste for

[1] Rashdall, *The Universities of Europe in the Middle Ages* 1. 44.
[2] Leach, *Educational Charters and Documents*, p. ix.
[3] Sandys, *A History of Classical Scholarship* 2. 171, 209, 223, 452.
[4] Leach, *Educational Charters and Documents*, p. xii. See also below, pp. 152-3.
[5] Leach, *Educational Charters and Documents*, pp. 10-1.

Greek culture may quickly be eradicated in a period of violence and disorder. During the tumult attendant upon the decline and fall of Rome, the British Isles, it is believed, afforded the last strongholds to Greek, if, in truth, it ever entirely died out. The incursions of the Danes, however, probably put an end to the study of it in England, and Alfred's restoration of learning seems to have contemplated only the reading of English and Latin. After the Norman Conquest, English education was more largely affected by the practice of the Continent, where scholasticism soon took the foremost place among purely intellectual studies. The Council of Vienne in 1311 provided for the teaching of Greek and other 'Oriental' languages at Oxford and at other universities;[1] but the purpose was to equip students for mission-work among the 'infidels,' and the provision seems not to have been connected with any tradition of scholarship.

One probably may say with truth that, through the labors of Selling, Grocyn, Linacre, and other 'traveling scholars,' toward the close of the fifteenth century, Greek was a second time brought from Italy into England; and that, as on the earlier occasion, it caused an immense quickening of intellectual life. 'It was not till the value of Greek thought became in any degree manifest that the New Learning awakened any enthusiasm in England.'[2] By 1491, probably, 'the teaching of Greek began to be effective in Oxford,'[3] and in 1499 Erasmus gives high praise to English scholarship in both Latin and Greek.[4] 'When in 1516 Bishop Fox, who had been Master of Pembroke College, Cambridge, founded Corpus Christi College, Oxford, he made provision for lecturers who were to give instruction in the Greek and Latin Classics. This was the first permanent establishment of a teacher of Greek in England.'[5]

[1] Leach, *Educational Charters and Documents*, pp. 268–9.
[2] Sandys, *A History of Classical Scholarship* 2. 223.
[3] *Ibid.* 2. 228.
[4] *Ibid.* 2. 229.
[5] *Ibid.* 2. 230.

It would probably be as unwise to attribute the progress of education in England solely to the study of Greek as to attribute the Revival of Learning in Italy to the fall of Constantinople. The intellectual movements that blossomed and bore fruit in Elizabeth's day struck deep roots into the soil of the Middle Ages; but all these movements were inspired and reinvigorated by the Hellenic culture that Englishmen in the fifteenth century had again begun largely to draw from its original sources. English national self-consciousness, after the Norman Conquest, probably began with Magna Charta, and came to vigorous expression in the thirteenth-century *Song of Lewes*.[1] But Leicester, Sidney, and Raleigh were friends and patrons of the poet Spenser, who fashioned his British hero upon the moral virtues of Aristotle and Plato. Mediæval 'Protestantism' had its English martyrs among the followers of Wyclif. But later the work of Erasmus, Tyndale, and Coverdale, in editing and translating the Greek text of the New Testament, and thereby making the Scriptures really known to the English people, was of incalculable moment to the English Church. The literary forerunners of the Elizabethan age knew, as Chaucer did, though not so well, how to use native material, and how to learn from the Italians. But even Shakespeare, for his full development, needed Plutarch, and Chapman's Homer, as well as Marlowe and British legend. Milton's debt to the Greek classics requires no comment here.

The effect, then, of the fifteenth-century Hellenic revival on English education, though eventually potent, was not so much creative as contributory to a growing interest of earlier date. This interest is most clearly to be observed in the founding or the re-endowing of colleges and grammar-schools. In the fourteenth century four colleges were founded at Oxford, and five at Cambridge. In the fifteenth century three were founded at Oxford, and four at Cambridge. 'It is not until the sixteenth century that we

[1] Kingsford, *The Song of Lewes*, pp. vii, xxviii, 1 (lines 9–12), 10 (lines 285–6).

can trace the influence of the Revival of Learning' in the foundation of new colleges at the two universities.[1]

At the beginning of the Renaissance, England, as we have seen, was reasonably well supplied with grammar-schools.[2] The educational reforms of Henry the Eighth and of Edward the Sixth consisted rather in re-founding and re-endowment than in the creation of new establishments.[3] The grammar-schools, too, had always adhered to a literary programme,[4] and so had carried on the classical tradition. The change produced in them by the Revival of Learning, therefore, and even by the bringing in of Greek, was probably less a modification of curriculum and method than the introduction of a new outlook upon life and a closer connection of studies with the affairs of the world.

A good example of English education under the impulse of the new learning is to be found in St. Paul's School, London, which, after an existence of four hundred years,[5] was re-endowed about 1512. Its new founder was John Colet, Dean of St. Paul's, the friend and teacher of Erasmus, and an eminent scholar and divine. To the new St. Paul's School Colet devoted his patrimony;[6] and he settled the details of the foundation with the greatest care. 'My intent,' said he, 'is by this school specially to increase knowledge, and worshiping of God and our Lord Jesus Christ, and good Christian life and manners in the children.'[7]

The boys were 'to be taught always in good literature, both Latin and Greek, and good authors, such as have the very Roman eloquence joined with the wisdom, specially Christian authors that wrote their wisdom with clean and chaste Latin, either in verse or prose; but, above all, the Catechism in English; after that

[1] Sandys, *A History of Classical Scholarship* 2. 238.
[2] See above, p. 25.
[3] Leach, *The Schools of Mediæval England*, pp. 277 ff.
[4] *Ibid.*, p. 248.
[5] *Ibid.*, p. 278.
[6] Seebohm, *The Oxford Reformers*, p. 208.
[7] *Ibid.*, p. 209.

the Accidence; then *Institutum Christiani Hominis*, which Erasmus made at my request, and the *Copia Verborum* of the same author; then other Christian authors, as, Lactantius, Prudentius and Proba, Sedulius, Juvencus, and Baptista Mantuanus, and such others as shall be thought convenient for the true Latin speech.'[1]

The grammar that Colet composed for the use of the pupils, with the aid of Erasmus and of William Lily, under whose name it appeared (1513), was later established by Royal authority as the uniform text-book of the schools throughout the realm, and is mentioned by Milton, in whose time it was still in use, as sufficient for the purposes of the school he proposed.[2] The provision that the boys were to learn the Articles of the Faith, and the Ten Commandments, in English, is an early instance of the recognition of the vernacular in teaching. The reorganization of St. Paul's School was probably the first important step toward introducing the new learning into the grammar-schools; and through the sound piety of Colet there was combined with it, as in the Mantuan school of Vittorino da Feltre, the simple and direct teaching of the Christian virtues.

Of the school as it was when Milton attended it, Masson says:

St. Paul's School, it is to be remembered, was strictly a grammar-school, or school for classical instruction only. But, since Colet's time, by reason of the great development which classical studies had received throughout the nation at large, the efficiency of the school within its assigned limits had immensely increased. Instead of peddling over Sedulius and other such small practitioners of later or middle-age Latinity, recommended as proper class-books by Colet, the scholars of St. Paul's, as of contemporary schools, were now led through very much the same list of Roman prose-writers and poets that are still honored in our academies. The practice of writing pure classical Latin, or what might pass for such, both in prose and in verse, was also carried to a perfection not known in Colet's time. But the improvement in Latin was as nothing compared with what had taken place in Greek. Although Colet in his testamentary recommendations to

---

[1] Masson, *Life of Milton* 1. 76. Reprinted by permission of The Macmillan Company, New York; Macmillan & Company, Ltd., London.
[2] See below, pp. 55–6.

the Mercers had mentioned it as desirable that the head-master should know Greek as well as Latin, he had added, 'if such a man can be gotten.' That, indeed, was the age of incipient Greek in England. Colet had none himself; and that Lily had mastered Greek, while residing in earlier life in Rhodes, was one of his distinctions. Since that time, however, the passion for Greek had spread; the battle between the Greeks and the Trojans, as the partisans of the new learning and its opponents were respectively called, had been fought out in the days of Ascham and Elizabeth; and, if Greek scholarship still lagged behind Latin, yet in such schools as St. Paul's there were Greek readings and exercises, in anticipation of the higher Greek at the Universities. Probably Hebrew also was taught optionally to a few of the highest boys.[1]

The progress of the new learning, however, was not unimpeded. In the universities, the study of Greek stimulated speculation on matters of politics and theology, and led to charges of heresy; and hence the opposition of the most conservative among the churchmen. The mediæval dialectic, too, which was as prominent in the university curriculum as natural science is at present in American institutions, was subjected by the humanists to unrelenting attack, which induced the most stubborn resistance in their opponents. The University Statutes of Elizabeth in 1561 confirmed the old dialectic in its position of importance. On the other hand, the statutes recognized the new learning by establishing Greek among the studies of the Triennium, or three-years' course following the Baccalaureate degree and leading to that of *Magister*. And, in fact, so liberally were the statutes interpreted that in Milton's time Greek studies might enter into any year even of the undergraduate course. At the same time, the practice of rhetoric and dialectic in public disputations was an important part of the university exercises as well as those of the several colleges;[2] and Milton, as a student, like many others, displayed his humanistic leanings in unsparing condemnation of it.[3]

---

[1] Masson, *Life of Milton* 1. 83-4.   Reprinted by permission of The Macmillan Company, New York; Macmillan & Company, Ltd., London.
[2] Masson, *Life of Milton* 1. 262-4.   [3] See below, pp. 65-7.

In the grammar-schools, too, the progress of humanism became involved in controversy. This centred chiefly in the study of Latin, which under the successors of the Italian and French humanists, and in Germany under Sturm (whose influence on English schools was very great),[1] tended toward excessive imitation of the classical style, especially that of Cicero. Such an aim, of course, placed the emphasis on Latin composition,[2] often to the detriment of classical reading, and consequently of that wide acquaintance with the instructive and inspiring matter of history and literature which is the very life of humanism.[3] The task of imparting to boys the precise command of Latin that was requisite to the desired facility in composition greatly lengthened the time spent in the grammar-schools,[4] and taxed the ingenuity of men like Ascham in devising methods for its attainment.[5] The early and excessive practice of composition in the schools is condemned by Milton in conjunction with the dialectic of the Universities.[6]

The influence of the new learning, as well as of national tradition, is also to be seen in certain treatises in English on education, that appeared in the sixteenth century, and in some degree anticipate the work of Milton.

The Boke Named the Governour, published in 1531 by Sir Thomas Elyot, a physician, and a courtier of King Henry the Eighth, was probably the first comprehensive educational treatise in English.[7] It professes to describe an ideal state or 'publike weale,' and is dedicated to the King. Inasmuch as the most important business of the State, in Elyot's estimation, as in that of Plato and Solomon, is the training of its rulers,[8] he devotes the work almost

---

[1] See below, p. 38.

[2] Woodward, *English Universities, Schools, and Scholarship in the Sixteenth Century*, in the *Cambridge History of English Literature* 3. 487–8.

[3] Bacon, *Advancement of Learning*, ed. by Wright, p. 30.

[4] Milton, *Accidence Commenced Grammar, Prose Works* 5. 432.

[5] Ascham, *English Works*, pp. 182–7.

[6] See below, pp. 53–4.

[7] Benndorf, *Die Englische Pädagogik im 16. Jahrhundert*, p. 1.

[8] Elyot, *The Governour* 1. cxcii, and note.

entirely to that subject. The matter of the treatise, he says, is gathered 'as well of the sayenges of moste noble autors (Grekes and Latines)' as from his own experience in affairs of state. His purpose was not to presume to instruct others in their duty, but to compile a handbook of information for those who might be interested in the subject.[1]

Elyot divides the upbringing of youth into four stages, beginning, like Quintilian, with the care of the child during his earliest years. At the age of seven the boy is to leave his nurse and pass under the care of a tutor, who should thus early begin to mould his character to the preference of all that is most commendable. At this age the pupil is to begin the study of Latin and Greek.[2] Grammar, which Elyot looks upon as a decidedly subordinate matter, is to be mastered with the aid of 'a few and quick rules,'[3] and to be made familiar by reading to the pupil Æsop's Fables in Greek;[4] after this he should at once proceed to the reading of the poets, especially Homer and Virgil. Between the ages of fourteen and seventeen, when the pupil's judgment has somewhat matured, he should study history and geography, and practise the arts of composition and oratory. At the age of seventeen he should begin the study of philosophy, with special regard to ethics,[5] finally reading Plato 'most studiously.' In addition to the philosophers, the pupil is expected to read the Scriptures, both of the Old and of the New Testament; and to Erasmus' *Institution of a Christian Prince* Elyot pays the high compliment of desiring that it be 'as familiar alway with gentlemen . . . as was Homer with the great king Alexander, or Xenophon with Scipio.'[6]

[1] *Ibid.* 1. cxcii.
[2] *Ibid.* 1. 53–4.
[3] *Ibid.* 1. 55. See below, p. 56.
[4] Elyot, *The Governour* 1. 56. See below, p. 56.
[5] Elyot, *The Governour* 1. 91. See below, p. 58; and see also Masson, *Life of Milton* 3. 247.
[6] Elyot, *The Governour* 1. 94–5.

Elyot's programme of studies, uniting, as it does, the classical with the Christian, is quite evidently humanistic. The attention that he gives to moral training, and even to deportment,[1] is also characteristic of the Renaissance. The national bias of the work is to be seen in the fact of its being written in English, and in its applicability to the education, not only of a sovereign, but also of all persons who may come to have authority in the State.[2] One also notes Elyot's recommendation of the distinctively English exercises, archery[3] and wrestling.[4] Unlike Milton, and the writers whom we are next to mention, Elyot would have his pupils instructed by private tutors, instead of in a school.

The next considerable English work on education was *The Scholemaster*, by Roger Ascham, pupil of Sir John Cheke, and tutor of Queen Elizabeth. Like Milton's treatise, *The Scholemaster* was written at the request of a friend to whom the writer had stated his views in conversation. It was not published, however, until 1570, about a year after Ascham's death. The occasion of the work, as related in the Preface,[5] was a conversation in which Ascham took part, with certain other members of the Queen's Privy Council, on the merits of the schoolmasters of their time. One of the noblemen present was so much pleased with Ascham's remarks that he requested him to set down his views in writing. In so doing, Ascham acknowledges his indebtedness to Sir John Cheke, his teacher at Cambridge, to John Sturm, the head of the school at Strassburg, and to Plato, Aristotle, and Cicero.

The work chiefly deals with the course of study in preparation for the university, and in particular with the method of teaching Latin. It thus applies more closely to the public schools than does the treatise by Elyot, and in various other details is like the Tractate of Milton.

[1] Elyot, *The Governour* 2. 38 ff.
[2] *Ibid.* 1. 25; 2. 447.
[3] *Ibid.* 1. 289, 290, and note.
[4] *Ibid.* 1. 173, and note.
[5] Ascham, *English Works*, p. 175.

34

Ascham first objects to the method of teaching Latin then in use, because it requires the pupil to practise composition before reading any good author. This is much the same fault that Milton refers to as a *'preposterous* exaction.'[1] In order to give the pupil facility in the use of Latin, Ascham recommends 'double translation,' the method enjoined in Cicero's *De Oratore,*[2] and employed under Ascham by Queen Elizabeth.[3] He also recommends, as does Elyot, the practice of reading to the pupil in the language studied, as soon as he has acquired the elements of grammar and a simple vocabulary. He remarks upon the general want of discipline in the upbringing of youth, and adduces the examples of ancient Greece and Persia by way of contrast. He then sums up from the point of view of discipline what he has said before: 'Meaning thereby,' says he, 'that, from seven year old to seventeen, love is the best allurement to learning; from seventeen to seven-and-twenty, that wise men should carefully see the steps of youth surely stayed by good order in that most slippery time, and specially in the Court.'[4] In his view of the age of seventeen as a critical point in the pupil's moral development, Ascham is in accord with Elyot and Milton. In connection with moral training he speaks of travel on the Continent, and delivers a long homily on the vices of Italian society and its demoralizing effect upon young Englishmen.[5] One is reminded of Milton's objection to sending young men into France under a French tutor. Ascham closes the 'Firste Booke' of his treatise with a promise not to leave the pupil until he has 'brought him a perfect scholar out of the school, and placed him in the university;'[6] he thus limits himself to the subject of the grammar-school. The 'Second Booke' contains a number of precepts and examples intended as an aid to the student in learning Latin.

[1] See below, p. 53.
[2] Ascham, *English Works,* p. 183; Cicero, *De Oratore* 1. 154.
[3] Ascham, *English Works,* p. 245.
[4] *Ibid.,* p. 222.
[5] *Ibid.,* pp. 223–37.
[6] *Ibid.,* p. 237.

The chief points of agreement between Ascham and Milton are the desire of a more compendious and effectual method of attaining a good Latin style, the 'special reinforcement' of moral teaching at the age when the pupil comes to years of discretion, and the insistence upon safeguards against vice, if the youth is to travel abroad. In addition to the normal programme of Renaissance education, as exhibited in Elyot, Ascham displays a vigorous Protestantism, a national prejudice which, one must admit, is somewhat narrow, and a deference to Cicero that is symptomatic of decadence.

In 1581, eleven years after the publication of Ascham's treatise, appeared the *Positions* of Richard Mulcaster; and in the following year, his *First Part of the Elementarie*. Mulcaster was the first head-master of the Merchant-Taylors' School in London, one of the grammar-schools refounded under the impulse given to education by the example of Colet.[1] He had served the Guild for twenty years in this capacity when he published his first treatise on education.[2] This work, which was dedicated to Queen Elizabeth, and entitled *Positions*—that is, grounds of argument, like the first principles of mathematics—was intended merely as an introduction to his main treatise.

Mulcaster does not advance his 'positions' as if they were axioms, to be accepted on their unsupported merits, or upon his authority alone. On the contrary, he says:

I have written in [support of] every one of those arguments enough, I think, for any reader whom reason will content; . . . for I have grounded them upon reading, and some reasonable experience; I have applied them to the use and custom of my country, nowhere enforcing her to any foreign or strange device. Moreover, I have conferred them with common sense, wherein long teaching hath not left me quite senseless.[3]

[1] Klähr, *Leben und Werke R. Mulcasters*, p. 1.
[2] Mulcaster, *Positions*, ed. by Quick, Appendix, p. 200.
[3] *Ibid.*, pp. 292–3.

Although these principles concern only the first stage in education, which Mulcaster calls the Elementary, they may be so interpreted, he believed, as to apply also to the Grammarian, or method for the grammar-school. His aim, as he says, is to improve the education of children with a view to learning; to furnish the teacher with a knowledge of the proper care of his pupil's health; and, so far as he is able, to improve the ordinary course of study, for the common good.[1]

Among other subjects, Mulcaster discusses the age at which a child should begin to study; the value of different kinds of physical exercise; and the education of girls as well as boys. He also insists throughout upon a consideration of the mental and physical capacity of the pupil. Under the disciplines of the Elementary, or primary part of education, he enumerates Reading (which should begin with English), Writing, Drawing, and Music.

Under his sixth principle Mulcaster discusses the subject that chiefly interested Elyot—the training of young gentlemen for the service of the State. He believes, however, that their education should be public rather than private, in order that they may practise among their fellow-students the virtues that they learn by precept. In Mulcaster's opinion, gentlemen ought, as a part of their duty to the State, to enter the learned professions, where their sense of honor will insure better service than that rendered by needy adventurers. Finally, he discusses the education of a Prince—whose elementary training should be the same with that of other children, except that the teacher should pay greater attention to cultivating a sense of honor in the pupil. The early breeding of the young Prince should inculcate a winning modesty, and develop such ability in affairs as will later command respect. To this should be added instruction in matters ecclesiastical, political, and military.

Mulcaster also proposes a number of reforms in the university. One of the most interesting of these is a more rational division of

[1] *Ibid.*, p. 295.

labor among the different faculties, so as to avoid the duplication of work within the several colleges.[1] This reform, if carried out, would have entirely changed the organization of the English universities.

Mulcaster's work as a whole is much more inclusive than that of either Elyot or Ascham. It is a fairly comprehensive handbook of theory and method, written by an experienced and imaginative teacher, and, in fact, is virtually encyclopædic in scope.

His wisdom appears, too, in his curriculum for the young. What a blessing for them, could he have arranged their studies all over Europe, instead of his contemporary, Sturm! He would have taught them to read and write their own language, to draw, to sing, and to play some musical instrument; and he maintains that if, instead of beginning with Latin, the child were put through a preliminary course in these five things, he would learn 'the tongue' sooner, and do more between twelve and sixteen than from seven to seventeen the other way.[2]

The chief point of similarity between Mulcaster's theories and those of Milton is the radical nature of the reforms proposed, especially in the university. This institution both Ascham and Elyot seem to accept as it was; neither proposes, like Mulcaster, to change its whole plan, or, like Milton, entirely to dispense with it for general studies. Yet the correspondence between Mulcaster and Milton is not close, existing only in so far as both recommend for the university a higher aim and a more efficacious method.

---

[1] Mulcaster, *Positions*, pp. 236–50; Rashdall, *The Universities of Europe in the Middle Ages* 2. 516.
[2] Quick, in Mulcaster, *Positions*, p. 308.

DISTINCTIVE FEATURES OF MILTON'S TREATISE

To the educational improvements which humanism and the Reformation were effecting in England, Milton's Tractate is in one sense a contribution. It emphasizes the chief principle represented in the achievements of Colet and Erasmus, and expressed in the writings of Elyot, Ascham, and Mulcaster—the provision, that is to say, of a better training for youth, especially in the affairs of practical life.

Milton's work also has its national aspect. The Tractate was undertaken from patriotic motives, and the time of its composition was hastened in compliance with the wishes of a public-spirited friend. Like Mulcaster and Elyot, Milton would educate young men for the public service.[1] He would revive the 'old admired virtues and excellencies' of the English people,[2] and he includes in his regimen of exercise the national art of wrestling.[3]

In the ardor of Milton's own devotion to classical studies, however, and in the personal responsibility that he felt as an interpreter of their true spirit to his people, there is the quality of original genius. This sense of responsibility directed him in the choice of a career.[4] It prompted his intellect to throw off the decadent Ciceronianism that had already developed, and to concentrate upon the deep and vital matters of scholarship. It enabled him, in the cause, as he believed, of English liberty, indefinitely to defer his chosen employment, and to endure with cheerfulness the loss of his eyesight. In all Milton's aims and

[1] See above, pp. 32, 37; below, p. 55.
[2] See below, p. 63.
[3] See below, p. 61.
[4] See below, pp. 89–92.

activities one may observe his conviction that he is the possessor of great gifts, entailing great responsibilities.[1]

It was this conviction, no doubt, that led Milton throughout his public life, and in his writings, to take an independent stand. Though severely critical of the Church, he was not identified with a particular sect; nor, while enunciating the principles of civil liberty, did he give unreserved support to a single political faction.[2] He gives, or withholds, his aid, refrains or applies himself, at will. He avoids overloading his argument with long citations, but threatens, at need, to turn and wind his adversary on his own ground of authority.[3] In the treatise that marks his last effort to establish republican institutions, he omits unnecessary detail, being mainly concerned with fundamental principles, which, as it seems to him, are too little regarded.[4] He is scornful of information that is undigested,[5] and of effort without purpose.[6] At all times Milton shows himself a true philosopher, having power over his own activities, to take them up, in varying degrees, and again to lay them aside.

Milton's characteristic independence and breadth of view dominate his Tractate *Of Education*. He is not restricted by existing establishments and methods. From the materials at hand he selects the best, and combines them in original fashion. Though he has in mind certain 'ancient and famous schools,'[7] it is difficult to trace at any length his indebtedness to a particular example. The physical plan he proposes is that of the ideal 'Academy,'[8] but it is modified by such innovations as he saw fit to introduce.[9] In the matter of curriculum, he is specific or general, as the case may

[1] See below, pp. 89–110.
[2] See below, pp. 267–76.
  See below, pp. 185–6.
[4] See below, p. 274.
[5] See below, pp. 176–7; 190–1.
[6] See below, p. 243.
[7] See below, p. 61.
[8] See above, pp. 8–11 and 15. See also Watson, *Vives on Education*, pp. cxlviii ff.
[9] See below, p. 61.

require. The Latin grammar is to be 'that now used, or any better.' The boys are to be practised in 'some chosen short book.' 'Some easy and delightful book of education' is to be read to them. The more substantial authors, on the other hand, are selected and arranged with such care as to convince one that Milton, as he wrote, bore in mind the intellectual contribution of each. Italian, again, is to be learned 'at any odd hour,'[1] Hebrew 'at a set hour.'[2] One item of training is probably supported by the authority of half-a-dozen of the ancients;[3] another, by a lesson from current affairs.[4] The underlying principle throughout is not deference to authority, or compromise with existing conditions, but the skilful adaptation of means to a noble and definite end.

One may form a better notion of Milton's plan by contrasting it with that of his contemporary, Charles Hoole. In *A New Discovery of the Old Art of Teaching School*, this author reveals himself to us as a teacher of sound scholarship, and of rare sympathy and tact. He devoted his entire life to the work of teaching, and attained to eminence in his profession. His *New Discovery* contains a valuable record of contemporary practice, and even to-day is full of vital suggestion for the teacher.

But Hoole's vision was limited to the English grammar-school as it was, or as it might become without radical change.[5] To train the child in conduct and deportment, to instruct him in the studies preliminary to a university career[6]—such is the extent of Hoole's purpose. He refers, indeed, to 'what a child of an extraordinary towardliness, and having a teacher at home, may attain unto, and in how short a space,'[7] and to adult private

---

[1] See below, p. 58.
[2] See below, p. 59.
[3] See below, p. 62, and note.
[4] See below, p. 62, and note.
[5] Hoole, *A New Discovery*, p. 224.
[6] *Ibid.*, p. 328.
[7] *Ibid.*, p. 29.

pupils;[1] but these matters lie outside his proper field. The true aim of the schoolmaster, in his view, is to teach the learned languages, oratory, and poetry.[2] He was wary of sudden changes.[3] No such vision seems to have entered his mind as an entirely new adjustment of humanistic education to the needs of the age.

Yet nothing less than such a vision is revealed in the design of Milton. Though he is indebted to antiquity for his material,[4] his complete 'Idea' is that of an education better in all respects than any that had 'been yet in practice.'[5] Most, if not all, of the individual elements in Milton's plan are to be found, I believe, in earlier writers. What is new is the plan itself—the method of combining these elements. By virtue of his power to select and organize the methods and materials of scholarship, Milton fully represents for England, as the preceding educational reformers had partially done, the main tendencies of humanism at its best, and regenerates from its original sources an educational movement of which the importance to later civilization can hardly be overestimated.[6]

Like other humanistic educators, Milton combines classical studies with direct religious instruction.[7] This process apparently consists of two distinct parts. In fact, Milton proposes two objects or ends of education, which do not at once seem to harmonize.[8] The one is Greek, the other Hebraic. One object— the ability 'to perform justly, skilfully, and magnanimously all the offices, both private and public, of peace and war'[9]—is not greatly different from the fourfold criterion of Isocrates,[10] who

[1] Hoole, *A New Discovery*, p. 162. See below, p. 144.
[2] Hoole, *A New Discovery*, p. 227.
[3] *Ibid.*, p. 325.
[4] See below, p. 52.
[5] See below, p. 52.
[6] See J. A. Symonds, *The Renaissance in Italy* 2.9: 'What the modern world would have been, if the Italian nation had not devoted its energies to the restoration of liberal learning, cannot even be imagined.'
[7] See above, pp. 10-1.
[8] Bundy, *Milton's View of Education in Paradise Lost*, in the *Journal of English and Germanic Philology* 21 (1922). 127-8.
[9] See below, p. 55.
[10] *Panathenæcus* 239.

would call men truly educated only in so far as they possess, first, good judgment in the affairs of everyday life, secondly, true courtesy, thirdly, self-control, and finally, modesty. The Greeks looked upon education as a preparation for service to the State;[1] the cultivation of 'virtue' was indeed a part of the process, but not in quite the sense that we find in the Christian humanists. Milton's plan includes another object, without which the pagan elements, though eminently noble, seem cold and barren. This object is the inculcation of practical piety, on the authority and by the precepts of revealed Christianity. 'The end . . . of learning,' says he, 'is to repair the ruins of our first parents by regaining to know God aright'[2]—in other words, to recover the health and power of the human soul that were lost through the Fall of Man. In thus assuming that human beings are imperfect to begin with and are in need of correction, and not of encouragement in all their natural impulses, Milton is following Hebraic tradition.[3]

Yet these two educational elements supplement each other, and unite in a single consummation. We must here carefully distinguish between the intellectual apprehension of the Deity, as a result of reasoning from universal principles, and the certainty of experience that comes to the believer through faith in Christianity and habitual obedience to its moral precepts. The one is Hellenic, and is perhaps best exemplified in Plato; the other is Hebraic, and attains to its complete development in the New Testament. Having designated as the end of education the right knowledge of God, with its consequent power to regenerate the soul and invigorate the will,[4] Milton combines two methods of attaining this end.

[1] Aristotle treats of the subject in his *Politics*; Plato in the *Republic* and the *Laws*. See above, p. 2.
[2] See below, p. 52.
[3] Romans 3. 23; Psalm 14. 1–3; see also Cooper, *Two Views of Education*, pp. 267–93.
[4] See below, p. 52

One of these methods is the systematic study of Nature, including man and his achievements. 'Our understanding,' says Milton, 'cannot in this body found itself but on sensible things, nor arrive so clearly to the knowledge of God and things invisible as by orderly conning over the visible and inferior creature.'[1] The same thought is expressed in *Paradise Lost*, when Adam thus addresses the archangel Raphael:

> O favorable Spirit, propitious guest,
> Well hast thou taught the way that might direct
> Our knowledge, and the scale of Nature set
> From centre to circumference, whereon
> In contemplation of created things
> By steps we may ascend to God.[2]

One may observe an analogy between this method and that of Plato, who would lead his prospective rulers from darkness to light by the study, first, of number, the universal or primary science, of which all the other arts and sciences are partakers, and, secondly, of dialectic, the instrument that would lead men to absolute truth.[3] Plato, however, would by this study gradually withdraw the soul from the dominion of the senses;[4] Milton, with a more hopeful view of sensory experience, would lead his pupils toward the beatific vision by the 'orderly,' or progressive, study of the Creation.

Milton, indeed, believed in a definite order among created things, with regard to their nearness to the Deity.

His views, as admirably summarized by Dr. Masson, amount to this—'that all created Being, whether called soul or body, consists of but one primordial matter, a direct efflux from the very substance of the Eternal and Infinite Spirit; . . . that there are graduated varieties or sorts of this first material efflux from

---

[1] See below, p. 52.
[2] *P.L.* 5. 507–12. Verity in his edition of *Paradise Lost* (p. 496) thus condenses Richardson's note on these lines: ' "Matter" (line 472) is the "centre," and "Nature" the "scale" which reaches to the utmost of our conceptions, all round. By ascending this ladder, that is, by the study of Nature, we are led to God.'
[3] Jowett, *The Dialogues of Plato* 3. ci., 222 ff.
[4] *Ibid.* 3. 227.

Deity, all radically one, but differentiated into an ascending series of forms, from the *inorganic* as the lowest, up to the *vegetable*, thence to the *animal*, thence to the *human*, and so to the *angelic*, or nearest in nature to the Divine original.'[1]

After a survey of external nature and the humblest arts, the pupils were to advance to the study of man and his loftiest aspirations, at the end of which stage [2] the two methods of approach may be said to converge and unite; for here the 'highest matters of theology,' the consummation of the religious teaching, are to be studied in conjunction with law, or the ethics of statecraft, as recorded both in Scripture and in ancient and modern statutes.[3]

Although Plato and Milton differ in their estimation of sensory experience, yet the idea of leading the soul progressively to the contemplation of Deity is sufficiently characteristic of both to place them in the same class of educational theorists, and thus to identify the one part of Milton's scheme with Hellenic tradition. In the other method of training which Milton employed in conjunction with the study of nature, we can recognize the Hebraic element.

It is characteristic of the Scriptural writers that they do not attempt to prove the existence of God. Whereas the Greek inferred it by a process of reasoning, the Hebrew assumed it as the basis of all thought and action. Upon this assumption Milton bases the part of his educational scheme which is complementary to the study of the visible creation.

In the earlier stages he keeps the two processes quite apart from each other. The day is spent in study and exercise; in the evening, until bedtime, the minds of the pupils are to be taken up with 'the easy grounds of religion, and the story of Scripture.'[4] These exercises, one may fancy, would be most like the relaxation

[1] Milton, *Paradise Lost*, ed. by Verity, p. 494. Verity's note.
[2] Masson, *Life of Milton* 3. 247–8.
[3] See below, p. 59.
[4] See below, p. 57.

afforded by music earlier in the day.[1] In the evening, when a wholesome weariness of mind and body has relieved the spirit of the eagerness, and perhaps the impatience, of earlier hours, religious thoughts make their strongest appeal to the mind. Such instruction would not necessarily be conducted with the rigor of the more formal lessons, or be expected to produce immediate results in the way of conduct. Such results are early provided for, much after the Greek fashion, by the reading of some 'delightful book of education,' and by the diligence of the teacher in winning his pupils 'to delight in manly and liberal exercises.'[2] The religious teaching is thus kept apart from the secular until the students have entered into the 'highest matters of theology, and Church-history, ancient and modern,'[3] and have had time to master the principles of natural science, history, moral philosophy for the individual, and justice in the State. It is here that the two processes may be said to unite. The Scriptures are now made the object of rational study, and in a twofold way— both as the divine sanction of human law and justice, and as the source of the wisdom that in this life most closely approaches the vision of absolute truth. Here the cycle of earthly knowledge, so much as is necessary for the good of man,[4] is complete. At this point are introduced as models the noblest specimens of the art of expression in language—the 'choice histories, heroic poems, and Attic tragedies';[5] henceforth, though not before, the students are to be trained even in the ambitious art of original composition, since they may now be considered as possessing an insight into all excellent and commendable ideas and affairs.

The Tractate *Of Education* belongs to the noblest of educational types; and, within its type, it is distinctive. It is an organic

[1] See below, p. 61.
[2] See below, p. 56.
[3] See below, p. 59.
[4] See below, p. 321.
[5] See below, p. 59.

product of the life and career of John Milton. It is an outgrowth
of the studies that he carried on in preparation for the writing
of his great epic poem. There can be little doubt that it reflects
his own intellectual development.[1] Its ideal of private conduct
and public service is the ideal that he represented in his own
person, and celebrated in others.[2] Rightly administered by the
teacher, and faithfully accepted by the student, Milton's plan of
education will lead one toward that universal insight which the
poet himself attained.

[1] See below, pp. 65–89.
[2] See below, pp. 121–9; 227–44.

OF EDUCATION

OF EDUCATION
To Master Samuel Hartlib

Mr. Hartlib: I am long since persuaded that to say or do aught worth memory and imitation, no purpose or respect should sooner move us than simply the love of God and of mankind. Nevertheless to write now the reforming of education, though it be one of the greatest and noblest designs that can be thought on, and for the want whereof this nation perishes, I had not yet at this time been induced but by your earnest entreaties and serious conjurements; as having my mind for the present half-diverted in the pursuance of some other assertions, the knowledge and the use of which cannot but be a great furtherance both to the enlargement of truth and honest living, with much more peace. Nor should the laws of any private friendship have prevailed with me to divide thus or transpose my former thoughts, but that I see those aims, those actions, which have won you with me the esteem of a person sent hither by some good providence from a far country to be the occasion and the incitement of great good to this island.

And, as I hear, you have obtained the same repute with men of most approved wisdom, and some of highest authority among us; not to mention the learned correspondence which you hold in foreign parts, and the extraordinary pains and diligence which you have used in this matter, both here and beyond the seas; either by the definite will of God so ruling, or the peculiar sway of nature, which also is God's working. Neither can I think that, so reputed and so valued as you are, you would, to the forfeit of your own discerning ability, impose upon me an unfit and over-ponderous argument; but that the satisfaction which you profess to have received from those incidental discourses which we have wandered into hath pressed and almost constrained you into a persuasion that what you require from me in this point I neither ought, nor can in conscience, defer beyond this time, both of so much need at once and so much opportunity, to try what God hath determined.

I will not resist, therefore, whatever it is either of divine or human obligement that you lay upon me; but will forthwith set down in writing, as you request me, that voluntary idea, which hath long in silence presented itself to me, of a better education, in extent and comprehension far more large, and yet of time far shorter and of attainment far more certain, than hath been yet in practice. Brief I shall endeavor to be; for that which I have to say, assuredly this nation hath extreme need should be done sooner than spoken. To tell you, therefore, what I have benefited herein among old renowned authors, I shall spare; and to search what many modern *Januas* and *Didactics*, more than ever I shall read, have projected, my inclination leads me not. But if you can accept of these few observations which have flowered off, and are as it were the burnishing of many studious and contemplative years altogether spent in the search of religious and civil knowledge, and such as pleased you so well in the re-lating, I here give you them to dispose of.

The end, then, of learning is to repair the ruins of our first parents by regaining to know God aright, and out of that knowledge to love Him, to imitate Him, to be like Him, as we may the nearest by possessing our souls of true virtue, which, being united to the heavenly grace of faith, makes up the highest perfection. But because our understanding cannot in this body found itself but on sensible things, nor arrive so clearly to the knowledge of God and things invisible as by orderly conning over the visible and inferior creature, the same method is neces-sarily to be followed in all discreet teaching. And seeing every nation affords not experience and tradition enough for all kind of learning, therefore we are chiefly taught the languages of those people who have at any time been most industrious after wisdom;

so that language is but the instrument conveying to us things useful to be known. And though a linguist should pride himself to have all the tongues that Babel cleft the world into, yet, if he have not studied the solid things in them as well as the words and lexicons, he were nothing so much to be esteemed a learned man as any yeoman or tradesman competently wise in his mother-dialect only.

Hence appear the many mistakes which have made learning generally so unpleasing and so unsuccessful. First, we do amiss to spend seven or eight years merely in scraping together so much miserable Latin and Greek as might be learned otherwise easily and delightfully in one year. And that which casts our proficiency therein so much behind is our time lost, partly in too oft idle vacancies given both to schools and universities, partly in a preposterous exaction, forcing the empty wits of children to compose themes, verses, and orations, which are the acts of ripest judgment, and the final work of a head filled, by long reading and observing, with elegant maxims and copious invention. These are not matters to be wrung from poor striplings, like blood out of the nose, or the plucking of untimely fruit; besides the ill habit which they get of wretched barbarizing against the Latin and Greek idiom with their untutored Anglicisms, odious to be read, yet not to be avoided without a well-continued and judicious conversing among pure authors digested, which they scarce taste. Whereas, if, after some preparatory grounds of speech, by their certain forms got into memory, they were led to the praxis thereof in some chosen short book lessoned throughly to them, they might then forthwith proceed to learn the substance of good things and arts in due order, which would bring the whole language quickly into their power. This I take to be the most rational and most profitable way of learning languages, and whereby we may best hope to give account to God of our youth spent herein.

53

And for the usual method of teaching arts, I deem it to be an old error of universities not yet well recovered from the scholastic grossness of barbarous ages, that instead of beginning with arts most easy (and those be such as are most obvious to the sense) they present their young unmatriculated novices, at first coming, with the most intellective abstractions of logic and metaphysics. So that they, having but newly left those grammatic flats and shallows where they stuck unreasonably to learn a few words with lamentable construction, and now on the sudden transported under another climate, to be tossed and turmoiled with their unballasted wits in fathomless and unquiet deeps of controversy, do for the most part grow into hatred and contempt of learning, mocked and deluded all this while with ragged notions and babblements, while they expected worthy and delightful knowledge; till poverty or youthful years call them importunately their several ways, and hasten them, with the sway of friends, either to an ambitious and mercenary, or ignorantly zealous, divinity. Some, allured to the trade of law, grounding their purposes, not on the prudent and heavenly contemplation of justice and equity (which was never taught them), but on the promising and pleasing thoughts of litigious terms, fat contentions, and flowing fees—others betake them to State-affairs, with souls so unprincipled in virtue and true generous breeding that flattery, and Court-shifts, and tyrannous aphorisms appear to them the highest points of wisdom; instilling their barren hearts with a conscientious slavery—if, as I rather think, it be not feigned. Others, lastly, of a more delicious and airy spirit, retire themselves (knowing no better) to the enjoyments of ease and luxury, living out their days in feast and jollity; which indeed is the wisest and the safest course of all these, unless they were with more integrity undertaken. And these are the errors, and these are the fruits, of misspending our prime youth at the schools and universities as we do, either in learning mere words, or such things chiefly as were better unlearned.

OF EDUCATION

I shall detain you no longer in the demonstration of what we should not do, but straight conduct you to a hill-side, where I will point you out the right path of a virtuous and noble education; laborious indeed at the first ascent, but else so smooth, so green, so full of goodly prospect and melodious sounds on every side, that the harp of Orpheus was not more charming. I doubt not but ye shall have more ado to drive our dullest and laziest youth, our stocks and stubs, from the infinite desire of such a happy nurture than we have now to hale and drag our choicest and hopefullest wits to that asinine feast of sow-thistles and brambles which is commonly set before them as all the food and entertainment of their tenderest and most docible age. I call therefore a complete and generous education that which fits a man to perform justly, skilfully, and magnanimously all the offices, both private and public, of peace and war. And how all this may be done between twelve and one-and-twenty, less time than is now bestowed in pure trifling at grammar and sophistry, is to be thus ordered.

First, to find out a spacious house and ground about it fit for an academy, and big enough to lodge a hundred and fifty persons, whereof twenty or thereabout may be attendants; all under the government of one, who shall be thought of desert sufficient, and ability, either to do all, or wisely to direct and oversee it done. This place should be at once both school and university, not needing a remove to any other house of scholarship, except it be some peculiar college of law or physic, where they mean to be practitioners. But as for those general studies which take up all our time from Lily to the commencing, as they term it, Master of Art, it should be absolute. After this pattern, as many edifices may be converted to this use as shall be needful, in every city throughout this land, which would tend much to the increase of learning and civility everywhere. This number, less or more, thus collected to the convenience of a foot-company, or interchangeably two troops of cavalry, should divide their day's work into three parts, as it lies orderly: their studies, their exercise, and their diet.

For their studies: First, they should begin with the chief and necessary rules of some good Grammar, either that now used, or any better; and, while this is doing, their speech is to be fashioned to a distinct and clear pronunciation, as near as may be to the Italian, especially in the vowels; for we Englishmen, being far northerly, do not open our mouths in the cold air wide enough to grace a southern tongue, but are observed by all other nations to speak exceeding close and inward; so that to smatter Latin with an English mouth is as ill a hearing as law-French. Next, to make them expert in the usefullest points of grammar, and withal to season them, and win them early to the love of virtue and true labor ere any flattering seducement or vain principle seize them wandering, some easy and delightful book of education would be read to them; whereof the Greeks have store, as Cebes, Plutarch, and other Socratic discourses; but in Latin we have none of classic authority extant, except the two or three first books of Quintilian and some select pieces elsewhere.

But here the main skill and groundwork will be to temper them such lectures and explanations upon every opportunity as may lead and draw them in willing obedience; inflamed with the study of learning and the admiration of virtue; stirred up with high hopes of living to be brave men and worthy patriots, dear to God and famous to all ages; that they may despise and scorn all their childish and ill-taught qualities, to delight in manly and liberal exercises—which he who hath the art and proper eloquence to catch them with, what with mild and effectual persuasions, and what with the intimation of some fear, if need be, but chiefly by his own example, might in a short space gain them to an incredible diligence and courage, infusing into their young breasts such an ingenuous and noble ardor as would not fail to make many of them renowned and matchless men. At the same time (some other hour of the day) might be taught them the rules of arithmetic, and, soon after, the elements of geometry, even playing, as the old manner was. After evening repast, till bedtime, their thoughts will be best taken up in the easy grounds of religion, and the story of Scripture.

The next step would be to the authors of agriculture—Cato, Varro, and Columella; for the matter is most easy, and, if the language be difficult, so much the better—it is not a difficulty above their years. And here will be an occasion of inciting and enabling them hereafter to improve the tillage of their country, to recover the bad soil, and to remedy the waste that is made of good; for this was one of Hercules' praises. Ere half these authors be read (which will soon be, with plying hard and daily), they cannot choose but be masters of any ordinary prose. So that it will be then seasonable for them to learn in any modern author the use of the globes and all the maps; first with the old names, and then with the new. Or they might be then capable to read any compendious method of natural philosophy; and at the same time might be entering into the Greek tongue, after the same manner as was before prescribed in the Latin. Whereby, the difficulties of grammar being soon overcome, all the historical physiology of Aristotle and Theophrastus are open before them, and, as I may say, under contribution. The like access will be to Vitruvius, to Seneca's *Natural Questions*, to Mela, Celsus, Pliny, or Solinus. And, having thus passed the principles of arithmetic, geometry, astronomy, and geography, with a general compact of physics, they may descend in mathematics to the instrumental science of trigonometry, and from thence to fortification, architecture, enginery, or navigation. And in natural philosophy they may proceed leisurely from the history of meteors, minerals, plants, and living creatures, as far as anatomy.

Then also in course might be read to them, out of some not tedious writer, the institution of physic, that they may know the tempers, the humors, the seasons, and how to manage a crudity;

which he who can wisely and timely do is not only a great physician to himself and to his friends, but also may at some time or other save an army by this frugal and expenseless means only; and not let the healthy and stout bodies of young men rot away under him for want of this discipline—which is a great pity, and no less a shame to the commander. To set forward all these proceedings in nature and mathematics, what hinders but that they may procure, as oft as shall be needful, the helpful experiences of hunters, fowlers, fishermen, shepherds, gardeners, apothecaries; and, in the other sciences, architects, engineers, mariners, anatomists, who doubtless would be ready, some for reward, and some to favor such a hopeful seminary? And this will give them such a real tincture of natural knowledge as they shall never forget, but daily augment with delight. Then also those poets which are now counted most hard will be both facile and pleasant: Orpheus, Hesiod, Theocritus, Aratus, Nicander, Oppian, Dionysius; and, in Latin, Lucretius, Manilius, and the rural part of Virgil.

By this time, years and good general precepts will have furnished them more distinctly with that act of reason which in ethics is called *proairesis*; that they may with some judgment contemplate upon moral good and evil. Then will be required a special reinforcement of constant and sound indoctrinating to set them right and firm, instructing them more amply in the knowledge of virtue and the hatred of vice; while their young and pliant affections are led through all the moral works of Plato, Xenophon, Cicero, Plutarch, Laertius, and those Locrian remnants; but still to be reduced in their nightward studies wherewith they close the day's work, under the determinate sentence of David or Solomon, or the Evangels and Apostolic Scriptures. Being perfect in the knowledge of personal duty, they may then begin the study of economics. And either now, or before this, they may have easily learned at any odd hour the Italian tongue. And soon after, but with wariness and good antidote, it would be wholesome enough to let them taste some choice comedies,

Greek, Latin, or Italian; those tragedies also that treat of household matters, as *Trachiniæ*, *Alcestis*, and the like.

The next remove must be to the study of politics; to know the beginning, end, and reasons of political societies, that they may not, in a dangerous fit of the Commonwealth, be such poor, shaken, uncertain reeds, of such a tottering conscience, as many of our great councilors have lately shown themselves, but steadfast pillars of the State. After this, they are to dive into the grounds of law and legal justice; delivered first and with best warrant by Moses; and as far as human prudence can be trusted, in those extolled remains of Grecian lawgivers, Lycurgus, Solon, Zaleucus, Charondas, and thence to all the Roman edicts and Tables with their Justinian; and so down to the Saxon and common laws of England, and the Statutes.

Sundays also and every evening may be now understandingly spent in the highest matters of theology, and Church-history ancient and modern. And ere this time the Hebrew tongue at a set hour might have been gained, that the Scriptures may be now read in their own original; whereto it would be no impossibility to add the Chaldee and the Syrian dialect. When all these employments are well conquered, then will the choice histories, heroic poems, and Attic tragedies of stateliest and most regal argument, with all the famous political orations, offer themselves; which if they were not only read, but some of them got by memory, and solemnly pronounced with right accent and grace, as might be taught, would endue them even with the spirit and vigor of Demosthenes or Cicero, Euripides or Sophocles.

And now, lastly, will be the time to read with them those organic arts which enable men to discourse and write perspicuously, elegantly, and according to the fitted style of lofty, mean, or lowly. Logic, therefore, so much as is useful, is to be referred to this due place, with all her well-couched heads and topics, until it be time to open her contracted palm into a graceful and ornate rhetoric taught out of the rule of Plato, Aristotle,

Phalereus, Cicero, Hermogenes, Longinus. To which poetry would be made subsequent, or, indeed, rather precedent, as being less subtile and fine, but more simple, sensuous, and passionate. I mean not here the prosody of a verse, which they could not but have hit on before among the rudiments of grammar; but that sublime art which in Aristotle's *Poetics*, in Horace, and the Italian commentaries of Castelvetro, Tasso, Mazzoni, and others, teaches what the laws are of a true epic poem, what of a dramatic, what of a lyric, what decorum is—which is the grand masterpiece to observe. This would make them soon perceive what despicable creatures our common rimers and playwriters be, and show them what religious, what glorious and magnificent, use might be made of poetry both in divine and human things.

From hence, and not till now, will be the right season of forming them to be able writers and composers in every excellent matter, when they shall be thus fraught with an universal insight into things. Or whether they be to speak in Parliament or council, honor and attention would be waiting on their lips. There would then also appear in pulpits other visages, other gestures, and stuff otherwise wrought than what we now sit under, oft-times to as great a trial of our patience as any other that they preach to us. These are the studies wherein our noble and our gentle youth ought to bestow their time in a disciplinary way from twelve to one-and-twenty; unless they rely more upon their ancestors dead than upon themselves living. In which methodical course, it is so supposed they must proceed by the steady pace of learning onward, as at convenient times for memory's sake to retire back into the middle-ward, and sometimes into the rear of what they have been taught, until they have confirmed and solidly united the whole body of their perfected knowledge, like the last embattling of a Roman legion.

Now will be worth the seeing what exercises and recreations may best agree, and become these studies.

The course of study hitherto briefly described is, what I can guess by reading, likest to those ancient and famous schools of Pythagoras, Plato, Isocrates, Aristotle, and such others, out of which were bred up such a number of renowned philosophers, orators, historians, poets, and princes, all over Greece, Italy, and Asia, besides the flourishing studies of Cyrene and Alexandria. But herein it shall exceed them, and supply a defect as great as that which Plato noted in the commonwealth of Sparta: whereas that city trained up their youth most for war, and these, in their Academies and Lyceum, all for the gown, this institution of breeding which I here delineate shall be equally good both for peace and war. Therefore, about an hour-and-a-half ere they eat at noon should be allowed them for exercise and due rest afterwards; but the time for this may be enlarged at pleasure, according as their rising in the morning shall be early.

The exercise which I commend first is the exact use of their weapon, to guard, and to strike safely with edge or point. This will keep them healthy, nimble, strong, and well in breath—is also the likeliest means to make them grow large and tall, and to inspire them with a gallant and fearless courage; which, being tempered with seasonable lectures and precepts to them of true fortitude and patience, will turn into a native and heroic valor, and make them hate the cowardice of doing wrong. They must be also practised in all the locks and grips of wrestling, wherein Englishmen were wont to excel, as need may often be in fight to tug or grapple and to close. And this, perhaps, will be enough wherein to prove and heat their single strength.

The interim of unsweating themselves regularly, and convenient rest before meat, may both with profit and delight be taken up in recreating and composing their travailed spirits with the solemn and divine harmonies of music, heard or learned; either while the skilful organist plies his grave and fancied descant in lofty fugues, or the whole symphony, with artful and unimaginable touches, adorn and grace the well-studied chords

61

of some choice composer; sometimes the lute, or soft organ-stop, waiting on elegant voices, either to religious, martial, or civil ditties; which, if wise men and prophets be not extremely out, have a great power over dispositions and manners, to smooth and make them gentle from rustic harshness and distempered passions. The like also would not be unexpedient after meat, to assist and cherish nature in her first concoction, and send their minds back to study in good tune and satisfaction. Where having followed it close under vigilant eyes till about two hours before supper, they are, by a sudden alarum or watchword, to be called out to their military motions, under sky or covert, according to the season, as was the Roman wont; first on foot, then, as their age permits, on horseback, to all the art of cavalry; that having in sport, but with much exactness and daily muster, served out the rudiments of their soldiership in all the skill of embattling, marching, encamping, fortifying, besieging, and battering, with all the helps of ancient and modern stratagems, tactics, and war-like maxims, they may, as it were out of a long war, come forth renowned and perfect commanders in the service of their country. They would not then, if they were trusted with fair and hopeful armies, suffer them for want of just and wise discipline to shed away from about them like sick feathers, though they be never so oft supplied. They would not suffer their empty and unrecruitable colonels of twenty men in a company to quaff out, or convey into secret hoards, the wages of a delusive list and a miserable remnant; yet in the mean while to be overmastered with a score or two of drunkards, the only soldiery left about them, or else to comply with all rapines and violences. No, certainly; if they knew aught of that knowledge that belongs to good men or good governors, they would not suffer these things.

But to return to our own institute. Besides these constant exercises at home, there is another opportunity of gaining experience, to be won from pleasure itself abroad. In those vernal seasons of the year, when the air is calm and pleasant, it were an injury and sullenness against nature not to go out and see her riches, and partake in her rejoicing with heaven and earth. I should not therefore be a persuader to them of studying much then, after two or three year that they have well laid their grounds, but to ride out in companies, with prudent and staid guides, to all the quarters of the land; learning and observing all places of strength, all commodities of building and of soil, for towns and tillage, harbors and ports for trade; sometimes taking sea as far as to our navy, to learn there also what they can in the practical knowledge of sailing and of sea-fight. These ways would try all their peculiar gifts of nature, and, if there were any secret excellence among them, would fetch it out and give it fair opportunities to advance itself by; which could not but mightily redound to the good of this nation, and bring into fashion again those old admired virtues and excellencies, with far more advantage now in this purity of Christian knowledge. Nor shall we then need the *Monsieurs* of Paris to take our hopeful youth into their slight and prodigal custodies, and send them over back again transformed into mimics, apes, and kickshaws. But if they desire to see other countries at three- or four-and-twenty years of age, not to learn principles, but to enlarge experience and make wise observation, they will by that time be such as shall deserve the regard and honor of all men where they pass, and the society and friendship of those in all places who are best and most eminent. And perhaps, then, other nations will be glad to visit us for their breeding, or else to imitate us in their own country.

Now, lastly, for their diet, there cannot be much to say, save only that it would be best in the same house; for much time else would be lost abroad, and many ill habits got. And that it should be plain, healthful, and moderate, I suppose is out of controversy. Thus, Mr. Hartlib, you have a general view in writing, as your desire was, of that which at several times I had discoursed with you concerning the best and noblest way of education; not beginning, as some have done, from the cradle, which yet might be worth many considerations, if brevity had not been my scope. Many other circumstances also I could have mentioned; but this, to such as have the worth in them to make trial, for light and direction may be enough. Only I believe that this is not a bow for every man to shoot in that counts himself a teacher, but will require sinews almost equal to those which Homer gave Ulysses; yet I am withal persuaded that it may prove much more easy in the assay than it now seems at distance, and much more illustrious—howbeit not more difficult than I imagine; and that imagination presents me with nothing but very happy and very possible according to best wishes, if God have so decreed, and this age have spirit and capacity enough to apprehend.

SUPPLEMENTARY EXTRACTS FROM OTHER WRITINGS OF MILTON

SUPPLEMENTARY EXTRACTS FROM OTHER WRITINGS OF MILTON

1. MILTON'S PERSONAL INTEREST IN STUDY AND HIS PREPARATION FOR WRITING [1]

FROM MILTON'S WRITINGS DURING HIS EARLY STUDIES —1625–1639[2]

From *Academic Exercise* 3. Against the Scholastic Philosophy. [3]

['This . . . is an oration of about half-an-hour before an audience in the Public Schools. . . . After a modest introduction, in which Cicero's observation is quoted, that a good speech ought at once to instruct, delight, and actively influence, the orator proceeds:']

I shall produce abundant active effect at present if I can induce you, my auditors, to turn over seldomer those huge and almost monstrous volumes of the subtle doctors, as they are called, and to indulge a little less in the warty controversies of the sophists.

['He undertakes to show that scholastic studies are neither pleasant nor fruitful. Under the first head he says:']

Often, my hearers, when there chanced to be imposed upon me now and then the necessity of investigating these subtle triviali-ties, after blunting both my mind and my eyesight with a day's reading—often, I say, I have stopped to take breath, and there-upon, measuring the task with my eyes, I have sought a wretched

---

[1] Although Milton did not, like Wordsworth in the *Prelude*, compose a unified history of his spiritual development, few great writers have left us a fuller account of their intellectual tastes, ambitions, and labors. The personal references in Milton's works are of inestimable aid in understanding his poetry. They naturally fall into three groups, generally corresponding to the three main periods of his life—his early studies and poetic aspirations, his political service, and, finally, his most important creative work.

[2] Among the earliest records of Milton's interest in study are his academic exercises. Like many other students of his time, he objects to the scholastic philos-ophy, preferring natural science, history, and literature.

[3] Translated and interpolated by Masson.

65

relief from my fatigue; but, as I always saw more remaining than
I had got through in my reading, I have wished again and again
that, instead of these enforced vanities, there had been assigned
me the task of a recleansing of the Augean cow-house, and have
called Hercules a happy fellow, to whom Juno in her good nature
had never commanded the endurance of this kind of toil. Nor is
this nerveless, languid, and earthy matter elevated or dignified
by any beauty of style. . . . I think there never can have
been any place for these studies on Parnassus, unless perhaps some
uncultivated nook at the foot of the hill, unlovely, rough and
horrid with brambles and thorns, overgrown with thistles and
thick nettles, far-removed from the dance and company of the
goddesses, producing neither laurel nor flowers, and never reached
by the sound of Apollo's lyre.

['Poetry, oratory, and history, he says, are all delightful, each
in its own way; but this scholastic philosophy does nothing but
irritate. He then passes to the second argument against it, that
from its inutility:']

By these two things in chief have I perceived a country to be
advanced and adorned: either noble speaking or brave action.
But this litigious battling of discordant opinions seems unable
either to qualify for eloquence, or to instruct in prudence, or to
incite to brave deeds. . . .

How much better would it be, Academicians, and how much
more worthy of your reputation, to walk as it were with the eyes
over the universe of earth as it is portrayed in the map, to see
places trodden by the ancient heroes, to traverse regions ennobled by wars, triumphs, and even the fables of illustrious poets
—now to cross the stormy Adriatic, now to approach safely the
flame-emitting Ætna; furthermore, to observe the manners of
men and the fairly-ordered states in which nations have arranged
themselves, and then to investigate and study the natures of all
living things, and from these again to direct the mind downward
to the secret virtues of stones and plants! Nor hesitate, my hearers,

even to soar into the heavens, and there contemplate the multiform shows of the clouds, and the collected power of the snow, and whence those morning tears, and then look into the coffers of the hail, and survey the magazines of the lightnings; nor let there be hidden from you what either Jupiter or Nature means when a dreadful and vast comet menaces the heaven with conflagration; nor let even the minutest little stars, in all their number, as they are scattered between the two poles, escape your notice; nay, follow the wandering sun as his companions, and call time itself to a reckoning, and demand an account of its eternal march. But let not your mind suffer itself to be contained and circumscribed within the same limits as the world, but let it stray even beyond the boundaries of the universe; and let it finally learn (which is yet the highest matter) to know itself, and at the same time those holy minds and intelligences with whom hereafter it is to enter into everlasting companionship. But why too much of this? Let your master in all this be that very same Aristotle who is so much delighted in, and who has left almost all these things scientifically and exquisitely written for our learning.[1]

From *Academic Exercise* 7. Art is more Conducive to Human Happiness than Ignorance.[2]

Although nothing is more agreeable and desirable to me, my hearers, than the sight of you, and the crowded attendance of gentlemen in gowns, and also this honorable office of speaking, which on more occasions than one I have with no unpleasant pains discharged among you, yet, to confess the actual truth, it always so happens that, though neither my genius nor the nature of my studies is at all out of keeping with the oratorical office, nevertheless I scarcely ever come to speak of my own free will and choice. Had it been in my power, I should not unwillingly have spared myself even this evening's labor; for, as I have learned

[1] Masson, *Life of Milton* I. 281–2. Reprinted by permission of The Macmillan Company, New York; Macmillan & Company, Ltd., London.
[2] Translated and interpolated by Masson.

from books and from the deliverances of the most learned men, that no more in the orator than in the poet can anything common or mediocre be tolerated, and that whoever would truly be and be reputed an orator must be instructed and finished with a certain circular subsidy of all the arts and of all science, so, my age not permitting this, I would rather be working with severe study for that true reputation by the preliminary acquisition of that subsidy than prematurely snatching a false reputation by a forced and precocious style. In such meditation and purpose daily chafed and kindled more and more, I have never experienced any hindrance and delay more grievous than this frequent mischief of interruption, and nothing more nutritive to my genius and conservative of its good health, as contradistinguished from that of the body, than a learned and liberal leisure. This I would fain believe to be the divine sleep of Hesiod; these to be Endymion's nightly meetings with the Moon; this to be that retirement of Prometheus, under the guidance of Mercury, to the steepest solitudes of Mount Caucasus, where he became the wisest of gods and men, so that even Jupiter himself is said to have gone to consult him about the marriage of Thetis. I call to witness for myself the groves and rivers, and the beloved village-elms under which in the last past summer (if it is right to speak the secrets of goddesses) I remember with such pleasure the supreme delight I had with the Muses; where I too, amid rural scenes and sequestered glades, seemed as if I could have vegetated through a hidden eternity. Here also I should have hoped for the same large liberty of retirement, had not this troublesome business of speech-making quite unseasonably interposed itself; which so disagreeably dispelled my sacred dreams, so wrenched my mind from other matters on which it was fixed, and proved such an impediment and burden among the precipitous difficulties of the arts, that losing all hope of continued repose, I began sorrowfully to think how far off I was from the tranquillity which letters first promised me—to think that life would be painful amid these heats and tossings, and that it would be better even to have parted with recollection of the arts altogether. And so, scarce master of myself, I undertook the rash design of appearing as the eulogist of an Ignorance that should have none of these inflictions to disturb her, and proposed accordingly for debate the question which of the two made her votaries happier, Art or Ignorance? But, what it is I know not, either fate or my genius has willed that I should not desert from my once begun love of the Muses; nay, blind Chance herself, as if suddenly become prudent and provident, seems to have set herself against the same result. Sooner than I could have anticipated, Ignorance has found her own advocate, and Knowledge is left to be defended by me. . . .

I regard it, my hearers, as known and accepted by all that the great Maker of the Universe, when He had constituted all things else fleeting and corruptible, did mingle up with Man, in addition to that of him which is mortal, a certain divine breath, as it were part of Himself, immortal, indestructible, free from death and extinction, which, after it had sojourned purely and holily for some time in the earth as a heavenly guest, should flutter aloft to its native Heaven, and return to its proper home and fatherland: accordingly, that nothing can deservedly be taken into account as among the causes of our happiness that does not somehow or other regard both that everlasting life and this civil life below. . . .

That many very learned men have been of bad character, slaves to anger, hatred, and evil lusts, and that, on the other hand, many men ignorant of letters have proved themselves good and excellent—what of that? Is Ignorance the more blessed state? By no means. . . . Where no arts flourish, where all learning is exterminated, there is no trace of a good man, but cruelty and horrid barbarism stalk abroad. I call as witness to this fact not one state, or province, or race, but Europe, the fourth part of the globe, over the whole of which during some bygone centuries all good arts had perished. The presiding Muses had then long left all the universities; blind inertness had invaded and occupied all things; nothing was heard in the schools except the impertinent dogmas of stupid monks; the profane and formless monster, Ignorance, having forsooth obtained a gown, capered boastingly through our empty reading-desks and pulpits, and through our squalid cathedrals. Then piety languished, and religion was extinguished and went to wreck, so that only of late, and scarce even at this day, has there been a recovery from the heavy wound. But truly, my hearers, it is sufficiently agreed upon, as an old maxim in philosophy, that the cognizance of every art and every science belongs only to the intellect, but that the home and abode of the virtues and of goodness is the will. Since, however, in the judgment of all, the human intellect shines eminent as chief and ruler over the other faculties of the mind, so it is this clearness of the intellect that tempers and illuminates the will itself, otherwise blind and dark—the will, like the moon, then shining with borrowed light. Wherefore, though we concede and grant most willingly that virtue without knowledge is better for a happy life than knowledge without virtue, yet, when once they have been mutually consociated in a happy union—as they generally ought to be, and as very often happens— then straightway Science appears and shines forth in her high superiority, with countenance erect and lofty, placing herself on high with king and emperor Intellect, and thence regarding as humble and low under foot whatever is done in the Will. . . .

The greatest share of civil happiness generally consists in human society and the formation of friendships. Now, many complain that the majority of those who pass for learned men are harsh, uncourteous, of ill-ordered manners, with no graciousness of speech for the conciliation of the minds of their fellows. I admit, indeed, that one who is almost wholly secluded and immersed in studies is readier to address the gods than men— whether because he is generally at home with the gods, but a stranger and pilgrim in human affairs, or because the mind, en-

larged by the constant contemplation of divine things, and so
wriggling with difficulty in the straits of the body, is less expert
than it might otherwise be in the nicer gestures of social saluta-
tion. But if worthy and suitable friendships are formed by such
a person, no one cherishes them more sacredly; for what can be
imagined pleasanter or happier than those colloquies of learned
and grave men, such as the divine Plato is said to have often and
often held under his plane-tree—colloquies worthy to have been
listened to with attentive silence by the whole human race together? But to talk together stupidly, to humor one another in
luxury and lusts—what is this but the friendship of ignorance,
or rather the ignorance of friendship?

Moreover, if civil happiness consists in the honorable and
liberal delectation of the mind, there is a pleasure in Learning and
Art which easily surpasses all pleasures besides. What a thing it
is to have compassed the whole humor of heaven and its stars;
all the motions and vicissitudes of the air, whether it terrifies
untaught minds by the august sound of its thunders, or by the
blazing hair of its comets, or whether it stiffens into snow and
hail, or whether it descends soft and placid in rain and dew; then
to have thoroughly learnt the alternating winds, and all the
exhalations or vapors which earth or sea gives forth; thereafter
to have become skilled in the secret forces of plants and metals,
and understanding in the nature and, if possible, the sensations,
of animals; further, to have studied the exact structure and medicine of the human body, and finally the divine *vis* and vigor of
the mind, and whether any knowledge reaches us of what are
called guardian spirits and genii and demons! There is an infini-
tude of things besides, a good part of which might be learnt before I could have enumerated them all. So, at length, my hearers,
when once universal learning has finished its circles, the soul, not
content with this darksome prison-house, will reach out far and
wide till it shall have filled the world itself, and space beyond
that, in the divine expatiation of its magnitude. . . . And

what additional pleasure it is to the mind to wing its way through all the histories and local sites of nations, and to turn to the account of prudence and of morals the conditions and mutations of kingdoms, states, cities, and peoples! This is nothing less, my hearers, than to be present as if living in every age, and have been born as it were coeval with Time herself; verily, while for the glory of our name we look forward into the future, this will be to extend and outstretch life backward from the womb, and to extort from unwilling fate a certain foregone immortality.

I omit that with which what can be counted equivalent? To be the oracle of many nations; to have one's house a kind of temple; to be such as kings and commonwealths invite to come to them, such as neighbors and foreigners flock to visit, such as to have even once seen shall be boasted of by others as something meritorious: these are the rewards, these the fruits, which learning both can and often does secure for her votaries in private life. But what in public life? It is true the reputation of learning has elevated few, nor has the reputation of goodness elevated many more, to the summit of actual majesty. And no wonder. Those men enjoy a kingdom in themselves, far more glorious than all dominion over realms; and who, without incurring the obloquy of ambition, affects a double sovereignty? I will add this more, however, that there have been but two men yet who have held in their possession as a gift from Heaven the universal globe, and shared, over all kings and dynasts, an empire equal to that of the gods themselves—to wit, Alexander the Great and Octavius Cæsar, both of them pupils of philosophy. It is as if a kind of model of election had been divinely exhibited to men, showing them to what sort of man, above all, the baton and reins of affairs ought to be entrusted. . . .

If, by living modestly and temperately, we choose rather to tame the first impulses of fierce youth by reason and persevering constancy in study, preserving the heavenly vigor of the mind pure and untouched from all contagion and stain, it would be

72

incredible, my hearers, to us, looking back after a few years, what a space we should seem to have traversed, what a huge sea of learning to have over-navigated with placid voyage. To which, however, this will be an important help—that one shall know the arts that are useful, and how rightly to select what is useful in the arts. How many despicable trifles there are, in the first place, among grammarians and rhetoricians! You may hear some talking like barbarians, and others like infants, in teaching their own art. What is logic? The queen, truly, of arts, if treated according to her worth. But alas! what madness there is in reason. Here it is not men that live, but only finches feeding on thistles and thorns. *O dura messorum ilia!* Why should I repeat that the art which the Peripatetics call metaphysics is not, as the authority of great men would have me believe, an extremely rich art— is not, I say, for the most part, an art at all, but an infamous tract of rocks, a kind of Lerna of sophisms, invented to cause shipwrecks and breed pestilence? . . . When all those things which can be of no profit have been deservedly contemned and cut off, it will be a matter of wonder how many whole years we shall save. . . . If from boyhood we allow no day to pass without its lessons and diligent study, if in art we wisely omit what is foreign, superfluous, useless, then certainly, within the age of Alexander the Great, we shall have made a greater and more glorious conquest than that of the globe, and so far shall we be from accusing the brevity of life or the fatigue of knowledge that I believe we shall be readier, like him of old, to weep and sob that there remain no more worlds for us to conquer.

['One last argument. . .Ignorance may still plead on her side. It is this:']

That, whereas a long series and onward course of years has celebrated the illustrious men of antiquity, we, on the other hand, are under a disadvantage by reason of the decrepit old age of the world and the fast approaching crash of all things; that, should we leave anything deserving to be spoken of with eternal praise, yet our name has but a narrow limit of time to have dealings with, inasmuch as there will be scarcely any posterity to inherit the memory of it; that already it is in vain that so many books and excellent monuments of genius are being produced, when that last fire of the world is so near that will burn them all in its conflagration. . . .

I do not deny that this may be likely; what I say is that the very habit of not hankering after glory when one has done well is itself above all glory. What a nothing has been the happiness conferred on those very heroes of the past by the empty speech of men, since no pleasure from it, no sense of it at all, could reach the absent and the dead! Let us expect an eternal life, in which at least the memory of our good deeds on earth shall never perish; in which, if we have done anything fairly here, we shall be present ourselves to hear of it; in which, as many have seriously speculated, those who have formerly, in a virtuously spent life on earth, given all their time to good acts, and by them been helpful to the human race, shall be aggrandized with singular and supreme science above all the rest of the immortals.[1]

From *At a Vacation Exercise.*

> Hail, native language! that by sinews weak
> Didst move my first endeavoring tongue to speak,
> And mad'st imperfect words with childish trips,
> Half-unpronounced, slide through my infant lips,
> Driving dumb silence from the portal door
> Where he had mutely sate two years before.
> Here I salute thee and thy pardon ask,
> That now I use thee in my latter task. . . .
> I pray thee, then, deny me not thy aid
> For this same small neglect that I have made;
> But haste thee straight to do me once a pleasure,
> And from thy wardrobe bring thy chiefest treasure—
> Not those newfangled toys, and trimming slight,

[1] Masson, *Life of Milton* 1. 297-302. Reprinted by permission of The Macmillan Company, New York; Macmillan & Company, Ltd., London.

Which takes our late fantastics with delight.
But cull those richest robes and gay'st attire
Which deepest spirits and choicest wits desire.
I have some naked thoughts that rove about,
And loudly knock to have their passage out,
And weary of their place, do only stay
Till thou hast decked them in thy best array;
That so they may, without suspect or fears,
Fly swiftly to this fair assembly's ears.
Yet I had rather, if I were to choose,
Thy service in some graver subject use,
Such as may make thee search thy coffers round,
Before thou clothe my fancy in fit sound;
Such where the deep transported mind may soar
Above the wheeling poles, and at Heaven's door
Look in, and see each blissful deity
How he before the thunderous throne doth lie,
Listening to what unshorn Apollo sings
To the touch of golden wires, while Hebe brings
Immortal nectar to her kingly sire;
Then, passing through the spheres of watchful fire,
And misty regions of wide air next under,
And hills of snow and lofts of piled thunder,
May tell at length how green-eyed Neptune raves,
In Heaven's defiance mustering all his waves;
Then sing of secret things that came to pass
When beldam Nature in her cradle was;
And last of kings and queens and heroes old,
Such as the wise Demodocus once told
In solemn songs at King Alcinous' feast,
While sad Ulysses' soul and all the rest
Are held with his melodious harmony,
In willing chains and sweet captivity.[1]

From a Letter to Alexander Gill [the younger—one of Milton's teachers at St. Paul's School]. Cambridge, July 2, 1628.

[How Milton spent his last Long Vacation.]

Since I find so few associates in study here, I should instantly direct my steps to London, if I had not determined to spend the

[1] *At a Vacation Exercise* 1–8; 15–52.

summer vacation in the depths of literary solitude, and, as it were, hide myself in the chamber of the Muses.[1]

From *Elegy* 6. To Charles Diodati (1629).[2]

[The Self-discipline of one who would be an Epic Poet.]

Truly light elegy is the care of many gods, and summons to its measures whom it will; to elegy Bacchus comes, and Erato, Ceres, and Venus, and tender Love with his mother, all will come. Such poets then may have abundant feasting, and full often may mellow themselves on old wine; but the poet who tells of wars, and of Heaven under Jove to manhood grown, of pious heroes, and of demigods, the leaders of men, who sings now of the sacred decrees of the gods above, and now of that deep realm guarded by the barking dog, he indeed must live sparely, after the manner of the Samian master, and herbs must supply his simple repast. Let only the crystal-clear water in a beechen bowl stand near him, and let him drink temperate draughts from the pure spring. More than this, his youth must be chaste and free from sin, his manners strict, and his hand without stain, even like you, O priest, when in sacred vestment, and gleaming with the waters of cleansing, you rise as augur to face the angry gods. After this manner, they say, wise Tiresias lived when the light of his eyes was gone; and Ogygian Linus, and Calchas, a fugitive from the doom of his household, and aged Orpheus when in their lonely caves he tamed the wild beasts. Thus sparing of food, and drinking but water, Homer bore Odysseus over the reaches of the sea, through Perseian Circe's magic hall, past the shoals made treacherous by the Siren's song, and through your house, infernal king, where with an offering of dark blood he is said to have held the flocks of shades. Truly the bard is sacred to the gods; he is their priest, and both his heart and lips mysteriously breathe the indwelling Jove.

[1] *Familiar Letters*, No. 3. *Prose Works* 3. 490.
[2] Translated by W. MacKellar.

But if you will know what I am doing—if indeed you think it of consequence to know that I am doing anything—I am singing of the peace-bearing King of heavenly race, and of that happy age promised in the sacred books, of the infant cries of Jesus, and His shelter beneath the humble roof, who with His Father now dwells in the realms above. I sing of the star-bearing firmament and melodious hosts in the heavens, of the gods suddenly shattered in their fanes. This is the gift that I have offered to Christ on His natal day, when the first light of dawn brought me my theme. These verses composed in my native tongue await you in close keeping, and when I recite them to you, you will be my judge. [1]

From *Elegy* 5, at the age of twenty. On the Approach of Spring. [2]

Time as it moves in its ceaseless round now with the warmth of spring recalls the zephyrs. Earth refreshed assumes her brief youth, and the ground released from the frost turns softly green. Is it only my fancy, or does fresh strength return to my song, and is it the gift of spring to inspire my genius? Yes, from spring comes genius waxing strong; and—who would believe it—my powers are already demanding for themselves some new task. Before my eyes hover the Castalian spring and the twin peaks of Parnassus, and dreams by night bear to me the fountain of Pieria. My heart burns, stirred by a secret throb, and a divine rapture and tumult within impel me. Phoebus himself comes; I see his locks encircled with the laurel of Daphne; Phoebus himself descends. My mind is quickly caught up into the heights of the limpid heavens, and free from the body I pass through the wandering clouds. Amid the shades and through the innermost shrines of the poets I am borne, and the secret fanes of the gods lie open before me. My soul perceives all that is done on Olympus, and the dark secrets of Tartarus escape not my sight. What lofty utterance will my soul pour from parted lips? What will this madness, what this sacred frenzy,

[1] *Elegy* 6. 48–90.
[2] Translated by W. MacKellar.

bring forth? Spring, that gave me inspiration, will my inspiration celebrate in song. His gifts repaid shall be his reward.[1]

From an English Letter to a Friend, [who had been remonstrating with him on his delay in choosing a profession.]

Sir: Besides that in sundry respects I must acknowledge me to profit by you whenever we meet, you are often to me, and were yesterday especially, as a good watchman to admonish that the hours of the night pass on (for so I call my life, as yet obscure and unserviceable to mankind), and that the day with me is at hand, wherein Christ commands all to labor while there is light. Which because I am persuaded you do to no other purpose than out of a true desire that God should be honored in every one, I therefore think myself bound, though unasked, to give you an account, as oft as occasion is, of this my tardy moving, according to the precept of my conscience, which I firmly trust is not without God. Yet now I will not strain for any set apology, but only refer myself to what my mind shall have at any time to declare herself at her best ease.

But if you think, as you said, that too much love of learning is in fault, and that I have given up myself to dream away my years in the arms of studious retirement, like Endymion with the Moon (as the tale of Latmus goes), yet consider that if it were no more but the mere love of learning, whether it proceed from a principle bad, good, or natural, it could not have held out thus long against so strong opposition on the other side of every kind. For, if it be bad, why should not all the fond hopes that forward youth and vanity are fledge with, together with gain, pride, and ambition, call me forward more powerfully than a poor, regardless, and unprofitable sin of curiosity should be able to withhold me; whereby a man cuts himself off from all action, and becomes the most helpless, pusillanimous, and unweaponed creature in the world, the most unfit and unable to do that which all mor-

[1] *Elegy* 5. 1–24.

tals most aspire to, either to be useful to his friends or to offend his enemies? Or, if it be to be thought a natural proneness, there is against that a much more potent inclination inbred, which about this time of a man's life solicits most—the desire of house and family of his own; to which nothing is esteemed more helpful than the early entering into credible employment, and nothing hindering than this affected solitariness. And, though this were enough, yet there is another act, if not of pure yet of refined nature, no less available to dissuade prolonged obscurity—a desire of honor and repute and immortal fame, seated in the breast of every true scholar; which all make haste to by the readiest ways of publishing and divulging conceived merits, as well those that shall as those that never shall obtain it. Nature, therefore, would presently work the more prevalent way, if there were nothing but this inferior bent of herself to restrain her. Lastly, the love of learning, as it is the pursuit of something good, it would sooner follow the more excellent and supreme good known and presented, and so be quickly diverted from the empty and fantastic chase of shadows and notions, to the solid good flowing from due and timely obedience to that command in the Gospel set out by the terrible feasing of him that hid the talent.

It is more probable, therefore, that not the endless delight of speculation, but this very consideration of that great commandment, does not press forward as soon as many do to undergo, but keeps off with a sacred reverence and religious advisement how *best* to undergo, not taking thought of being *late*, so it give advantage to be more *fit*; for those that were latest lost nothing when the master of the vineyard came to give each one his hire. And here I am come to a stream-head, copious enough to disburden itself like Nilus, at seven mouths, into an ocean. But then I should also run into a reciprocal contradiction of ebbing and flowing at once, and do that which I excuse myself for not doing, preach and not preach. Yet, that you may see that I am something suspicious of myself, and do take notice of a certain belated-ness in me, I am the bolder to send you some of my nightward thoughts some while since, because they come in not altogether unfitly, made up in a Petrarchian stanza, which I told you of:

> How soon hath Time, the subtle thief of youth
> Stolen on his wing my three-and-twentieth year!
> My hasting days fly on with full career;
> But my late spring no bud or blossom shew'th.
> Perhaps my semblance might deceive the truth
> That I to manhood am arrived so near;
> And inward ripeness doth much less appear,
> That some more timely-happy spirits endu'th.
> Yet, be it less or more, or soon or slow,
> It shall be still in strictest measure even
> To that same lot, however mean or high,
> Toward which Time leads me, and the will of Heaven.
> All is, if I have grace to use it so,
> As ever in my great Task-Master's eye.

By this I believe you may well repent of having made mention at all of this matter; for, if I have not all this while won you to this, I have certainly wearied you of it. This, therefore, alone may be a sufficient reason for me to keep me as I am, lest, having thus tired you singly, I should deal worse with a whole congregation, and spoil all the patience of a parish; for I myself do not only see my own tediousness, but now grow offended with it, that has hindered me thus long from coming to the last and best *period* of my letter, and that which must now chiefly work my pardon—that I am

Your true and unfeigned friend, etc.[1]

From *To My Father* (1632?).[2]

Scorn not the poet's song, a work divine, which more than aught else reveals our ethereal origin, and heavenly race. Nothing so much as its origin does grace to the human mind,

[1] Masson, *Life of Milton* I. 323–5. Reprinted by permission of the Macmillan Company, New York; Macmillan & Company, Ltd., London.
[2] Translated by W. MacKellar.

possessing yet some sacred traces of the Promethean fire. The gods love song, song that has power to move the trembling depths of Tartarus, to bind the nether gods, and restrain the cruel shades with triple adamant. The priestesses of Apollo and the pale trembling Sibyl disclose in song the secrets of the distant future. The sacrificing priest composes verses before the solemn altars, whether he strikes the tossing head of the bull between its golden horns, or sagely consults the destinies hidden in the reeking flesh, and reads fate in the entrails still warm with life. When I too return to my native Olympus, and when the changeless ages of eternity stretch for ever before me, I shall go through the temples of Heaven crowned with gold, accompanying my sweet songs with the gentle beat of the plectrum, wherewith the stars and the arch of Heaven shall resound. Even now that fiery spirit who encircles the swift orbs himself sings with the starry choirs in an immortal melody, an ineffable song, while the glittering serpent checks his angry hissing, and fierce Orion with lowered sword grows gentle, and Maurusian Atlas no longer feels the burden of the stars.

Poems were wont to grace the banquets of kings, when as yet luxury and the vast gulf of gluttony were unknown, and at dinner Lyæus flowed in moderation. Then, according to custom, the bard, seated at the festal board, his unshorn locks wreathed with a garland from the oak, used to sing the feats of heroes and their emulable deeds, sang of chaos and the broadly laid foundations of the world, of the creeping gods that fed upon acorns, and of the thunderbolt not yet brought from the cavern of Ætna. And finally, what will the empty modulation of the voice avail, void of words and sense, and of eloquent numbers? That song will do for the sylvan choirs, but not for Orpheus, who with song and not with lute held back the rivers, and gave ears to the oaks, and moved the shades of the dead to tears; these praises he has from song.

Do not, I pray, persist in contemning the sacred Muses; think them not vain and poor, by whose gift you yourself are skilled in setting a thousand sounds to fitting numbers, and are trained to vary the singing voice through a thousand modulations, you who by merit should be heir to the name of Arion. Now if it has happened that I have been born a poet, why is it strange to you that we, so closely joined by the loving bond of blood, should pursue related arts and kindred ways of life? Phoebus, wishing to divide himself in two, gave some gifts to me, others to my father; and we, father and son, possess the divided god.

Although you pretend to hate the gentle Muses, I do not believe you hate them, for you did not bid me go, father, where the broad way lies open, where the field of gain is easier, and where the certain hope of laying up money shines golden; neither do you drag me to the bar, to the laws of the nation so ill observed, nor do you condemn my ears to silly clamorings. But, wishing my already nurtured mind to grow more rich, you permit me in deep retreats, far from the city's uproar, to pass my pleasant leisure by the Aonian stream, and to go a happy companion by Apollo's side.

I pass in silence over the common kindness of a loving parent —greater matters demand me. When at your cost, dear father, I had become fluent in the tongue of Romulus, and had mastered the graces of Latin, and the lofty words of the magniloquent Greeks, which became the lips of Jove himself; you then persuaded me to add to these the flowers that Gallia boasts, and the language which the modern Italian pours from his degenerate mouth—a witness by his speech of the barbarian tumults—and the mysteries which the prophet of Palestine utters. Finally, whatever is contained in the heavens, in mother Earth beneath, and in the air that flows between earth and heaven, whatever is hidden by the waves and the restless surface of the sea—this through you I may learn, through you, if I care to learn. From the parted cloud appears Science, and naked bends her lovely face to my kisses, unless I wish to flee, and if it be not dangerous to taste.

Go, gather wealth, fool, whoever you are, that prefer the ancestral treasures of Austria, and of the Peruvian realms. But what more than learning could my father have given, or Jove himself had he given all but heaven? He who committed to his young son the common lights, the chariots of Hyperion, the reins of day, and the tiara radiant with light, gave not more potent gifts, however safe they had been. Therefore, since I am one, though the humblest, of the learned company, I shall sit among the victor's ivy and laurels, and no longer obscurely mingle with the dull rabble; my footsteps will avoid the gaze of profane eyes. Away sleepless cares, away complaints, and the wry glance of envy with sidelong goatish leer. Fierce Calumny, open not your serpent's jaws. O most detestable band, you can cause me no unhappiness; I am not under your law. Safe may I walk, my breast secure, high above your viper stroke.

But as for you, dear father, since it is not granted me to make a just return for your deserts, nor to recompense your gifts with my deeds, let it suffice that I remember, and with gratitude count over, your repeated gifts, and treasure them in a faithful mind.

You too, my youthful verses, my pastime, if only you dare hope for endless years, dare think to survive your master's pyre and look upon the light, and if dark oblivion does not drag you down to crowded Orcus, perchance you will treasure these praises and a father's name rehearsed in song as an example to a distant age.[1]

From a Letter to Alexander Gill. December 4, 1634.

If you had made me a present of a piece of plate, or any other valuable which excites the admiration of mankind, I should not be ashamed in my turn to remunerate you, as far as my circum-

[1] *To My Father* 17–120.

stances would permit. But since you the day-before-yesterday presented me with an elegant and beautiful poem in hendecasyllabic verse, which far exceeds the worth of gold, you have increased my solicitude to discover in what manner I may requite the favor of so acceptable a gift. I had by me at the time no compositions in a like style which I thought at all fit to come in competition with the excellence of your performance. I send you therefore a composition which is not entirely my own, but the production of a truly inspired bard, from whom I last week rendered this ode into Greek heroic verse, as I was lying in bed before the day dawned, without any previous deliberation, but with a certain impelling faculty, for which I know not how to account. By his help who does not less surpass you in his subject than you do me in the execution, I have sent something which may serve to restore the equilibrium between us. If you see reason to find fault with any particular passage, I must inform you that, from the time I left your school, this is the first and the last piece I have ever composed in Greek; since, as you know, I have attended more to Latin and to English composition. He who at this time employs his labor and his time in writing Greek is in danger of writing what will never be read.

Adieu, and expect to see me, God willing, at London on Monday, among the booksellers.[1]

From a Letter to Charles Deodati. London, September 2, 1637.

I clearly see that you are determined not to be overcome in silence; if this be so, you shall have the palm of victory, for I will write first. Though, if the reasons which make each of us so long in writing to the other should ever be judicially examined, it will appear that I have many more excuses for not writing than you. For it is well known, and you well know, that I am naturally slow in writing, and averse to write; while you, either from

---

[1] *Familiar Letters*, No. 5. *Prose Works* 3. 491.

disposition or from habit, seem to have little reluctance in engaging in these literary προσφωνήσεις (allocutions). It is also in my favor that your method of study is such as to admit of frequent interruptions, in which you visit your friends, write letters, or go abroad; but it is my way to suffer no impediment, no love of ease, no avocation whatever, to chill the ardor, to break the continuity, or to divert the completion, of my literary pursuits. From this and no other reasons it often happens that I do not readily employ my pen in any gratuitous exertions: but I am not, nevertheless, my dear Deodati, a very sluggish correspondent; nor has it at any time happened that I ever left any letter of yours unanswered till another came. . . .

I have much to say to you concerning myself and my studies, but I would rather do it when we meet; and as to-morrow I am about to return into the country, and am busy in making preparations for my journey, I have but just time to scribble this.[1]

From a Letter to Charles Deodati. London, September 23, 1637.

Whatever the Deity may have bestowed upon me in other respects, He has certainly inspired me, if any ever were inspired, with a passion for the good and fair. Nor did Ceres, according to the fable, ever seek her daughter Proserpine with such unceasing solicitude as I have sought this τοῦ καλοῦ ἰδέαν, this perfect model of the beautiful in all the forms and appearances of things (πολλαὶ γὰρ μορφαὶ τῶν Δαιμονίων—many are the forms of the divinities). I am wont day and night to continue my search; and I follow in the way in which you go before. Hence, I feel an irresistible impulse to cultivate the friendship of him who, despising the prejudices and false conceptions of the vulgar, dares to think, to speak, and to be that which the highest wisdom has in every age taught to be the best. But if my disposition or my destiny were such that I could without any conflict or any toil emerge to the highest pitch of distinction and of praise, there

---

[1] *Familiar Letters*, No. 6. *Prose Works* 3. 492–3.

would nevertheless be no prohibition, either human or divine, against my constantly cherishing and revering those who have either obtained the same degree of glory, or are successfully laboring to obtain it. But now I am sure that you wish me to gratify your curiosity, and to let you know what I have been doing, or am meditating to do. Hear me, my Deodati, and suffer me for a moment to speak, without blushing, in a more lofty strain. Do you ask what I am meditating? By the help of Heaven, an immortality of fame. But what am I doing? Πτεροφυῶ: I am letting my wings grow and preparing to fly, but my Pegasus has not yet feathers enough to soar aloft in the fields of air. I will now tell you seriously what I design—to take chambers in one of the Inns of Court, where I may have the benefit of a pleasant and shady walk; and where with a few associates I may enjoy more comfort when I choose to stay at home, and have a more elegant society when I choose to go abroad. In my present situation you know in what obscurity I am buried, and to what inconveniences I am exposed.

You shall likewise have some information respecting my studies. I went through the perusal of the Greek authors to the time when they ceased to be Greeks; I was long employed in unraveling the obscure history of the Italians under the Lombards, the Franks, and Germans, to the time when they received their liberty from Rodolphus, King of Germany. From that time it will be better to read separately the particular transactions of each state. But how are you employed? How long will you attend to your domestic ties and forget your city connections? But unless this novercal hostility be more inveterate than that of the Dacian or Sarmatian, you will feel it a duty to visit me in my winter quarters. In the meantime, if you can do it without inconvenience, I will thank you to send me Giustiniani, the historian of Venice. I will either keep it carefully till your arrival, or, if you had rather, will soon send it back again.[1]

[1] *Familiar Letters*, No. 7. *Prose Works* 3. 494-5.

From *Lycidas*. (November, 1637.)

> Who would not sing for Lycidas? He knew
> Himself to sing, and build the lofty rime. . . .
> For we were nursed upon the self-same hill,
> Fed the same flock, by fountain, shade and rill;
> Together both, ere the high lawns appeared
> Under the opening eyelids of the Morn,
> We drove afield, and both together heard
> What time the gray-fly winds her sultry horn,
> Battening our flocks with the fresh dews of night,
> Oft till the star that rose at evening bright
> Toward Heaven's descent had sloped his westering wheel.
> Meanwhile the rural ditties were not mute,
> Tempered to the oaten flute;
> Rough Satyrs danced, and Fauns with cloven heel
> From the glad sound would not be absent long,
> And old Damœtas loved to hear our song.[1]

From *An Epitaph on Damon* (1639).[2]

Ah, what wandering fancy lured me to traverse lofty cliffs and snowy Alps to unknown shores! Was there any such need to see buried Rome—even had it been what it was when Tityrus left his sheep and his pastures to see it—that I could part with so charming a companion, that I could put between us so many deep seas, so many mountains, forests, rocks, and roaring streams? Surely, had I staid, I might at the last have touched the hand, and closed the eyes of him who was peacefully dying, might have said: 'Farewell; remember me when you go to the stars.'

Go home unfed, my lambs, your troubled master is not free to tend you. Even though I shall never weary of remembering you, O Tuscan shepherds, youths devoted to the Muses, yet here too were grace and charm; and you too, Damon, were a Tuscan tracing your lineage from the ancient city of Lucumo. O how elated I was when, stretched on the softest grass in the poplar grove by

[1] *Lycidas* 10-1; 23-36.
[2] Translated by W. MacKellar.

the cool murmuring Arno, I listened to Menalcas contending with Lycidas in song! Even I myself ventured to enter the contest, nor do I think I greatly displeased you, for I still have with me your gifts—reed-baskets, bowls, and shepherd's pipes with waxen stops. Nay, both Dati and Francini, renowned for their eloquence and their learning, and both of Lydian blood, have taught my name to their beeches.

Go home unfed, my lambs, your troubled master is not free to tend you. These things the dewy moon used to tell me, when happy and alone I was shutting my tender kids in their wattled cotes. Ah! how often have I said, when already you were but dark ashes:

'Now Damon is singing, or stretching nets for the hare; now he is plaiting osiers for his various uses.'

What I then with easy mind hoped for the future, with the wish I lightly seized and fancied present.

'Ho, good friend, have you anything to do? If nothing prevents, let us go and lie down awhile in the murmuring shade, by the waters of Colne, or in the fields of Cassibelaunus. You shall go over to me your healing herbs and juices, hellebore, the lowly crocus, and the leaf of the hyacinth, whatever plants the marshes yield, and tell me of the physician's art.'

Ah! perish the herbs and medicines, perish the physician's art, since they have profited their master nothing! And I—for I know not what my pipe was grandly sounding—it is now eleven nights and a day—and then perhaps I had put my lips to new pipes, but they burst asunder, broken at my touch, and could no more bear the deep tones—I hesitate too lest I seem puffed up, yet I will tell the tale. Give place then, O forests.

Go home unfed, my lambs, your troubled master is not free to tend you. I would tell of Dardanian ships along the Rutupian sea, and of the ancient realm of Imogen, Pandras' daughter, of the leaders Brennus and Arviragus, and old Belinus, and of colonists in Armorica under British laws; then I would tell of Igraine pregnant with Arthur by a fatal fraud, of the seeming face and counterfeited arms of Gorloïs, Merlin's artifice. Ah! then if life remain, you, my pipe, shall hang on some aged pine far off and forgotten, unless forsaking your native songs you shrilly sound a British theme. Why not a British theme? One man cannot do all things, cannot hope to do all things. Sufficient my reward, my honors ample—even if I am for ever unknown and without fame in foreign parts—if yellow-haired Ouse reads me, and he who drinks the waters of Alaun, and Abra full of eddies, and all the woods of Trent, and above all my own Thames, and Tamar stained with metals, and if the Orkneys and their remotest waves but learn my songs.[1]

From Milton's Political Writings—1641–1659

From *The Reason of Church-Government* (1641).

I[2] must say, therefore, that after I had for my first years, by the ceaseless diligence and care of my father, (whom God recompense!) been exercised to the tongues, and some sciences, as my age would suffer, by sundry masters and teachers, both at home and at the schools, it was found that whether aught was imposed me by them that had the overlooking, or betaken to of mine own choice in English, or other tongue, prosing or versing, but chiefly this latter, the style, by certain vital signs it had, was likely to live. But much latelier in the private academies of Italy, whither I was favored to resort, perceiving that some trifles which I had in memory, composed at under twenty or thereabout (for the manner is that every one must give some proof of his wit and reading there), met with acceptance above what was looked for; and other things, which I had shifted in scarcity of books and conveniences to patch up amongst them, were received

---

[1] *An Epitaph on Damon* 112–78.

[2] In several of his earlier pamphlets, Milton introduces himself to the public as one who, having dedicated his life to the service of poetry, might justly assume the office of prophet.

with written encomiums, which the Italian is not forward to bestow on men of this side the Alps; I began thus far to assent both to them and divers of my friends here at home, and not less to an inward prompting which now grew daily upon me, that by labor and intent study (which I take to be my portion in this life) joined with the strong propensity of nature, I might perhaps leave something so written to aftertimes as they should not willingly let it die. These thoughts at once possessed me, and these other: that if I were certain to write as men buy leases, for three lives and downward, there ought no regard be sooner had than to God's glory, by the honor and instruction of my country. For which cause, and not only for that I knew it would be hard to arrive at the second rank among the Latins, I applied myself to that resolution which Ariosto followed against the persuasions of Bembo—to fix all the industry and art I could unite to the adorning of my native tongue; not to make verbal curiosities the end (that were a toilsome vanity), but to be an interpreter and relater of the best and sagest things, among mine own citizens throughout this island, in the mother-dialect; that what the greatest and choicest wits of Athens, Rome, or modern Italy, and those Hebrews of old, did for their country, I, in my proportion, with this over and above, of being a Christian, might do for mine; not caring to be once named abroad, though perhaps I could attain to that, but content with these British islands as my world; whose fortune hath hitherto been that, if the Athenians, as some say, made their small deeds great and renowned by their eloquent writers, England hath had her noble achievements made small by the unskilful handling of monks and mechanics.

Time serves not now—and perhaps I might seem too profuse— to give any certain account of what the mind at home, in the spacious circuits of her musing, hath liberty to propose to herself, though of highest hope and hardest attempting: whether that epic form whereof the two poems of Homer and those other two of Virgil and Tasso are a diffuse, and the Book of Job a brief, model; or whether the rules of Aristotle herein are strictly to be kept, or nature to be followed—which in them that know art, and use judgment, is no transgression, but an enriching of art; and, lastly, what king or knight, before the Conquest, might be chosen in whom to lay the pattern of a Christian hero. And as Tasso gave to a prince of Italy his choice whether he would command him to write of Godfrey's expedition against the Infidels, or Belisarius against the Goths, or Charlemagne against the Lombards; if to the instinct of nature and the emboldening of art aught may be trusted, and that there be nothing adverse in our climate, or the fate of this age, it haply would be no rashness, from an equal diligence and inclination, to present the like offer in our own ancient stories; or whether those dramatic constitutions, wherein Sophocles and Euripides reign, shall be found more doctrinal and exemplary to a nation. The Scripture also affords us a divine pastoral drama in the Song of Solomon, consisting of two persons and a double chorus—as Origen rightly judges; and the Apocalypse of St. John is the majestic image of a high and stately tragedy, shutting up and intermingling her solemn scenes and acts with a sevenfold chorus of hallelujahs and harping symphonies—and this my opinion the grave authority of Paræus, commenting that book, is sufficient to confirm. Or, if occasion shall lead, to imitate those magnific odes and hymns wherein Pindarus and Callimachus are in most things worthy, some others in their frame judicious, in their matter most an end faulty. But those frequent songs throughout the law and prophets beyond all these, not in their divine argument alone, but in the very critical art of composition, may be easily made appear over all the kinds of lyric poesy to be incomparable.[1]

The thing which I had to say, and those intentions which have lived within me ever since I could conceive myself anything worth to my country, I return to crave excuse that urgent reason hath plucked from me, by an abortive and foredated discovery. And the accomplishment of them lies not but in a power above

[1] *Prose Works* 2. 477–9.

man's to promise; but that none hath by more studious ways endeavored, and with more unwearied spirit that none shall, that I dare almost aver of myself, as far as life and free leisure will extend; and that the land had once enfranchised herself from this impertinent yoke of prelaty, under whose inquisitorious and tyrannical duncery no free and splendid wit can flourish. Neither do I think it shame to covenant with any knowing reader that for some few years yet I may go on trust with him toward the payment of what I am now indebted, as being a work not to be raised from the heat of youth, or the vapors of wine, like that which flows at waste from the pen of some vulgar amorist, or the trencher-fury of a riming parasite; nor to be obtained by the invocation of dame memory and her siren daughters, but by devout prayer to that eternal Spirit Who can enrich with all utterance and knowledge, and sends out His seraphim, with the hallowed fire of His altar, to touch and purify the lips of whom He pleases. To this must be added industrious and select reading, steady observation, insight into all seemly and generous arts and affairs.[1]

From *An Apology for Smectymnuus* (1642).

I fear it would but harm the truth for me to reason in her behalf, so long as I should suffer my honest estimation to lie unpurged from these insolent suspicions. And if I shall be large, or unwonted in justifying myself to those who know me not, for else it would be needless, let them consider that a short slander will oft-times reach farther than a long apology; and that he who will do justly to all men must begin from knowing how, if it so happen, to be not unjust to himself.

I must be thought, if this libeller (for now he shows himself to be so) can find belief, after an inordinate and riotous youth spent at the university, to have been at length 'vomited out thence.' For which commodious lie, that he may be encouraged

[1] *Prose Works* 2. 480–1.

in the trade another time, I thank him; for it hath given me an apt occasion to acknowledge publicly, with all grateful mind, that more than ordinary favor and respect which I found above any of my equals at the hands of those courteous and learned men, the Fellows of that college wherein I spent some years; who, at my parting, after I had taken two degrees, as the manner is, signified many ways how much better it would content them that I would stay; as by many letters full of kindness and loving respect, both before that time, and long after, I was assured of their singular good affection towards me. Which being likewise propense to all such as were for their studious and civil life worthy of esteem, I could not wrong their judgments and upright intentions so much as to think I had that regard from them for other cause than that I might be still encouraged to proceed in the honest and laudable courses of which, they apprehended, I had given good proof. And to those ingenuous and friendly men, who were ever the countenancers of virtuous and hopeful wits, I wish the best and happiest things that friends in absence wish one to another.

As for the common approbation or dislike of that place, as now it is—that I should esteem or disesteem myself or any other the more for that, too simple and too credulous is the confuter if he think to obtain with me, or any right discerner. Of small practice were that physician who could not judge, by what both she or her sister hath of long time vomited, that the worser stuff she strongly keeps in her stomach, but the better she is ever kecking at, and is queasy. She vomits now out of sickness; but ere it be well with her, she must vomit by strong physic. In the meantime that suburb sink—as this rude scavanger calls it, and more than scurrilously taunts it with the plague— . . . that suburb wherein I dwell shall be, in my account, a more honorable place than his university; which, as in the time of her better health and mine own younger judgment, I never greatly admired, so now much less.

But he follows me to the city, still usurping and forging beyond his book-notice, which only he affirms to have had; and where my morning haunts are, he wisses not. . . . Those morning haunts are where they should be, at home—not sleeping, or concocting the surfeits of an irregular feast, but up and stirring; in winter often ere the sound of any bell awake men to labor, or to devotion; in summer as oft with the bird that first rouses, or not much tardier, to read good authors, or cause them to be read, till the attention be weary, or memory have his full fraught; then, with useful and generous labors preserving the body's health and hardiness to render lightsome, clear, and not lumpish obedience to the mind, to the cause of religion, and our country's liberty, when it shall require firm hearts in sound bodies to stand and cover their stations, rather than to see the ruin of our protestation, and the enforcement of a slavish life.[1]

But because . . . he would seem privily to point me out to his readers as one whose custom of life were not honest but licentious, I shall entreat to be borne with, though I digress; and, in a way not often trod, acquaint ye with the sum of my thoughts in this matter, through the course of my years and studies; although I am not ignorant how hazardous it will be to do this under the nose of the envious, as it were in skirmish to change the compact order, and, instead of outward actions, to bring inmost thoughts into front. And I must tell ye, readers, that by this sort of men I have been already bitten at; yet shall they not for me know how slightly they are esteemed, unless they have so much learning as to read what in Greek ἀπειροκαλία is, which, together with envy, is the common disease of those who censure books that are not for their reading. With me it fares now as with him whose outward garment hath been injured and ill-bedighted; for, having no other shift, what help but to turn the

[1] *Prose Works* 3. 110–3.

inside outwards, especially if the lining be of the same, or, as it is sometimes, much better? So if my name and outward demeanor be not evident enough to defend me, I must make trial if the discovery of my inmost thoughts can; wherein of two purposes, both honest and both sincere, the one perhaps I shall not miss; although I fail to gain belief with others of being such as my perpetual thoughts shall here disclose me, I may yet not fail of success in persuading some to be such really themselves, as they cannot believe me to be more than what I feign.

I had my time, readers, as others have who have good learning bestowed upon them, to be sent to those places where the opinion was it might be soonest attained; and, as the manner is, was not unstudied in those authors which are most commended. Whereof some were grave orators and historians, whose matter methought I loved indeed, but, as my age then was, so I understood them; others were the smooth elegiac poets whereof the schools are not scarce, whom—both for the pleasing sound of their numerous writing, which in imitation I found most easy, and most agreeable to nature's part in me, and for their matter, which what it is there be few who know not—I was so allured to read that no recreation came to me better welcome. For that it was then those years with me which are excused, though they be least severe, I may be saved the labor to remember ye. Whence having observed them to account it the chief glory of their wit, in that they were ablest to judge, to praise, and by that could esteem themselves worthiest to love those high perfections which under one or other name they took to celebrate; I thought with myself, by every instinct and presage of nature (which is not wont to be false) that what emboldened them to this task might, with such diligence as they used, embolden me; and that what judgment, wit, or elegance was my share would herein best appear, and best value itself, by how much more wisely and with more love of virtue I should choose (let rude ears be absent) the object of not unlike praises. For albeit these thoughts to some will seem virtuous and commendable, to others only pardonable, to a third sort perhaps idle; yet the mentioning of them now will end in serious.

Nor blame it, readers, in those years to propose to themselves such a reward as the noblest dispositions above other things in this life have sometimes preferred; whereof not to be sensible, when good and fair in one person meet, argues both a gross and shallow judgment, and withal an ungentle and swainish breast. For by the firm settling of these persuasions, I became, to my best memory, so much a proficient that, if I found those authors anywhere speaking unworthy things of themselves, or unchaste of those names which before they had extolled, this effect it wrought with me: from that time forward their art I still applauded, but the men I deplored; and, above them all, preferred the two famous renowners of Beatrice and Laura, who never write but honor of them to whom they devote their verse, displaying sublime and pure thoughts, without transgression. And long it was not after, when I was confirmed in this opinion: that he who would not be frustrate of his hope to write well hereafter in laudable things ought himself to be a true poem—that is, a composition and pattern of the best and honorablest things; not presuming to sing high praises of heroic men or famous cities unless he have in himself the experience and the practice of all that which is praiseworthy. These reasonings, together with a certain niceness of nature, an honest haughtiness, and self-esteem either of what I was or what I might be (which let envy call pride), and lastly that modesty, whereof, though not in the title-page, yet here, I may be excused to make some beseeming profession; all these, uniting the supply of their natural aid together, kept me still above those low descents of mind beneath which he must deject and plunge himself that can agree to saleable and unlawful prostitutions.

Next (for hear me out now, readers, that I may tell ye whither my younger feet wandered), I betook me among those lofty fables and romances which recount in solemn cantos the deeds of knighthood founded by our victorious kings, and from hence had in renown over all Christendom. There I read it, in the oath of every knight, that he should defend to the expense of his best blood, or of his life if it so befell him, the honor and chastity of virgin or matron; from whence even then I learned what a noble virtue chastity sure must be, to the defence of which so many worthies, by such a dear adventure of themselves, had sworn. And, if I found in the story afterward any of them by word or deed breaking that oath, I judged it the same fault of the poet as that which is attributed to Homer—to have written undecent things of the gods. Only this my mind gave me—that every free and gentle spirit, without that oath, ought to be born a knight, nor needed to expect the gilt spur or the laying of a sword upon his shoulder to stir him up both by his counsel and his arm to secure and protect the weakness of any attempted chastity. So that even those books, which to many others have been the fuel of wantonness and loose living, I cannot think how, unless by divine indulgence, proved to me so many incitements, as you have heard, to the love and steadfast observation of that virtue which abhors the society of bordelloes.

Thus, from the laureate fraternity of poets, riper years and the ceaseless round of study and reading led me to the shady spaces of philosophy, but chiefly to the divine volumes of Plato, and his equal Xenophon. Where, if I should tell ye what I learnt of chastity and love—I mean that which is truly so, whose charming cup is only virtue, which she bears in her hand to those who are worthy (the rest are cheated with a thick intoxicating potion, which a certain sorceress, the abuser of love's name, carries about); and how the first and chiefest office of love begins and ends in the soul, producing those happy twins of her divine generation, knowledge and virtue, with such abstracted sublimities as these; it might be worth your listening, readers, as I may one day hope to have ye in a still time, when there shall be no chiding; not in these noises—the adversary, as ye know, barking at the door, or searching for me at the bordelloes, where, it may be, he has lost himself, and raps up without pity the sage and rheumatic old prelatess with all her young Corinthian laity, to inquire for such a one.

Last of all, not in time, but as perfection is last, that care was ever had of me, with my earliest capacity, not to be negligently trained in the precepts of the Christian religion. This that I have hitherto related hath been to show that, though Christianity had been but slightly taught me, yet a certain reservedness of natural disposition, and moral discipline learnt out of the noblest philosophy, was enough to keep me in disdain of far less incontinences than this of the bordello. But having had the doctrine of Holy Scripture unfolding those chaste and high mysteries, with timeliest care infused, that 'the body is for the Lord, and the Lord for the body'; thus also I argued to myself that, if unchastity in a woman, whom St. Paul terms the glory of man, be such a scandal and dishonor, then certainly in a man, who is both the image and glory of God, it must, though commonly not so thought, be much more deflowering and dishonorable; in that he sins both against his own body, which is the perfecter sex, and his own glory, which is in the woman, and, that which is worst, against the image and glory of God, which is in himself. Nor did I slumber over that place expressing such high rewards of ever accompanying the Lamb with those celestial songs to others inapprehensible, but not to those who were not defiled with women—which doubtless means fornication, for marriage must not be called a defilement.

Thus large I have purposely been that, if I have been justly taxed with this crime, it may come upon me after all this my confession with a tenfold shame; but if I have hitherto deserved no such opprobrious word or suspicion, I may hereby engage myself now openly to the faithful observation of what I have professed.[1]

[1] *Prose Works* 3. 115-22.

MILTON'S INTEREST IN STUDY

From *The Second Defence of the People of England* (1654).

I must, therefore, crave the indulgence of the reader if I have said already, or shall say hereafter, more of myself than I wish to say; that, if I cannot prevent the blindness of my eyes, the oblivion or the defamation of my name, I may at least rescue my life from that species of obscurity which is the associate of unprincipled depravity. This it will be necessary for me to do on more accounts than one: First, that so many good and learned men among the neighboring nations, who read my works, may not be induced by this fellow's calumnies to alter the favorable opinion which they have formed of me; but may be persuaded that I am not one who ever disgraced beauty of sentiment by deformity of conduct, or the maxims of a freeman by the actions of a slave; and that the whole tenor of my life has, by the grace of God, hitherto been unsullied by enormity or crime. Next, that those illustrious worthies, who are the objects of my praise, may know that nothing could afflict me with more shame than to have any vices of mine diminish the force or lessen the value of my panegyric upon them. And, lastly, that the people of England, whom fate, or duty, or their own virtues have incited me to defend, may be convinced from the purity and integrity of my life that my defence, if it do not redound to their honor, can never be considered as their disgrace.

I will now mention who and whence I am. I was born at London, of an honest family; my father was distinguished by the undeviating integrity of his life; my mother, by the esteem in which she was held, and the alms which she bestowed. My father destined me from a child to the pursuits of literature; and my appetite for knowledge was so voracious that from twelve years of age I hardly ever left my studies or went to bed before midnight. This primarily led to my loss of sight. My eyes were naturally weak, and I was subject to frequent headaches; which, however, could not chill the ardor of my curiosity, or retard the progress of my improvement. My father had me daily instructed

99

in the grammar-school, and by other masters at home. He then, after I had acquired a proficiency in various languages, and had made a considerable progress in philosophy, sent me to the University of Cambridge. Here I passed seven years in the usual course of instruction and study, with the approbation of the good, and without any stain upon my character, till I took the degree of Master of Arts. After this I . . . retired to my father's house, whither I was accompanied by the regrets of most of the Fellows of the college, who showed me no common marks of friendship and esteem.

On my father's estate, where he had determined to pass the remainder of his days, I enjoyed an interval of uninterrupted leisure, which I entirely devoted to the perusal of the Greek and Latin classics; though I occasionally visited the metropolis, either for the sake of purchasing books, or of learning something new in mathematics or in music, in which I, at that time, found a source of pleasure and amusement. In this manner I spent five years till my mother's death. I then became anxious to visit foreign parts, and particularly Italy. My father gave me his permission, and I left home with one servant. . . . Taking ship at Nice, I arrived at Genoa, and afterward visited Leghorn, Pisa, and Florence. In the latter city, which I have always more particularly esteemed for the elegance of its dialect, its genius, and its taste, I stopped about two months; when I contracted an intimacy with many persons of rank and learning, and was a constant attendant at their literary parties; a practice which prevails there, and tends so much to the diffusion of knowledge and the preservation of friendship. . . . When I was preparing to pass over into Sicily and Greece, the melancholy intelligence which I received of the civil commotions in England made me alter my purpose; for I thought it base to be traveling for amusement abroad, while my fellow-citizens were fighting for liberty at home. . . . By the favor of God I got safe back to Florence, where I was received with as much affection as if I had returned to my native country. There I stopped as many months as I had done before, except that I made an excursion for a few days to Lucca; and, crossing the Apennines, passed through Bologna and Ferrara to Venice. After I had spent a month in surveying the curiosities of this city, and had put on board a ship the books which I had collected in Italy, I proceeded through Verona and Milan, and along the Leman lake to Geneva. The mention of this city brings to my recollection the slandering More, and makes me again call the Deity to witness that, in all those places in which vice meets with so little discouragement and is practised with so little shame, I never once deviated from the paths of integrity and virtue, and perpetually reflected that, though my conduct might escape the notice of men, it could not elude the inspection of God. At Geneva I held daily conferences with John Deodati, the learned professor of theology. Then, pursuing my former route through France, I returned to my native country, after an absence of one year and about three months. . . .

As soon as I was able, I hired a spacious house in the city for myself and my books; where I again with rapture renewed my literary pursuits, and where I calmly awaited the issue of the contest, which I trusted to the wise conduct of Providence, and to the courage of the people. . . . I saw that a way was opening for the establishment of real liberty; that the foundation was laying for the deliverance of man from the yoke of slavery and superstition; that the principles of religion, which were the first objects of our care, would exert a salutary influence on the manners and constitution of the Republic; and, as I had from my youth studied the distinction between religious and civil rights, I perceived that, if I ever wished to be of use, I ought at least not to be wanting to my country, to the Church, and to so many of my fellow-Christians, in a crisis of so much danger; I therefore determined to relinquish the other pursuits in which I was engaged, and to transfer the whole force of my talents and my industry to this one important object.

I accordingly wrote two books to a friend concerning the reformation of the Church of England. Afterwards, when two bishops of superior distinction vindicated their privileges against some principal ministers, I thought that on those topics, to the consideration of which I was led solely by my love of truth, and my reverence for Christianity, I should not probably write worse than those who were contending only for their own emoluments and usurpations. I therefore answered the one in two books, of which the first is inscribed *Concerning Prelatical Episcopacy*, and the other, *Concerning the Mode of Ecclesiastical Government;* and I replied to the other in some *Animadversions*, and soon after in an *Apology*. On this occasion it was supposed that I brought a timely succor to the ministers, who were hardly a match for the eloquence of their opponents; and from that time I was actively employed in refuting any answers that appeared.

When the bishops could no longer resist the multitude of their assailants, I had leisure to turn my thoughts to other subjects; to the promotion of real and substantial liberty, which is rather to be sought from within than from without, and whose existence depends, not so much on the terror of the sword, as on sobriety of conduct and integrity of life. When, therefore, I perceived that there were three species of liberty which are essential to the happiness of social life—religious, domestic, and civil—and as I had already written concerning the first, and the magistrates were strenuously active in obtaining the third, I determined to turn my attention to the second, or the domestic, species. As this seemed to involve three material questions—the conditions of the conjugal tie, the education of the children, and the free publication of the thoughts—I made them objects of distinct consideration. I explained my sentiments, not only concerning the solemnization of the marriage, but the dissolution, if circumstances rendered it necessary; and I drew my arguments from the divine law, which Christ did not abolish, or publish another more grievous than that of Moses.

I stated my own opinions, and those of others, concerning the exclusive exception of fornication, which our illustrious Selden has since, in his *Hebrew Wife*, more copiously discussed; for he in vain makes a vaunt of liberty in the senate or in the forum who languishes under the vilest servitude to an inferior at home. On this subject, therefore, I published some books which were more particularly necessary at that time, when man and wife were often the most inveterate foes—when the man often stayed to take care of his children at home, while the mother of the family was seen in the camp of the enemy, threatening death and destruction to her husband. I then discussed the principles of education in a summary manner, but sufficiently copious for those who attend seriously to the subject; than which nothing can be more necessary to principle the minds of men in virtue—the only genuine source of political and individual liberty, the only true safeguard of states, the bulwark of their prosperity and renown. Lastly, I wrote my *Areopagitica*, in order to deliver the press from the restraints with which it was encumbered; that the power of determining what was true and what was false, what ought to be published and what to be suppressed, might no longer be entrusted to a few illiterate and illiberal individuals, who refused their sanction to any work which contained views or sentiments at all above the level of the vulgar superstition. On the last species of civil liberty I said nothing, because I saw that sufficient attention was paid to it by the magistrates; nor did I write anything on the prerogative of the Crown, till the King, voted an enemy by the Parliament, and vanquished in the field, was summoned before the tribunal which condemned him to lose his head. But when, at length, some Presbyterian ministers, who had formerly been the most bitter enemies to Charles, became jealous of the growth of the Independents and of their ascendancy in the Parliament, most tumultuously clamored against the sentence, and did all in their power to prevent the execution—though they were not angry so much on account of the act itself as because it was not the act of their party—and when they dared to affirm that the doctrine of the Protestants and of all the reformed churches was abhorrent to such an atrocious proceeding against kings, I thought that it became me to oppose such a glaring falsehood; and accordingly, without any immediate or personal application to Charles, I showed, in an abstract consideration of the question, what might lawfully be done against tyrants; and, in support of what I advanced, produced the opinions of the most celebrated divines, while I vehemently inveighed against the egregious ignorance or effrontery of men who professed better things, and from whom better things might have been expected. That book did not make its appearance till after the death of Charles, and was written rather to reconcile the minds of the people to the event than to discuss the legitimacy of that particular sentence— which concerned the magistrates, and which was already executed.

Such were the fruits of my private studies, which I gratuitously presented to the Church and to the State, and for which I was recompensed by nothing but impunity; though the actions themselves procured me peace of conscience and the approbation of the good, while I exercised that freedom of discussion which I loved. Others, without labor or desert, got possession of honors and emoluments; but no one ever knew me either soliciting anything myself or through the medium of my friends, ever beheld me in a supplicating posture at the doors of the senate or the levees of the great. I usually kept myself secluded at home, where my own property, part of which had been withheld during the civil commotion, and part of which had been absorbed in the oppressive contributions which I had to sustain, afforded me a scanty subsistence. When I was released from these engagements, and thought that I was about to enjoy an interval of uninterrupted ease, I turned my thoughts to a continued history of my country, from the earliest times to the present period. I had already finished four books when, after the subversion of the monarchy and the establishment of a republic, I was surprised by an invitation from the council of state, who desired my services in the office for foreign affairs. A book appeared soon after, which was ascribed to the King, and contained the most invidious charges against the Parliament. I was ordered to answer it, and opposed the *Iconoclast* to his *Icon*. I did not insult over fallen majesty, as is pretended; I only preferred Queen Truth to King Charles. The charge of insult, which I saw that the malevolent would urge, I was at some pains to remove in the beginning of the work, and as often as possible in other places. Salmasius then appeared, to whom they were not, as More says, long in looking about for an opponent, but immediately appointed me, who happened at that time to be present in the council. I have thus, Sir, given some account of myself, in order to stop your mouth, and to remove any prejudices which your falsehoods and misrepresentations might cause even good men to entertain against me.[1]

From *Considerations Touching the Likeliest Means to Remove Hirelings out of the Church* (1659).

That I, though among many others in this common concernment, interpose to your deliberations what my thoughts also are, your own judgment and the success thereof hath given me the confidence; which requests but this: that, if I have prosperously, God so favoring me, defended the public cause of this Commonwealth to foreigners, ye would not think the reason and ability whereon ye trusted once (and repent not) your whole reputation to the world, either grown less by more maturity and longer study, or less available in English than in another tongue.[2]

FROM MILTON'S LATER POEMS

On his Blindness (1655).

When I consider how my light is spent
    Ere half my days, in this dark world and wide,
    And that one talent which is death to hide

[1] *Prose Works* 1. 253-61.
[2] *Ibid.* 3. 2.

Lodged with me useless, though my soul more bent
To serve therewith my Maker, and present
  My true account, lest He returning chide;
  'Doth God exact day-labor, light denied?'
  I fondly ask. But Patience, to prevent
That murmur, soon replies: 'God doth not need
  Either man's work or his own gifts. Who best
  Bear His mild yoke, they serve Him best. His state
Is kingly: thousands at His bidding speed,
  And post o'er land and ocean without rest;
  They also serve who only stand and wait.'[1]

To Mr. Cyriack Skinner, upon his Blindness (1655).

Cyriack, this three-years' day these eyes, though clear
  To outward view, of blemish or of spot,
  Bereft of light, their seeing have forgot;
  Nor to their idle orbs doth sight appear
Of sun, or moon, or star, throughout the year,
  Or man, or woman. Yet I argue not
  Against Heaven's hand or will, nor bate a jot
Of heart or hope, but still bear up and steer
Right onward. What supports me, dost thou ask?
  The conscience, friend, to have lost them overplied
  In Liberty's defence, my noble task,
Of which all Europe talks from side to side.
  This thought might lead me through the world's vain mask
  Content, though blind, had I no better guide.[2]

From *Paradise Lost* (1667).

  Sing Heavenly Muse,[3] that on the secret top
Of Oreb, or of Sinai, didst inspire
That shepherd, who first taught the chosen seed
In the beginning how the Heavens and Earth
Rose out of Chaos.[4]

  And chiefly thou, O Spirit, that dost prefer
Before all temples the upright heart and pure,

[1] *Sonnet* 19.
[2] *Sonnet* 22.
[3] The personal allusions in *Paradise Lost* mostly concern Milton's notion of the true source of inspiration, and the difficulties that must be overcome.
[4] *Paradise Lost* I. 6–10.

Instruct me, for thou know'st; . . .
     What in me is dark
Illumine, what is low raise and support.[1]
With other notes than to the Orphean lyre
I sung of Chaos and eternal Night;
Taught by the Heavenly Muse to venture down
The dark descent, and up to reascend,
Though hard and rare. Thee I revisit safe,
And feel thy sovran vital lamp; but thou
Revisit'st not these eyes, that roll in vain
To find thy piercing ray, and find no dawn—
So thick a drop serene hath quenched their orbs,
Or dim suffusion veiled. Yet not the more
Cease I to wander where the Muses haunt
Clear spring, or shady grove, or sunny hill,
Smit with the love of sacred song; but chief
Thee, Sion, and the flowery brooks beneath,
That wash thy hallowed feet, and warbling flow,
Nightly I visit; nor sometimes forget
Those other two equaled with me in fate
(So were I equaled with them in renown)
Blind Thamyris and blind Mæonides,
And Tiresias and Phineus, prophets old:
Then feed on thoughts that voluntary move
Harmonious numbers; as the wakeful bird
Sings darkling, and, in shadiest covert hid,
Tunes her nocturnal note.—Thus with the year
Seasons return; but not to me returns
Day, or the sweet approach of even or morn,
Or sight of vernal bloom, or summer's rose,
Or flocks, or herds, or human face divine;
But cloud instead and ever-during dark
Surrounds me, from the cheerful ways of men
Cut off, and for the book of knowledge fair,
Presented with a universal blank
Of Nature's works, to me expunged and rased,
And wisdom at one entrance quite shut out.
So much the rather thou, celestial Light,
Shine inward, and the mind through all her powers

---

[1] *Ibid.* I. 17–23.

Irradiate: there plant eyes, all mist from thence
Purge and disperse, that I may see and tell
Of things invisible to mortal sight.[1]

Descend from Heaven, Urania, by that name
If rightly thou art called, whose voice divine
Following, above the Olympian hill I soar,
Above the flight of Pegasean wing!
The meaning, not the name, I call; for thou
Nor of the Muses nine, nor on the top
Of old Olympus dwell'st; but Heavenly-born,
Before the hills appeared or fountain flowed,
Thou with eternal Wisdom didst converse,
Wisdom thy sister, and with her didst play
In presence of the Almighty Father, pleased
With thy celestial song. Up led by thee,
Into the Heaven of Heavens I have presumed,
An earthly guest, and drawn empyreal air,
Thy tempering; with like safety guided down,
Return me to my native element;
Lest from this flying steed unreined (as once
Bellerophon, though from a lower clime)
Dismounted, on the Aleian field I fall,
Erroneous there to wander and forlorn.[2]

Standing on Earth, not rapt above the pole,
More safe I sing with mortal voice, unchanged
To hoarse or mute, though fallen on evil days,
On evil days though fallen, and evil tongues;
In darkness, and with dangers compassed round,
And solitude; yet not alone, while thou
Visit'st my slumbers nightly, or when morn
Purples the east. Still govern thou my song,
Urania, and fit audience find, though few.
But drive far off the barbarous dissonance
Of Bacchus and his revellers, the race
Of that wild rout that tore the Thracian bard
In Rhodope, where woods and rocks had ears
To rapture, till the savage clamor drowned
Both harp and voice; nor could the Muse defend

[1] *Paradise Lost* 3. 17-55.
[2] *Ibid.* 7. 1-20.

Her son. So fail not thou who thee implores;
For thou art Heavenly, she an empty dream.[1]

    Sad task! yet argument
Not less but more heroic than the wrath
Of stern Achilles on his foe pursued
Thrice fugitive about Troy wall; or rage
Of Turnus for Lavinia disespoused;
Or Neptune's ire, or Juno's, that so long
Perplexed the Greek, and Cytherea's son:
If answerable style I can obtain
Of my celestial patroness, who deigns
Her nightly visitation unimplored,
And dictates to me slumbering, or inspires
Easy my unpremeditated verse,
Since first this subject for heroic song
Pleased me, long choosing and beginning late,
Not sedulous by nature to indite
Wars, hitherto the only argument
Heroic deemed, chief mastery to dissect
With long and tedious havoc fabled knights
In battles feigned (the better fortitude
Of patience and heroic martyrdom
Unsung), or to describe races and games
Or tilting furniture, imblazoned shields,
Impresses quaint, caparisons and steeds
Bases and tinsel trappings, gorgeous knights,
At joust and tournament; then marshaled feast
Served up in hall with sewers and seneschals:
The skill of artifice or office mean;
Not that which justly gives heroic name
To person or to poem. Me, of these
Nor skilled nor studious, higher argument
Remains, sufficient of itself to raise
That name, unless an age too late, or cold
Climate, or years, damp my intended wing
Depressed; and much they may, if all be mine,
Not hers who brings it nightly to my ear.[2]

[1] *Ibid.* 7. 23-39.
[2] *Ibid.* 9. 13-47.

2. MILTON AS PUPIL AND AS TEACHER[1]

From *Comus* (1634).

> How charming is divine Philosophy!
> Not harsh and crabbed, as dull fools suppose,
> But musical as is Apollo's lute,
> And a perpetual feast of nectared sweets,
> Where no crude surfeit reigns.[2]

From a Letter to Thomas Young [Milton's tutor]. London, March 26, 1625.

Though I had determined, my excellent tutor, to write you an epistle in verse, yet I could not satisfy myself without sending also another in prose, for the emotions of my gratitude, which your services so justly inspire, are too expansive and too warm to be expressed in the confined limits of poetical metre; they demand the unconstrained freedom of prose, or rather the exuberant richness of Asiatic phraseology; though it would far exceed my power accurately to describe how much I am obliged to you, even if I could drain dry all the sources of eloquence, or exhaust all the topics of discourse which Aristotle or the famed Parisian logician has collected. You complain with truth that my letters have been very few and very short; but I do not grieve at the omission of so pleasurable a duty so much as I rejoice at having such a place in your regard as makes you anxious often to hear from me. I beseech you not to take it amiss that I have not now written to you for more than three years; but, with your usual benignity, to impute it rather to circumstances than to inclination. For Heaven knows that I regard you as a parent, that I have always treated you with the utmost respect, and that I

[1] Chiefly in Milton's letters may one find interesting records of his attachment to his studies, his teachers, and, later, his pupils.
[2] *Comus* 476–80. Milton's lifelong devotion to study—the logic of the Schoolmen always excepted—is well summed up in these lines.

was unwilling to tease you with my compositions. And I was anxious that, if my letters had nothing else to recommend them, they might be recommended by their rarity. And, lastly, since the ardor of my regard makes me imagine that you are always present, that I hear your voice and contemplate your looks; and, as thus (which is usually the case with lovers) I charm away my grief by the illusion of your presence, I was afraid when I wrote to you the idea of your distant separation should forcibly rush upon my mind; and that the pain of your absence, which was almost soothed into quiescence, should revive and disperse the pleasurable dream.

I long since received your desirable present of the Hebrew Bible.

I wrote this at my lodgings in the city, not, as usual, surrounded by my books. If, therefore, there be anything in this letter which either fails to give pleasure, or which frustrates expectation, it shall be compensated by a more elaborate composition as soon as I return to the dwelling of the Muses.[1]

From *Elegy* 1. To Charles Deodati (1626).[2]

I am now[3] in the city that is washed by the ebbing and flowing Thames, tarrying, not unwilling, under my father's kindly roof. Meanwhile I care not to revisit reedy Cam; I suffer from no longing for my forbidden hearth; I find no pleasure in bare fields that afford no gentle shade. How ill that place befits the cult of Phœbus! Nor does it suit me always to endure the threats of a harsh master, and other wrongs to which my nature will not submit. If this be exile, to have retired to my father's house, and there care-free to live in pleasant leisure, then I refuse neither the name nor the lot of an exile, and gladly enjoy such banishment. Would that no heavier blow had fallen on the lamentable bard

---

[1] *Familiar Letters*, No. 1. *Prose Works* 3. 487–8.

[2] Translated by W. MacKellar.

[3] Milton's pleasant relations with his teachers suffered one interruption. These lines were written while he was at home, and possibly in rustication from the University. See Rand, *Milton in Rustication*, in *Studies in Philology* 19 (1922). 109–35.

who was exiled to the land of Tomis! In naught would he then have yielded to Ionian Homer, nor would the first praise be yours, O vanquished Maro.

Here I may freely give my time to the tranquil Muses; and here my books, which are my life, absorb me wholly. When I am weary, the splendors and the mazes of the theatre engross me, and the babbling stage summons me to its applause. Sometimes it is the grasping old man or spendthrift heir who speaks, the lover or the soldier with helmet doffed who is present; again it is an advocate grown rich on a ten-years' suit who thunders forth his barbarous expressions to the untutored court. Often the sly servant aids the enamoured son, and on every side cheats the stern father under his very nose; there often the maiden, marveling at the unwonted glow of passion, knows not what love is—yet, not knowing, loves. Then raging Tragedy brandishes her gory sceptre, and rolls her eyes beneath disheveled locks. As I look upon her the sight pains me, yet in the pain there is pleasure. Sometimes in tears the sweet and the bitter are mingled: as when perchance an unhappy boy leaves his joy untasted, and, torn from his love, perishes in sorrow; or when the cruel avenger has crossed again from the gloom of Styx, stirring with baleful torch the hearts that are conscious of sin; or when the House of Pelops, or of noble Ilus, mourns, or Creon's Court suffers for its incestuous sires.

But not always do I live secluded within doors, nor even within the city; neither do I let the spring pass by in vain. I visit, too, the neighboring grove thick-set with elms, and the suburban haunts noted for their shade. There one may often see the bands of maidens pass, stars that breathe seductive flames. Ah, how often have I stood amazed at the marvelous beauty of some form which might rejuvenate even the old age of Jove; ah, how often have I seen eyes brighter than jewels, brighter than all the stars that turn about either pole; necks which surpass the arms of twice-living Pelops, and the galaxy that flows with pure nectar; how often seen the surpassing beauty of brow and light-blown hair, golden snares set by deceiving Love; and how often seen alluring cheeks, to which hyacinthine purple, and even the blush of your flower, O Adonis, are pale. . . .

But as for me, while yet the indulgence of the blind boy permits, I am preparing with what haste I can to leave these happy walls, and with the aid of divine moly to guide my steps far from the infamous halls of faithless Circe. It is also fixed that I return to the sedgy marshes of Cam, and once more enter the hoarse murmur of the schools. Meanwhile accept the small tribute of a faithful friend, even these few words coaxed into alternate measures.[1]

From *Elegy* 4. At the Age of Eighteen. To his tutor, Thomas Young, now performing the duties of Chaplain to the English merchants at Hamburg.[2]

Away, my letter, speed through the boundless sea; go, seek the Teutonic lands over the smooth expanse of the deep; have done with lingering delays, and let nothing, I pray, thwart your going, nothing stay the haste of your course. I shall myself implore Æolus, who restrains the winds in his Sicilian cave, and the green gods, and cerulean Doris with her company of nymphs, to give you a peaceful journey through their realms. But, if possible, procure for yourself the swift team wherewith Medea in flight rode from the face of her husband, or that with which young Triptolemus reached the Scythian shores, a welcome messenger from the city of Eleusis. And when you descry the yellow sands of Germany, turn your course to the walls of rich Hamburg, which, as the legend runs, derives its name from Hama, slain, it is said, by a Cimbrian club. There dwells a pastor, renowned for his simple piety, instructed to feed the flocks of Christ. In truth he is more than half my soul, and I am forced to live half my life without him. Alas, how many seas, how many mountains, intervene and part me from my other dearer self!

[1] *Elegy* 1. 9–62; 85–92.
[2] Translated by W. MacKellar.

Dearer is he to me than you, Socrates, wisest of the Greeks, were to Alcibiades of the stock of Telamon; dearer even than the great Stagirite to his noble pupil, whom a Chaonian mother bore to Libyan Jove. What the son of Amyntor and what the half-divine son of Philyra were to the king of the Myrmidons, such is this man to me. He was my guide when I was first threading the Aonian shades, and the sacred greenswards of the cloven hill; he first led me to drink of the Pierian water, and favored by Clio I thrice wet my lips with Castalian wine. But thrice has flaming Æthon passed the sign of the Ram, and newly clothed his fleecy back with gold; and twice, Chloris, you have bestrewn the old earth with new grass, and twice Auster has swept away your wealth, since my eyes were permitted to feast on his face, or my ears to drink in the sweet music of his voice.

Go, then, and in your course outstrip the roaring East Wind. Whatever admonition you may need, circumstance will teach and you yourself will see. You will find him perhaps sitting with his charming wife, fondling on his knee the pledges of their love; or perchance turning over some stout volume of the ancient Fathers, or the Holy Scriptures of the one true God; or shedding the heavenly dew upon the souls of feeble men, which is religion's sublime work of healing. But only let it be your care to greet him, as the custom is, and to speak as would befit your master were he present. Fix your shy glances for a brief space on the ground, then remember with modest lips to speak these words:

'If in the midst of battles there is leisure for the gentle Muses, a faithful hand sends you these verses from the shores of England. Though it be late, accept this cordial greeting.'[1]

From a Letter to Alexander Gill. London, May 20, 1628.

I received your letters and your poem, with which I was highly delighted, and in which I discover the majesty of a poet and the style of Virgil. I knew how impossible it would be for a person of

---

[1] *Elegy* 4. 1–53.

your genius entirely to divert his mind from the culture of the Muses, and to extinguish those heavenly emotions, and that sacred and ethereal fire which is kindled in your heart; for what Claudian said of himself may be said of you, your 'whole soul is instinct with the fire of Apollo.'[1]

From a Letter to Alexander Gill. Cambridge, July 2, 1628.

When your letter arrived, I was strenuously engaged in that work concerning which I had given you some obscure hints, and the execution of which could not be delayed. One of the Fellows of our college, who was to be the respondent in a philosophical disputation for his degree, engaged me to furnish him with some verses, which are annually required on this occasion; since he himself had long neglected such frivolous pursuits, and was then intent on more serious studies. Of these verses I sent you a printed copy, since I knew both your discriminating taste in poetry and your candid allowances for poetry like mine. If you will in your turn deign to communicate to me any of your productions, you will, I can assure you, find no one to whom they will give more delight, or who will more impartially endeavor to estimate their worth; for as often as I recollect the topics of your conversation (the loss of which I regret even in this seminary of erudition) I cannot help painfully reflecting on what advantages I am deprived by your absence, since I never left your company without an increase of knowledge, and always had recourse to your mind as to an emporium of literature.[2]

From a Letter to Thomas Young. Cambridge, July 21, 1628.

Your many recent services must prevent me from entertaining any suspicion of your forgetfulness or neglect. Nor do I see how you could possibly forget one on whom you had conferred so many favors. Having an invitation into your part of the country in the spring, I shall readily accept it, that I may enjoy the

[1] *Familiar Letters*, No. 2. *Prose Works* 3. 488.
[2] *Familiar Letters*, No. 3. *Prose Works* 3. 489.

deliciousness of the season as well as that of your conversation; and that I may withdraw myself for a short time from the tumult of the city to your rural mansion, as to the renowned portico of Zeno, or Tusculan of Tully, where you live on your little farm, with a moderate fortune, but a princely mind; and where you practise the contempt, and triumph over the temptations, of ambition, pomp, luxury, and all that follows the chariot of fortune or attracts the gaze and admiration of the thoughtless multitude.[1]

From a Letter to Richard Heth. Westminster, December 13, 1652.

If I were able, my excellent friend, to render you any service in the promotion of your studies, which at best could have been but very small, I rejoice, on more accounts than one, that that service, though so long unknown, was bestowed on so fruitful and so genial a soil, which has produced an honest pastor to the Church, a good citizen to our country, and to me a most acceptable friend. Of this I am well aware not only from the general habits of your life but from the justness of your religious and political opinions, and particularly from the extraordinary ardor of your gratitude, which no absence, no change of circumstances or lapse of time, can either extinguish or impair. Nor is it possible, till you have made a more than ordinary progress in virtue, in piety, and the improvement of the mind and heart, to feel so much gratitude towards those who have in the least assisted you in the acquisition. Wherefore, my pupil, a name which with your leave I will employ, be assured that you are among the first objects of my regard; nor would anything be more agreeable to me, if your circumstances permit as much as your inclination, than to have you take up your abode somewhere in my neighborhood, where we may often see each other, and mutually profit by the reciprocations of kindness and of literature. But this must be as God pleases, and as you think best. Your future communications may, if you

---

[1] *Familiar Letters*, No. 4. *Prose Works* 3. 490.

please, be in our own language, lest (though you are no mean proficient in Latin composition) the labor of writing should make each of us more averse to write; and that we may freely disclose every sensation of our hearts without being impeded by the shackles of a foreign language.[1]

From a Letter to the noble Youth, Richard Jones. Westminster, September 21, 1656.

As often as I have taken up the pen to answer your last letter, some sudden interruptions have occurred to prevent the completion of my purpose. I afterwards heard that you had made an excursion to the adjoining country. As your excellent mother is on the eve of departing for Ireland, whose loss we have both no small occasion to regret, and who has to me supplied the place of every relative, she will herself be the bearer of these letters to you. You may rest assured of my regard, and be persuaded it will increase in proportion as I see an increasing improvement in your heart and mind. This, by the blessing of God, you have solemnly pledged yourself to accomplish. I am pleased with this fair promise of yourself, which I trust you will never violate.

Though you write that you are pleased with Oxford, you will not induce me to believe that Oxford has made you wiser or better. Of that I require very different proof. I would not have you lavish your admiration on the triumphs of the chiefs whom you extol, and things of that nature in which force is of most avail. For why need we wonder if the wethers of our country are born with horns which may batter down cities and towns? Do you learn to estimate great characters, not by the quantity of their animal strength, but by the habitual justice and temperance of their conduct.

Adieu, and make my best respects to the accomplished Henry Oldenburgh, your college chum.[2]

[1] *Familiar Letters*, No. 13. *Prose Works*. 3. 505.
[2] *Familiar Letters*, No. 19. *Prose Works* 3. 511.

From a Letter to the accomplished Youth, Peter Heimbach. Westminster, November 8, 1656.

You have done all I desired respecting the Atlas, of which I wished to know the lowest price. You say it is a hundred and thirty florins, which I think is enough to purchase the mountain of that name. But such is the present rage for typographical luxury that the furniture of a library hardly costs less than that of a villa. Paintings and engravings are of little use to me. While I roll my blind eyes about the world, I fear lest I should seem to lament the privation of sight in proportion to the exorbitance of the price for which I should have purchased the book. Do you endeavor to learn in how many volumes the entire work is contained; and, of the two editions, whether that of Blaeu or Janson be the more accurate and complete.[1]

From a Letter to the noble Youth, Richard Jones.

With pleasure I perceive the emotions of your attachment and your gratitude. I have never ceased to promote the culture of your genius, and to justify the favorable opinion which your excellent mother entertains of me, and the confidence she places in me, by benevolence the most pure and counsels the most sincere. In that agreeable and healthy spot to which you have retired, there are books enough for the purposes of academical education. If beauty of situation contributed as much to improve the wit of the inhabitants as it does to please the eye, the felicity of that place would be complete. The library there is rich in books; but, unless the minds of the students be improved by a more rational mode of education, it may better deserve the name of a book-repository than of a library. You justly acknowledge that all these helps to learning should be associated with a taste for literature, and with diligence in the cultivation. Take care I may never have occasion to blame you for deviating from that opinion. And this you will

[1] *Familiar Letters*, No. 20. *Prose Works* 3. 511-2.

readily avoid if you will diligently obey the weighty and friendly precepts of the accomplished Henry Oldenburgh, your associate and friend.

Adieu, my dearest Richard; and let me incite you, like another Timothy, to the practice of virtue and piety by the example of your mother, who is the best of women.[1]

From a Letter to the noble Youth, Richard Jones. Westminster, August 1, 1657.

I rejoice to hear that you accomplished so long a journey with so little inconvenience, and, what redounds so much to your credit, that, despising the luxuries of Paris, you hastened with so much celerity where you might enjoy the pleasures of literature with the conversation of the learned. As long as you please you will there be in a haven of security; in other places you will have to guard against the shoals of treachery and the siren's songs. I would not wish you to thirst too much after the vintage of Saumur, but to resolve to dilute the Bacchanalian stream with more than a fifth part of the crystal liquor of the Parnassian fount. But in this respect without my injunction you have an excellent preceptor whom you cannot do better than obey; and by obeying whom you will give the highest satisfaction to your excellent mother, and daily increase in her regard and love. That you may have power to do this, you should daily ask help from above.

Adieu, and endeavor to return as much improved as possible, both in virtue and erudition. This will give me more than ordinary pleasure.[2]

From a Letter to the noble Youth, Richard Jones. Westminster, December 20, 1659.

I shall perceive all the ardor of your gratitude (since you will extol the merit of my services) not so much in the frequency of your letters as in the excellence of your habits and the degree of

---

[1] *Familiar Letters*, No. 22. *Prose Works* 3. 513-4.
[2] *Familiar Letters*, No. 25. *Prose Works* 3. 517.

your moral and intellectual proficiency. On the theatre of the world on which you have entered, you have rightly chosen the path of virtue; but know there is a path common to virtue and to vice; and that it behoves you to advance where the way divides. Leaving the common track of pleasure and amusement, you should cheerfully encounter the toils and the dangers of that steep and rugged way which leads to the pinnacle of virtue. This, believe me, you will accomplish with more facility since you have got a guide of so much integrity and skill.[1]

From Milton's *Commonplace Book*.

De liberis educandis

Natura cuiusque imprimis inspicienda nec torquenda aliorsum; deum enim non omnes ad singula destinat, sed ad suum quemque opus proprium; unde Dantes

> E se il mondo laggiù ponesse mente
> Al fondamento che natura pone, etc.

Vide *Paradiso*, Cant. 8. . . .

Not to labor, as most men do, to make them bold and pert while they are young, which ripens them too soon; and true boldness and spirit is not bred but of virtuous causes, which are wrought in them by sober discipline. To this purpose Chaucer, speaking of feasts, and revels and dances:

> Swich thinges maken children for to be
> To sone rype and bold, as men may see,
> Which is ful perilous.[2]

Doctor of Phis. Tale, fol. 58.

[1] *Familiar Letters*, No. 30. *Prose Works*. 3. 521.
[2] *Commonplace Book*, p. 111.

3. MILTON'S RELATIONS WITH OTHER SCHOLARS

From *Manso* (1639).[1]

Therefore, father Manso, in the name of Clio and of mighty Phoebus, I, a youthful traveler sent from beneath the Hyperborean heaven, wish you good health through a long life. You are kind, and will not spurn a foreign Muse, which, but sparely nourished under the frozen Bear, of late has indiscreetly ventured to fly through the cities of Italy. Methinks through the dusky shades of night I too have heard the swans singing in our own river, where silvery Thames with clear urns lets her gleaming locks flow wide in the waters of ocean. Indeed Tityrus once came to these shores.

But we, a race that through long nights endures the wintry Boötes in that region of the world that is furrowed by the sevenfold Triones, we are not untaught and useless to Phœbus. We even worship Phoebus, and—unless age renders void the tale— we have sent him gifts—yellowing ears, rosy apples in baskets, crocuses breathing fragrance, and troops of maidens chosen from the Druid race. The Druids, an ancient people skilled in the rites of the gods, used to sing the praises of heroes and their emulable deeds. Hence as often as they circle the altars in festive song, as is their wont, the Greek maidens on grassy Delos in joyful verses commemorate Corinedian Loxo, prophetic Upis, with yellow-haired Hecaerge, their bare breasts stained with Caledonian paint. . . .

Aged man, beloved of the gods, Jupiter must have been friendly to you at birth; Phœbus and the grandson of Atlas must have shone with kindly light; for no one, unless from his birth he were dear to the gods above, could have befriended a great poet. Hence your old age blooms with lingering flowers, and, still full

[1] Translated by W. MacKellar.

121

of life, has the benefit of the Æsonian spindles, keeping the honors of your brow unshed, your genius flourishing, and the keenness of your mind in its prime. If ever I recall in song my native kings, and Arthur setting wars in motion even beneath the earth; if ever I tell of the high-souled heroes in the social bond of the invincible Table; and—let the spirit be present to aid me—if ever I break the Saxon phalanxes with British war; then may my lot grant me such a friend, one who knows so well how to honor the sons of Phœbus. At last when I had measured the span of a life not mute, and, sated with years, should leave to ashes their due, with tear-stained eyes he would stand by my bed; and as he stood there I need only say, 'Let me be under thy care.' He would see that my limbs, relaxed in livid death, were gently gathered in a little urn. Perchance he would also draw my features from marble, binding the locks on my brow with Paphian myrtle or with laurel of Parnassus, and I should rest in heedless peace. Then, if there be any faith, and if there be sure rewards for the righteous, I myself, removed to the ethereal realms of the heaven-dwelling gods, whither labor, a pure mind, and ardent courage convey us, even I shall see these things from some part of that secret world—as the Fates permit—and with mind all serene, my smiling face suffused with a purple light, I shall joyfully clap my hands on ethereal Olympus.[1]

From *The Second Defence of The People of England* (1654).

[How Milton's first *Defence* was welcomed.]

In the mean time not one hair of my head is singed by the conflagrations which you kindle, but those affronts are balanced by much delight and many sweets. One tribunal, perhaps, or a single Parisian executioner, under some unlucky bias, burnt my book; but, nevertheless, how many good and wise men through all France read it, cherished and admired it? How many through the spacious tracts of Germany, the domicile of freedom, and

---

[1] *Manso* 24–48; 70–100.

wherever any traces of freedom yet remain? Moreover, Greece it-self, and Athens, the eye of Greece, mingles its applause in the voice of its noble Philaras. And this I can truly say—that as soon as my *Defence* appeared, and had begun to excite the public curiosity, there was no public functionary of any prince or state then in the city who did not congratulate me when we accident-ally met, who did not desire my company at his house or visit me at mine. But it would be wrong not to mention you, O Adrian Paul, the honor and the ornament of Holland, who, dispatched on a splendid embassy to us, thought I had never the pleasure of seeing you, sent me frequent assurances of your extraordinary pre-dilection and regard. This it often delights me to recollect and—which could never have happened without the special appoint-ment of the Deity—that royalty itself courteously favored me who had apparently written against kings, and afforded to my integ-rity and veracity a testimony next to the divine; for why should I fear to say this, when I consider how zealously and how highly all persons extol that illustrious Queen?[1] Nor do I think that he who was the wisest of the Athenians—and with whom I by no means wish to compare myself—was more honored by the testi-mony of the Pythian oracle than I am by the approbation of such a Queen. If this had happened to me when a young man, and orators might have taken the same liberties as poets, I should not have hesitated to prefer my fate to that of some of the gods themselves; for, while they contended for the prize of beauty or harmony before a human judge, I, in the most glorious of all con-tests, had the palm of victory adjudged to me by the voice of an immortal.[2]

From a Letter to Luke Holstein, in the Vatican at Rome. Florence, March 30, 1639.

I know not, most learned Holstein, whether I am the only Englishman to whom you have shown so much friendship and regard, or whether you are led to show the same to all my

[1] Christina, of Sweden.   [2] *Prose Works* I. 278-9.

countrymen, from a recollection of the three years which you passed at the University of Oxford. If this be the case, you generously pay to our dear England the fees of her education. . . . It would indeed have been far more grateful to me if I could have been at all instrumental in promoting those honorable and illustrious pursuits in which you are engaged; and which it behoves all men, on all occasions, and in all circumstances, to promote. . . .

Adieu, most learned Holstein, and, if you think me worthy of the honor, rank me, I beseech you, for the future, wherever I may be, among those who are most attached to you and to your studies in which you are engaged.[1]

From a Letter to Carolo Deodati, a Florentine Noble. London, April 21, 1647.

But you, by first addressing me in a manner so truly friendly, and by a triple repetition of epistolary kindness, have laid me under an obligation to write to you, and have exonerated me from the censure of those to whom I do not write; though I must confess that I found other reasons for silence in these convulsions which my country has experienced since my return home, which necessarily diverted my attention from the prosecution of my studies to the preservation of my property and my life. For can you imagine that I could have leisure to taste the sweets of literary ease while so many battles were fought, so much blood shed, and while so much ravage prevailed among my fellow-citizens? But even in the midst of this tempestuous period I have published several works in my native language, which, if they had not been written in English, I should have pleasure in sending to you, whose judgment I so much revere. My Latin poems I will soon send as you desire; and this I should have done long ago without being desired, if I had not suspected that some rather harsh expressions which they contained against the Roman Pontiff would have rendered them less pleasing to your ears.

[1] *Familiar Letters*, No. 9. *Prose Works* 3. 499–500.

Now I request, whenever I mention the rites of your religion in my own way, that you will prevail on your friends (for I am under no apprehensions from you) to show me the same indulgence not only which they did to Aligerius and to Petrarch on a similar occasion, but which you did formerly with such singular benevolence to the freedom of my conversation on topics of religion. With pleasure I perused your description of the funeral of King Louis. I do not acknowledge the inspiration of that vulgar and mercenary Mercury whom you jocosely profess to worship, but of that Mercury who excels in eloquence, who is dear to the Muses, and the patron of men of genius.[1]

From a Letter to the renowned Leonard Philaras, the Athenian. London, January, 1652.

I was in some measure made acquainted, most accomplished Philaras, with your goodwill towards me, and with your favorable opinion of my *Defence of the People of England*, by your letters to the Lord Auger, a person so renowned for his singular integrity in executing the embassies of the Republic. I then received your compliments with your picture and a eulogy worthy of your virtues; and, lastly, a letter full of civility and kindness. I, who am not wont to despise the genius of the German, the Dane, and the Swede, could not but set the highest value on your applause who [were] born at Athens itself, and who, after having happily finished your studies in Italy, obtained the most splendid distinctions and the highest honors. For if Alexander the Great, when waging war in the distant East, declared that he encountered so many dangers and so many trials for the sake of having his praises celebrated by the Athenians, ought not I to congratulate myself on receiving the praises of a man in whom alone the talents and the virtues of the ancient Athenians seem to recover their freshness and their strength after so long an interval of corruption and decay? To the writings of those illustrious men

[1] *Familiar Letters*, No. 10. *Prose Works* 3. 501–2.

[whom] your city has produced, in the perusal of which I have been occupied from my youth, it is with pleasure I confess that I am indebted for all my proficiency in literature. Did I possess their command of language and their force of persuasion, I should feel the highest satisfaction in employing them to excite our armies and our fleets to deliver Greece, the parent of eloquence, from the despotism of the Ottomans. Such is the enterprise in which you seem to wish to implore my aid. And what did formerly men of the greatest courage and eloquence deem more noble, or more glorious, than by their orations or their valor to assert the liberty and independence of the Greeks? But we ought besides to attempt, what is, I think, of the greatest moment, to inflame the present Greeks with an ardent desire to emulate the virtue, the industry, the patience, of their ancient progenitors; and this we cannot hope to see effected by any one but yourself, and for [this] you seem adapted by the splendor of your patriotism, combined with so much discretion, so much skill in war, and such an unquenchable thirst for the recovery of your ancient liberty.[1]

From a Letter to Henry Oldenburgh, Aulic Counselor to the Senate of Bremen. Westminster, July 6, 1654.

I should not have sent you my *Defence* without any compliment or apology; and I have since received another letter from you, in which you return me more ample acknowledgments than the present deserved. And I had more than once an intention of substituting our English for your Latin, that you, who have studied our language with more accuracy and success than any foreigner with whom I am acquainted, might lose no opportunity of writing it, which I think that you would do with equal elegance and correctness. . . . If my health and the deprivation of my sight (which is more grievous than all the infirmities of age), or the cries of these impostors, will permit, I shall readily be led to engage in other undertakings, though I know not whether they

---

[1] *Familiar Letters*, No. 12. *Prose Works* 3. 503-4.

can be more noble or more useful; for what can be more noble or more useful than to vindicate the liberty of man? An inactive indolence was never my delight; but this unexpected contest with the enemies of liberty has involuntarily withdrawn my attention from very different and more pleasurable pursuits.[1]

From a Letter to Henry Oldenburgh, Aulic Counselor to the Senate of Bremen. Westminster, June 25, 1656.

I congratulate you on your retirement because it gives pleasure to you, though it is a loss to me; and I admire that felicity of genius which can so readily leave the factions or the diversions of the city for contemplations the most serious and sublime. I see not what advantage you can have in that retirement except in an access to a multitude of books. The associates in study whom you have found there, were, I believe, rather made students by their own natural inclinations than by the discipline of the place. But perhaps I am less partial to the place because it detains you, whose absence I regret. You rightly observe that there are too many there who pollute all learning, divine and human, by their frivolous subtleties and barren disputations, and who seem to do nothing to deserve the salary which they receive. But you are not so unwise.

Those ancient records of the Chinese from the period of the deluge, which you say are promised by the Jesuit Martinius, are, no doubt, on account of their novelty, expected with avidity; but I do not see what authority or support they can add to the books of Moses.[2]

From a Letter to the accomplished Emeric Bigot. Westminster, March 24, 1658.

Many have been celebrated for their compositions whose common conversation and intercourse have betrayed no marks of sublimity or genius. But, as far as possible, I will endeavor to

---

[1] *Familiar Letters*, No. 14. *Prose Works.* 3. 506.
[2] *Familiar Letters*, No. 18. *Prose Works* 3. 510-1.

seem equal in thought and speech to what I have well written, if I have written anything well; and, while I add to the dignity of what I have written, I will at the same time derive from my writings a greater splendor of reputation. Thus I shall not seem to have borrowed the excellence of my literary compositions from others so much as to have drawn it pure and unmingled from the resources of my own mind and the force of my own conceptions.

It gives me pleasure that you are convinced of the tranquillity which I possess under this afflicting privation of sight, as well as of the civility and kindness with which I receive those who visit me from other countries. And indeed why should I not submit with complacency to this loss of sight, which seems only withdrawn from the body without to increase the sight of the mind within? Hence, books have not incurred my resentment, nor do I intermit the study of books, though they have inflicted so heavy a penalty on me for my attachment; the example of Telephus, King of Mysia, who did not refuse to receive a cure from the same weapon by which he had been wounded, admonished me not to be so morose.[1]

From a Letter to Henry Oldenburgh. Westminster, December 20, 1659.

The indulgence which you beg for yourself you will rather have to bestow on me, whose turn, if I remember, it was to write. My regard for you has, believe me, suffered no diminution; but either my studies or my domestic cares, or perhaps my indolence in writing, have made me guilty of this omission of duty. I am, by God's help, as well as usual.

I am not willing, as you wish me, to compile a history of our troubles, for they seem rather to require oblivion than commemoration; nor have we so much need of a person to compose a history of our troubles as happily to settle them. I fear with you

---

[1] *Familiar Letters*, No. 21. *Prose Works* 3. 512–3.

lest our civil dissensions, or rather maniacal agitation, should expose us to the attack of the lately confederated enemies of religion and of liberty; but those enemies could not inflict a deeper wound upon religion than we ourselves have long since done by our follies and our crimes. But whatever disturbances kings and cardinals may meditate and contrive, I trust that God will not suffer the machinations and the violence of our enemies to succeed according to their expectations.[1]

[1] *Familiar Letters*, No. 29. *Prose Works* 3. 520.

4. MILTON ON PLEASURE AND RECREATION

From *Academic Exercise* 6. That Sportive Exercises on Occasion are not Inconsistent with the Studies of Philosophy.[1]

I entreat you, my hearers, that none of you repent of giving yourselves a brief holiday with these frivolities of mine; for the report is that all the gods themselves have often, the care of their heavenly polity laid aside for the time, been present at the spectacle of pygmies fighting; sometimes even they are related, not disdaining humble cottages, and received with a poor hospitality, to have made a meal of beans and leeks. I, in like manner, beseech and beg you, my excellent hearers, that this poor little entertainment of mine, such as it is, may pass for a feast to your subtle and knowing palates. Truly, though I know very many sciolists with whom it is a constant custom, if they are ignorant of anything, haughtily and foolishly to contemn that same in others as a thing not worth *their* bestowing pains upon — this one for example impertinently carping at dialectics, which he never could acquire, and this other making no account of philosophy, because Nature, that fairest of the goddesses, never deemed him worthy of such an honor as that she should let him behold her naked charms — yet I will not grudge to praise, to the extent of my power, festivities and jest, in which I do acknowledge my faculty to be very slight, premising only this, that it seems an arduous and far from easy task for me this day to praise jocularity in serious terms.

Nor are my praises undeserved. What is there that sooner conciliates and longer retains friendship than a pleasant and festive disposition? Let there be a person who has no jests, nor fun, nor nice little *facetiæ* in him, and you will hardly find one to whom he is agreeable and welcome. And, were it our daily

[1] Translated by Masson.

custom, Academicians, to go to sleep and as it were die in philosophy, and to grow old among the thickets and thorns of logic,
without any relaxation or any breathing-time granted, what
else, pray, would philosophizing be but prophesying in the cave
of Trophonius and following Cato's too rigid sect? The very
rustics themselves would say that we lived on mustard. Add that,
as those who accustom themselves to field strife and sports are
rendered much stronger than others, and readier for all work, so
in like manner it happens that by this intellectual gymnastic the
sinews of the mind are strengthened, and better blood and juice,
as it were, is procured, and the genius becomes clearer and acuter,
and nimble and versatile for everything. But, if there is any one
who would rather not be considered urbane and gay, let him not
take it to heart if he is called country-bred and clownish. Well
do we know a certain illiberal kind of fellows, who, utterly
morose and unfestive themselves, and silently taking measure of
their own meanness and ignorance, can never hear any remark of a
sprightly nature without immediately thinking it is leveled at
them — deserving, in fact, to have that happen to them which they
wrongly suspect, and to be pelted with the jeers of all till they
almost think of hanging themselves. Those riff-raff gentry, however, avail nothing against the freedom of elegant politeness.

Do you wish, my hearers, that on this foundation of reason I
should pile an argument from instances? Such are supplied me
abundantly. First of all there is Homer, that morning star of
civilized literature, with whom all learning was born as a twin;
for he, sometimes recalling his divine mind from the counsels of
the gods and the deeds in heaven, and turning aside into the
humorous, described most amusingly the battles of the mice and
the frogs. Moreover, Socrates, the wisest of mortals, the Pythian
himself being witness, is said often to have baffled with pleasantry
the brawling bad temper of his wife. Then we read reports everywhere of the pithy sayings of the old philosophers, well sprinkled
with salt and classic wit; and surely it was this alone that

conferred an eternity of name on all the ancient writers of comedies and epigrams, both Grecian and Latin. Moreover, we hear of Cicero's jokes and *facetiæ* as having filled three books, when collected by a disciple. And every one now has in his hands that most ingenious *Encomium of Folly*, the work of no low writer; . . . and many other not unamusing essays of very celebrated speakers of late times are extant on laughable topics. Will you have the greatest commanders, kings, and warriors? Take Pericles, Epaminondas, Agesilaus, and Philip of Macedon, who (if I may speak in the Gellian manner) are related by historians to have abounded in jocosities and witty sayings, and, with them, Caius Lælius, Publius Cornelius Scipio, Cnæus Pompeius, Caius Julius Cæsar, and also Octavius Cæsar, who are said, on the authority of M. Tullius, to have excelled all their contemporaries in this sort of thing. Will you have yet greater names? The poets, most sagacious in shadowing forth the truth, bring in Jupiter himself and the rest of the celestials abandoning themselves to joviality amid their feasts and cups. . . .

But perchance there are not wanting certain Bearded Masters, very crabbed and harsh, who, thinking themselves great Catos, and not little Catos, and composing their countenances to a Stoic severity, and shaking their stiff polls, will tetchily complain that everything nowadays is in confusion and tending to the worse, and that, in place of an exposition of the *Prior Analytics* of Aristotle by the recently initiated Bachelors, scurrilities and empty trivialities are shamelessly and unseasonably bandied about; this day's exercise too, doubtless rightly and faithfully established by our ancestors with a view to some signal benefit whether in rhetoric or in philosophy, now of late giddily changing itself into a display of insipid witticisms. But I have an answer at hand and ready for such. Let them know, if they do not know, that letters had hardly been brought from foreign countries to these coasts at the time when the laws of our Literary Republic were first framed; on which account, as skill in the Greek and

Latin tongues was then exceedingly rare and unusual, it was fitting that men should labor and aspire after them by all the harder study and all the more assiduous exercises. But we, worse moraled than our predecessors, but better instructed, ought to leave studies that have not much difficulty, and go on to those to which they would have betaken themselves if they had had leisure. Nor has it escaped you that all early legislators are wont always to promulgate edicts a little harder and more severe than can be borne, so that men by deviating and gradually relapsing may hit the right mean. . . . But truly I think that the man who is wont to be so taken with jests as plainly to neglect for them what is serious and more useful—I think, I say, that such a man cannot make much progress either in this line or in that; certainly not in serious matters, because, were he equipped and fashioned by nature for treating serious things, I believe he would not so easily suffer himself to be drawn away from them; nor yet in lightsome affairs, because scarce any one can jest well and gracefully unless he has first learned to act seriously.[1]

From *Elegy* 6. To Charles Deodati (1629). [2]

[While staying in the country he had written to the author on the thirteenth of December, and asked him to excuse his verses, if they were not so good as usual, because, amid the festivities with which he had been received by his friends, he was unable favorably to devote himself to the Muses; he received the following reply.]

I who am not surfeited with feasting wish you good health, which perhaps you may need because of an overtaxed stomach. But why should your Muse lure mine forth and permit it not to seek the shades it loves? You would hear in song how much I love and cherish you? But believe me, you can hardly learn that from a song, for neither is my love bound in strict measures, nor does it come unimpaired on halting feet.

[1] Masson, *Life of Milton* I. 286-9. Reprinted by permission of The Macmillan Company, New York; Macmillan & Company, Ltd., London.
[2] Translated by W. MacKellar.

How well you describe the banquets, the December merriment, the pleasures and the cheer, that do honor to the God who flees from Heaven and seeks the earth! How well you recount the joys of winter in the country, and the French must quaffed by the comfortable fireside! But why do you complain that poetry shuns wine and feasting? Song loves Bacchus, and Bacchus loves song. Nor was Phoebus ashamed to have worn the green corymbus, and to have preferred the ivy to his own laurel. Often on the Aonian hills, have the nine Muses in a crowd shouted 'Evoe!' and mingled with the Bacchic revels. Naso sent bad verses from the Corallian fields, because there he had not enough of dainties and of wine. Of what but wine and roses, and Bacchus crowned with clusters, did the Teian Muse sing in his brief measures? Teumesian Euan inspires the Pindaric numbers, and every page breathes the fragrance of outpoured wine, as with loud crash the heavy chariot lies overturned, and the horseman speeds on, swarthy with the Elean dust. The Roman lyrist drank deep of the four-year-old wine when he sweetly sang of Glycera and golden-haired Chloe. The rich board with its sumptuous provision now fosters the strength of your mind and your genius. Your Massic cups foam rich with song, and from the jar itself you pour the treasures of your verse. To these influences let us add the arts, and give Phœbus freedom of the inmost heart, and let Bacchus, Apollo, and Ceres lend as one their favor. Small wonder then that your songs are so sweet, brought forth as they were by the common will of three gods.

For you too now sounds the Thracian lute, inwrought with gold, and gently touched by the nimble hand. In tapestried rooms is heard the lyre that guides in sprightly rhythm the maidens' feet. At least let such sights as these stay your Muse, and let them recall whatever inspiration idle indulgence in wine has banished. Be assured, when the ivory keys resound, and the accompanying festive band fills the perfumed chambers, you will feel Phœbus

silently steal into your breast, like a sudden glow that penetrates
the very bones; and, through the eyes and hands of the girlish
player, swift Thalia will fill your whole breast.[1]

From *L'Allegro*.[2]

> Thus done the tales, to bed they creep,
> By whispering winds soon lulled asleep.
> Towered cities please us then,
> And the busy hum of men,
> Where throngs of knights and barons bold,
> In weeds of peace, high triumphs hold,
> With store of ladies, whose bright eyes
> Rain influence, and judge the prize
> Of wit, or arms, while both contend
> To win her grace whom all commend.
> There let Hymen oft appear
> In saffron robe, with taper clear,
> And pomp, and feast, and revelry,
> With masque and antique pageantry;
> Such sights as youthful poets dream
> On summer eves by haunted stream.
> Then to the well-trod stage anon,
> If Jonson's learned sock be on,
> Or sweetest Shakespeare, Fancy's child,
> Warble his native wood-notes wild.
> And ever, against eating cares,
> Lap me in soft Lydian airs
> Married to immortal verse,
> Such as the meeting soul may pierce,
> In notes with many a winding bout
> Of linked sweetness long drawn out
> With wanton heed and giddy cunning,
> The melting voice through mazes running,
> Untwisting all the chains that tie
> The hidden soul of harmony;
> That Orpheus' self may heave his head

[1] *Elegy* 6. 1–48.

[2] 'The probability is that these two celebrated pieces [*L'Allegro* and *Il Penseroso*] were written at Horton in the autumn or latter part of 1632, and were the first exercises of Milton's Muse in his rustic retirement there.' Masson, *Life of Milton* 1. 569.

From golden slumber on a bed
Of heaped Elysian flowers, and hear
Such strains as would have won the ear
Of Pluto to have quite set free
His half-regained Eurydice.[1]

From *Il Penseroso*.

Or let my lamp at midnight hour
Be seen in some high lonely tower,
Where I may oft outwatch the Bear,
With thrice-great Hermes, or unsphere
The spirit of Plato to unfold
What worlds or what vast regions hold
The immortal mind that hath forsook
Her mansion in this fleshly nook;
And of those demons that are found
In fire, air, flood, or under-ground,
Whose power hath a true consent
With planet, or with element.
Some time let gorgeous Tragedy
In sceptred pall come sweeping by,
Presenting Thebes, or Pelops' line,
Or the tale of Troy divine,
Or what (though rare) of later age
Ennobled hath the buskined stage.
But, O sad Virgin, that thy power
Might raise Musæus from his bower,
Or bid the soul of Orpheus sing
Such notes as warbled to the string
Drew iron tears down Pluto's cheek,
And made Hell grant what Love did seek.
Or call up him that left half-told
The story of Cambuscan bold,
Of Camball, and of Algarsife,
And who had Canace to wife,
That owned the virtuous ring and glass,
And of the wondrous horse of brass
On which the Tartar king did ride;
And if aught else great bards beside
In sage and solemn tunes have sung,

[1] *L'Allegro* 115-50.

Of turneys, and of trophies hung,
Of forests, and enchantments drear,
Where more is meant than meets the ear. . . .
But let my due feet never fail
To walk the studious cloister's pale,
And love the high embowèd roof,
With antique pillars massy-proof,
And storied windows richly dight,
Casting a dim religious light.
There let the pealing organ blow
To the full-voiced quire below,
In service high and anthems clear,
As may with sweetness, through mine ear,
Dissolve me into ecstasies,
And bring all Heaven before mine eyes.[1]

From *Arcades* (1633).

But else, in deep of night, when drowsiness
Hath locked up mortal sense, then listen I
To the celestial Sirens' harmony,
That sit upon the nine infolded spheres,
And sing to those that hold the vital shears,
And turn the adamantine spindle round
On which the fate of gods and men is wound.
Such sweet compulsion doth in music lie,
To lull the daughters of Necessity,
And keep unsteady Nature to her law,
And the low world in measured motion draw
After the heavenly tune, which none can hear
Of human mould with gross unpurgèd ear.[2]

Canzone (1639). [3]

They mock my toil—the nymphs and am'rous swains—
'And whence this fond attempt to write,' they cry,
'Love-songs in language that thou little know'st?
How dar'st thou risk to sing these foreign strains?
Say truly. Find'st not oft thy purpose crossed,
And that thy fairest flow'rs here fade and die?'
Then with pretence of admiration high—

[1] *Il Penseroso* 85-120; 155-66.
[2] *Arcades* 61-73.
[3] Translated by Cowper.

'Thee other shores expect, and other tides,
Rivers, on whose grassy sides
Her deathless laurel-leaf, with which to bind
Thy flowing locks, already Fame provides;
Why then this burthen, better far declined?'
Speak, Muse! for me.—The fair one said who guides
My willing heart, and all my fancy's flights,
'This is the language, in which Love delights.'

From *The Reason of Church-Government* (1641).

But, because the spirit of man cannot demean itself lively in this body without some recreating intermission of labor and serious things, it were happy for the Commonwealth if our magistrates, as in those famous governments of old, would take into their care, not only the deciding of our contentious law-cases and brawls, but the managing of our public sports and festival pastimes; that they might be not such as were authorized a while since, the provocations of drunkenness and lust, but such as may inure and harden our bodies by martial exercises to all warlike skill and performance; and may civilize, adorn, and make discreet our minds by the learned and affable meeting of frequent academies, and the procurement of wise and artful recitations, sweetened with eloquent and graceful enticements to the love and practice of justice, temperance, and fortitude, instructing and bettering the nation at all opportunities, that the call of wisdom and virtue may be heard everywhere. . . . Whether this may not be not only in pulpits, but, after another persuasive method, at set and solemn paneguries, in theatres, porches, or what other place or way may win most upon the people to receive at once both recreation and instruction, let them in authority consult.[1]

From *Tetrachordon* (1645).

No mortal nature can endure, either in the actions of religion or study of wisdom, without some time slackening the cords of intense thought and labor; which lest we should think faulty,

[1] *Prose Works* 2. 480.

God Himself conceals us not His own recreations before the world was built: 'I was,' saith the Eternal Wisdom, 'daily His delight, playing always before Him.' And to Him, indeed, wisdom is as a high tower of pleasure, but to us a steep hill, and we toiling ever about the bottom. He executes with ease the exploits of His omnipotence, as easy as with us it is to will; but no worthy enterprise can be done by us without continual plodding and wearisomeness to our faint and sensitive abilities. We cannot, therefore, always be contemplative, or pragmatical abroad, but have need of some delightful intermissions wherein the enlarged soul may leave off awhile her severe schooling and, like a glad youth in wandering vacancy, may keep her holidays to joy and harmless pastime.[1]

To Mr. Lawrence (1656).

Lawrence, of virtuous father virtuous son,
    Now that the fields are dank, and ways are mire,
    Where shall we sometimes meet, and by the fire
    Help waste a sullen day, what may be won
From the hard season gaining? Time will run
    On smoother, till Favonius reinspire
    The frozen earth, and clothe in fresh attire
    The lily and rose, that neither sowed nor spun.
What neat repast shall feast us, light and choice,
    Of Attic taste, with wine, whence we may rise
    To hear the lute well touched, or artful voice
Warble immortal notes and Tuscan air?
    He who of those delights can judge, and spare
    To interpose them oft, is not unwise.

To Cyriack Skinner (1656).

Cyriack, whose grandsire on the royal bench
    Of British Themis, with no mean applause,
    Pronounced, and in his volumes taught our laws,
    Which others at their bar so often wrench;
To-day deep thoughts resolve with me to drench
    In mirth that after no repenting draws;
    Let Euclid rest, and Archimedes pause,

[1] *Prose Works* 3. 331.

And what the Swede intend, and what the French.
To measure life learn thou betimes, and know
 Toward solid good what leads the nearest way;
 For other things mild Heaven a time ordains,
And disapproves that care, though wise in show,
 That with superfluous burden loads the day,
 And, when God sends a cheerful hour, refrains.

From *Paradise Lost* (1667).

 Yet not so strictly hath our Lord imposed
 Labor as to debar us when we need
 Refreshment, whether food, or talk between,
 Food of the mind, or this sweet intercourse
 Of looks and smiles; for smiles from reason flow,
 To brute denied, and are of love the food—
 Love, not the lowest end of human life.
 For not to irksome toil, but to delight,
 He made us, and delight to reason joined.[1]

[1] *Paradise Lost* 9. 235-43.

5. MILTON ON THE STUDY OF LANGUAGE

To Benedetto Buommattei, of Florence.[1] Florence, September 10, 1638.

By this work of yours, Benedetto Buommattei—the compilation of new institutes of your native tongue—now so far advanced that you are about to give it the finishing touch, you are entering on a path to renown shared with you by some intellects of the highest order, and have also, as I see, raised a hope and an opinion of yourself among your fellow-citizens, as of one that is to confer, by his own easy effort, either lucidity or richness, or, at least, polish and order, on what has been handed down by others. Under what extraordinary obligation you have laid your countrymen by this, they must be ungrateful if they do not perceive.

For whoever in a state knows how to form wisely the manners of men and to rule them at home and in war with excellent institutes, him in the first place, above others, I should esteem worthy of all honor; but next to him the man who strives to establish in maxims and rules the method and habit of speaking and writing received from a good age of the nation, and, as it were, to fortify the same round with a kind of wall, any attempt to overleap which ought to be prevented by a law only short of that of Romulus. Should we compare the two in respect of utility, it is the former alone that can make the social existence of the citizens just and holy, but it is the latter alone that can make it splendid and beautiful—which is the next thing to be wished. The one, as I believe, supplies a noble courage and intrepid counsels against an enemy invading the territory; the other takes to himself the task of extirpating and defeating, by means of a learned detective police of ears and a light cavalry of good authors, that barbarism which makes large inroads upon the minds of men, and is a destructive intestine enemy to genius.

[1] Translated by Masson.

Nor is it to be considered of small consequence what language, pure or corrupt, a people has, or what is their customary degree of propriety in speaking it—a matter which oftener than once involved the salvation of Athens: nay, while it is Plato's opinion that, by a change in the manner and habit of dressing, serious commotions and mutations are portended in a commonwealth, I, for my part, would rather believe that the fall of that city and its low and obscure condition were consequent on the general vitiation of its usage in the matter of speech. For, let the words of a country be in part unhandsome and offensive in themselves, in part debased by wear and wrongly uttered, and what do they declare but, by no light indication, that the inhabitants of that country are an indolent, idly-yawning race, with minds already long prepared for any amount of servility? On the other hand, we have never heard that any empire, any state, did not flourish moderately at least as long as liking and care for its own language lasted.

Therefore, Benedetto, if only you proceed to perform vigorously this labor of yours for your native state, behold clearly, even from this, what a fair and solid affection you will necessarily win from your countrymen. All this I say, not because I suppose you to be ignorant of any of it, but because I persuade myself that you are much more intent on the consideration of what you yourself can do for your country than of what your country will, by the best right, owe to you. I will now speak of foreigners. For obliging *them*, if that is at your heart, most certainly at present an ample opportunity is offered—since what one is there among them that, happening to be more blooming than the rest in genius or in pleasing and elegant manners, and so counting the Tuscan tongue among his chief delights, does not also consider that it ought to have a place for him in the solid part of his literature, especially if he has imbibed Greek and Latin either not at all or but in slight tincture? I, certainly, who have not wet merely the tips of my lips with both those tongues, but have, as much as any, to the full allowance of my years, drained their deeper draughts, can yet sometimes willingly and eagerly go for a feast to that Dante of yours, and to Petrarch, and a good few more; nor has Attic Athens herself, with her pellucid Ilissus, nor that old Rome with her bank of the Tiber, been able so to hold me but that I love often to visit your Arno and these hills of Fæsule. See now, I entreat, whether it has not been with enough of providential cause that *I* have been given to you for these few days, as your latest guest from the ocean, who am so great a lover of your nation that, as I think, there is no other more so.

Wherefore you may, with more reason, remember what I am wont so earnestly to request of you—to wit, that to your work already begun, and in greater part finished, you would, to the utmost extent that the case will permit, add yet, in behalf of us foreigners, some little appendix concerning the right pronunciation of the language; for with other authorities in your tongue hitherto the intention seems to have been to satisfy only their own countrymen, without care for us. Although, in my opinion, they would have consulted both their own fame and the glory of the Italian tongue much more certainly had they so delivered their precepts as if it concerned all mankind to acquire the knowledge of that language, yet, in so far as has depended on them, you might seem, you Italians, to regard nothing beyond the bounds of the Alps. This praise, therefore, untasted by any one before, will be wholly your own, and keeps itself till now untouched and entire for you; nor less another which I will venture to mention. Would you consider it too much trouble if you were to give information separately on such points as these: who, in such a crowd of writers, can justly claim for himself the second place, next after the universally celebrated authors of the Florentine tongue; who is illustrious in Tragedy; who happy and sprightly in Comedy; who smart or weighty in Epistles or Dialogues; who noble in History? By this means the choice of the best in each kind would not be difficult for the willing student, while, whenever it might please him to range more widely, he would have ground on which to step intrepidly. In this matter you will have, among the ancients, Cicero and Fabius for examples; but whether any of your own men I know not. Though I believe I have already (unless my memory deceive me) made these demands of you every time we have fallen on the matter in talk—such is your politeness and kindly disposition—I am unwilling to regard that as any reason for not entreating the same in set phrase, so to speak, and in an express manner. For while your own worth and candor would assign the lowest value and the lowest estimation to your own labors, my wish is that both their inherent dignity and my individual respect should set the just and exact value upon them; and certainly it is but fair everywhere that, the more easily one admits a request, the less defect should there be of due honor to his compliance.

For the rest, should you perchance wonder why, on such a subject, I use the Latin tongue rather than yours, please to understand that it is precisely because I wish to have this Italian tongue of yours cleared up for me in precepts by yourself that I employ Latin openly in my confession of poverty and want of skill. By this very method I have hoped to prevail more with you—not without a belief at the same time that, by the very act of bringing with me that hoary and venerable mother from Latium as my helper in her daughter's cause, I should make sure that you would deny nothing to her venerable authority, her majesty august through so many ages.[1]

From *Accidence Commenced Grammar* (1669).

Accidence Commenced Grammar; Supplied with Sufficient Rules for the Use of such as, Younger or Elder, are Desirous, without more Trouble than Needs, to Attain the Latin Tongue; the Elder sort Especially, with little Teaching and their own Industry.

[1] Masson, *Life of Milton* 1. 789–92. Reprinted by permission of The Macmillan Company, New York; Macmillan & Company, Ltd., London.

THE STUDY OF LANGUAGE

To the Reader

It hath been long a general complaint, not without cause, in the bringing up of youth, and still is, that the tenth part of man's life, ordinarily extended, is taken up in learning, and that very scarcely, the Latin tongue. Which tardy proficience may be attributed to several causes: in particular, the making two labors of one, by learning first the Accidence, then the Grammar, in Latin, ere the language of those rules be understood. The only remedy of this was to join both books into one, and in the English tongue; whereby the long way is much abbreviated, and the labor of understanding much more easy; a work supposed not to have been done formerly, or, if done, not without such difference here, in brevity and alteration, as may be found of moment. That of Grammar, touching letters and syllables, is omitted, as learnt before, and little different from the English Spelling-book; especially since few will be persuaded to pronounce Latin otherwise than their own English. What will not come under rule, by reason of the much variety in declension, gender, or construction, is also here omitted, lest the course and clearness of method be clogged with catalogues instead of rules, or too much interruption between rule and rule; which Linacre, setting down the various idioms of many verbs, was forced to do by alphabet, and therefore, though very learned, not thought fit to be read in schools. But in such words a dictionary stored with good authorities will be found the readiest guide. Of figurate construction, what is useful is digested into several rules of Syntaxis; and Prosody, after this Grammar well learned, will not need to be Englished for him who hath a mind to read it. Account might be now given what addition or alteration from other Grammars hath been here made, and for what reason. But he who would be short in teaching must not be long in prefacing. The book itself follows, and will declare sufficiently to them who can discern. . . .

Latin Grammar is the art of right understanding, speaking, or writing Latin, observed from them who have spoken or written it best.[1]

[1] *Prose Works* 5. 432–3.

6. MILTON ON THE STUDY AND WRITING OF HISTORY

From a Letter to the illustrious Lord Henry De Bras. Westminster, July 15, 1657.

I see, my Lord, that you, unlike most of our modern youth who pass through foreign countries, wisely travel, like the ancient philosophers, for the sake of completing your juvenile studies, and of picking up knowledge wherever it may be found. . . . I wish it were as easy for me in every way to promote the increase of your knowledge, and the improvement of your intellect, as it is pleasing and flattering to me to have that assistance requested by talents and genius like yours. . . .

Of Sallust I will speak, as you desire, without any hesitation or reserve. I prefer him to any of the Latin historians; which was also the general opinion of the ancients. Your favorite Tacitus deserves his meed of praise; but his highest praise, in my opinion, consists in his having imitated Sallust with all his might. By my conversation with you on this subject, I seem, as far as I can guess from your letter, to have inspired you with sentiments very similar to my own, concerning that most energetic and animated writer.

As he in the beginning of his *Catilinarian War* asserted that there was the greatest difficulty in historical composition, because the style should correspond with the nature of the narrative, you ask me how a writer of history may best attain that excellence. My opinion is that he who would describe actions and events in a way suited to their dignity and importance ought to write with a mind endued with a spirit, and enlarged by an experience, as extensive as the actors in the scene, that he may have a capacity properly to comprehend and to estimate the most momentous affairs, and to relate them, when comprehended, with energy and distinctness, with purity and perspicuity of diction.

The decorations of style I do not greatly heed; for I require a historian, and not a rhetorician. I do not want frequent interspersions of sentiment, or prolix dissertations on transactions, which interrupt the series of events, and cause the historian to entrench on the office of the politician, who, if, in explaining counsels and explaining facts, he follows truth rather than his own partialities and conjectures, excites the disgust or the aversion of his party. I will add a remark of Sallust, and which was one of the excellencies he himself commends in Cato, that he should be able to say much in few words; a perfection which I think no one can attain without the most discriminating judgment and a peculiar degree of moderation. There are many in whom you have not to regret either elegance of diction or copiousness of narrative, who have yet united copiousness with brevity; and among these Sallust is, in my opinion, the chief of the Latin writers. Such are the virtues which I think every historian ought to possess who would proportion his style to the facts which he records.[1]

From a Letter to the illustrious Lord Henry De Bras. Westminster, December 16, 1657.

Your letter, so full of erudition, left me less occasion for sending you my advice . . . than my congratulations. First, I congratulate myself on having been so fortunate in characterizing the merits of Sallust as to have excited you to the assiduous perusal of that author, who is so full of wisdom, and who may be read with so much advantage. Of him I will venture to assert what Quintilian said of Cicero—that he who loves Sallust is no mean proficient in historical composition.

That precept of Aristotle in the third book of his *Rhetoric*, which you wish me to explain, relates to the morality of the reflections and the fidelity of the narrative. It appears to me to need little comment, except that it should be appropriated not to the composition of rhetoric but of history; for the offices of

[1] *Familiar Letters*, No. 23. *Prose Works* 3. 514-5.

a rhetorician and a historian are as different as the arts which they profess. Polybius, Halicarnassus, Diodorus, Cicero, Lucian, and many others, whose works are interspersed with precepts on the subject, will better teach you what are the duties of a historian.[1]

From *The History of Britain* (1670).

The History of Britain, that Part especially now called England; from the First traditional Beginning, Continued to the Norman Conquest; Collected out of the Ancientest and Best Authors thereof.

The beginning of nations, those excepted of whom sacred books have spoken, is to this day unknown—nor only the beginning, but the deeds also of many succeeding ages, yea, periods of ages, either wholly unknown, or obscured and blemished with fables; whether it were that the use of letters came in long after, or were it the violence of barbarous inundations, or they themselves, at certain revolutions of time, fatally decaying and degenerating into sloth and ignorance, whereby the monuments of more ancient civility have been, some destroyed, some lost. Perhaps disesteem and contempt of the public affairs then present, as not worth recording, might partly be in cause. Certainly oft-times we see that wise men, and of best ability, have foreborne to write the acts of their own days, while they beheld with a just loathing and disdain not only how unworthy, how perverse, how corrupt, but often how ignoble, how petty, how below all history, the persons and their actions were; who, either by fortune or some rude election, had attained, as a sore judgment and ignominy upon the land, to have chief sway in managing the commonwealth.

But, that any law or superstition of our old philosophers, the Druids, forbade the Britons to write their memorable deeds, I know not why any out of Cæsar should allege. He indeed saith that their doctrine they thought not lawful to commit to letters; but in most matters else, both private and public, among which

---

[1] *Familiar Letters*, No. 26. *Prose Works* 3. 517–8.

well may history be reckoned, they used the Greek tongue; and
that the British Druids who taught those in Gaul would be ignorant of any language known and used by their disciples, or, so
frequently writing other things, and so inquisitive into highest,
would for want of recording be ever children in the knowledge of
times and ages, is not likely. Whatever might be the reason, this
we find—that of British affairs, from the first peopling of the island to the coming of Julius Cæsar, nothing certain, either by
tradition, history, or ancient fame hath hitherto been left us.
That which we have of oldest seeming hath by the greater part
of judicious antiquaries been long rejected for a modern fable.

Nevertheless, there being others besides the first supposed
author, men not unread, nor unlearned in antiquity, who admit
that for approved story which the former explode for fiction, and
seeing that oft-times relations heretofore accounted fabulous have
been after found to contain in them many footsteps and relics of
something true, as what we read in poets of the Flood and
Giants, little believed till undoubted witnesses taught us that all
was not feigned; I have therefore determined to bestow the telling
over even of these reputed tales, be it for nothing else but in favor
of our English poets and rhetoricians, who by their art will know
how to use them judiciously.

I might also produce example, as Diodorus among the Greeks,
Livy and others among the Latins, Polydore and Virunnius accounted among our own writers. But I intend not with controversies and quotations to delay or interrupt the smooth course of
history; much less to argue and debate long who were the first
inhabitants, with what probabilities, what authorities, each
opinion hath been upheld; but shall endeavor that which hitherto hath been needed most—with plain and lightsome brevity to
relate well and orderly things worth the noting, so as may best
instruct and benefit them that read. Which, imploring divine
assistance, that it may redound to His glory and the good of the
British nation, I now begin.[1]

[1] *Prose Works* 5. 164–5.

Thus far, though leaning only on the credit of Geoffrey Monmouth and his assertors, I yet, for the specified causes, have thought it not beneath my purpose to relate what I found. Whereto I neither oblige the belief of other person, nor overhastily subscribe mine own. Nor have I stood with others computing or collating years and chronologies, lest I should be vainly curious about the time and circumstance of things whereof the substance is so much in doubt. By this time, like one who had set out on his way by night and traveled through a region of smooth or idle dreams, our history now arrives on the confines where daylight and truth meet us with a clear dawn, representing to our view, though at a far distance, true colors and shapes.[1]

I am now to write of what befell the Britons from fifty-and-three years before the birth of our Saviour, when first the Romans came in, till the decay and ceasing of that empire; a story of much truth, and, for the first hundred years and somewhat more, collected without much labor; so many and so prudent were the writers which those two, the civilest and the wisest of European nations, both Italy and Greece, afforded to the actions of that puissant city. For worthy deeds are not often destitute of worthy relators; as, by a certain fate, great acts and great eloquence have most commonly gone hand in hand, equaling and honoring each other in the same ages. It is true that in obscurest times, by shallow and unskilful writers, the indistinct noise of many battles and devastations of many kingdoms, overrun and lost, hath come to our ears. For what wonder if in all ages ambition and the love of rapine hath stirred up greedy and violent men to bold attempts in wasting and ruining wars, which to posterity have left the work of wild beasts and destroyers, rather than the deeds and monuments of men and conquerors? But he whose just and true valor uses the necessity of war and dominion, not to destroy, but to prevent destruction, to bring in liberty against tyrants, law and

[1] *Prose Works* 5. 184.

civility among barbarous nations (knowing that, when he conquers all things else, he cannot conquer time or detraction—wisely conscious of this his want, as well as of his worth not to be forgotten or concealed), honors and hath recourse to the aid of eloquence, his friendliest and best supply; by whose immortal record his noble deeds, which else were transitory, become fixed and durable against the force of years and generations. He fails not to continue through all posterity, over envy, death, and time also victorious.[1]

As for these, the only authors we have of British matters, while the power of Rome reached hither (for Gildas affirms that of the Romans' times no British writer was in his days extant, or if any were, either burnt by enemies or transported with such as fled the Pictish and Saxon invasions); these, therefore, only Roman authors there be who in the Latin tongue have laid together as much, and perhaps more, than was requisite to a history of Britain. So that, were it not for leaving an unsightly gap so near to the beginning, I should have judged this labor, wherein so little seems to be required above transcription, almost superfluous. Notwithstanding, since I must through it, if aught by diligence may be added or omitted, or by other disposing may be more explained or more expressed, I shall assay. . . .

If . . . the Druid learning, honored so much among them, were first taught them out of Britain, and they who soonest would attain that discipline sent hither to learn, it appears not how Britain at that time should be so utterly unknown in Gallia.[2]

I affect not set speeches in a history, unless known for certain to have been so spoken in effect as they are written; nor then, unless worth rehearsal; and to invent such, though eloquently, as some historians have done, is an abuse of posterity, raising, in them that read, other conceptions of those times and persons than were true. Much less therefore do I purpose here or elsewhere to copy

[1] *Ibid.* 5. 185.
[2] *Ibid.* 5. 186–7.

out tedious orations without decorum, though in their authors composed ready to my hand.[1]

Henceforth we are to steer by another sort of authors: near enough to the things they write, as in their own country, if that would serve; in time not much belated—some of equal age; in expression barbarous; and to say how judicious I suspend awhile. This we must expect: in civil matters to find them dubious relaters, and still to the best advantage of what they term the Holy Church—meaning indeed themselves; in most other matters of religion blind, astonished, and struck with superstition as with a planet; in one word—Monks. Yet these guides, where can be had no better, must be followed; in gross, it may be, true enough, in circumstances, each man, as his judgment gives him, may reserve his faith or bestow it.[2]

This third book, having to tell of accidents as various and exemplary as the intermission or change of government hath anywhere brought forth, may deserve attention more than common, and repay it with like benefit to them who can judiciously read; . . . for, if it be a high point of wisdom in every private man, much more is it in a nation, to know itself; rather than, puffed up with vulgar flatteries and encomiums for want of self-knowledge, to enterprise rashly and to come off miserably in great undertakings.[3]

Thus representing the state of things in this island, Bede surceased to write. Out of whom chiefly has been gathered, since the Saxon's arrival, such as hath been delivered: a scattered story picked out here and there, with some trouble and tedious work, from among his many legends of visions and miracles; toward the latter end so bare of civil matters as what can be thence collected may seem a calendar rather than a history, taken up for the most part with succession of kings and computation of years, yet those hard to be reconciled with the Saxon annals.

[1] *Prose Works* 5. 210-1.
[2] *Ibid.* 5. 235.
[3] *Ibid.* 5. 235.

Their actions we read of were most commonly wars; but for what cause waged, or by what counsels carried on, no care was had to let us know; whereby their strength and violence we understand, of their wisdom, reason, or justice little or nothing; the rest, superstition and monastical affectation: kings one after another leaving their kingly charge to run their heads fondly into a monk's cowl—which leaves us uncertain whether Bede was wanting to his matter, or his matter to him. Yet from hence to the Danish invasion it will be worse with us, destitute of Bede, left only to obscure and blockish chronicles; whom Malmesbury and Huntingdon (for neither they than we had better authors of those times), ambitious to adorn the history, make no scruple oft-times, I doubt, to interline with conjectures and surmises of their own. Them rather than imitate, I shall choose to represent the truth naked, though as lean as a plain journal. Yet William of Malmesbury must be acknowledged, both for style and judgment, to be by far the best writer of them all; but what labor is to be endured turning over volumes of rubbish in the rest—Florence of Worcester, Huntingdon, Simeon of Durham, Hoveden, Matthew of Westminster, and many others of obscurer note, with all their monachisms—is a penance to think. Yet these are our only registers, transcribers one after another for the most part, and sometimes worthy enough of the things they register. This travail, rather than not to know at once what may be known of our ancient story, sifted from fables and impertinences, I voluntarily undergo; and to save others, if they please, the like unpleasing labor; except those who take pleasure to be all their lifetime raking the foundations of old abbeys and cathedrals. But to my task now as it befalls.[1]

I am sensible how wearisome it may likely be to read of so many bare and reasonless actions, so many names of kings one after another, acting little more than mute persons in a scene. What would it be to have inserted the long bead-roll of

[1] *Ibid.* 5. 295–6.

archbishops, bishops, abbots, abbesses, and their doings neither to religion profitable nor to morality, swelling my authors each to a voluminous body—by me studiously omitted?[1]

The year following [794] was remarkable for the death of Offa the Mercian, a strenuous and subtile king. He had much intercourse with Charles the Great; at first enmity, to the interdicting of commerce on either side; at length much amity and firm league, as appears by the letter of Charles himself yet extant, procured by Alcuin, a learned and prudent man, though a monk, whom the kings of England in those days had sent orator into France, to maintain good correspondence between them and Charles the Great.[2]

From *A Brief History of Moscovia* (1682).

The study of geography is both profitable and delightful; but the writers thereof, though some of them exact enough in setting down longitudes and latitudes, yet, in those other relations of manners, religion, government, and such-like, accounted geographical, have for the most part missed their proportions. Some, too brief and deficient, satisfy not; others, too voluminous and impertinent, cloy and weary out the reader while they tell long stories of absurd superstitions, ceremonies, quaint habits, and other petty circumstances little to the purpose. Whereby, that which is useful, and only worth observation, in such a wood of words is either over-slipped or soon forgotten; which perhaps brought into the mind of some men more learned and judicious, who had not the leisure or purpose to write an entire geography, yet at least to assay something in the description of one or two countries, which might be as a pattern or example to render others more cautious hereafter who intended the whole work. And this, perhaps, induced Paulus Jovius to describe only Moscovy and Britain.

[1] *Prose Works* 5. 299.
[2] *Ibid.* 5. 302.

Some such thoughts, many years since, led me at a vacant time to attempt the like argument, and I began with Moscovy, as being the most northern region of Europe reputed civil, and the more northern parts thereof first discovered by English voyagers; wherein I saw I had by much the advantage of Jovius. What was scattered in many volumes, and observed at several times by eyewitnesses, with no cursory pains I laid together, to save the reader a far longer travail of wandering through so many desert authors; who yet with some delight drew me after them, from the eastern bounds of Russia to the walls of Cathay, in several late journeys made thither overland by Russians who describe the countries in their way far otherwise than our common geographers. From proceeding further other occasions diverted me. This Essay, such as it is, was thought by some who knew of it not amiss to be published; that so many things remarkable, dispersed before, now brought under one view might not hazard to be otherwise lost, nor the labor lost of collecting them.[1]

[1] *Ibid.* 5. 394–5.

7. OBSERVATIONS ON LITERATURE

On Shakespeare, 1630.

> What needs my Shakespeare for his honored bones
> The labor of an age in pilèd stones,
> Or that his hallowed relics should be hid
> Under a star-ypointing pyramid?
> Dear son of memory, great heir of fame,
> What need'st thou such weak witness of thy name?
> Thou in our wonder and astonishment
> Hast built thyself a livelong monument.
> For whilst to th' shame of slow-endeavoring art
> Thy easy numbers flow, and that each heart
> Hath from the leaves of thy unvalued book
> Those Delphic lines with deep impression took,
> Then thou, our fancy of itself bereaving,
> Dost make us marble with too much conceiving;
> And so sepulchred in such pomp dost lie,
> That kings for such a tomb would wish to die.

From *An Apology for Smectymnuus* (1642).

[True Eloquence.]

For me, readers, although I cannot say that I am utterly untrained in those rules which best rhetoricians have given, or unacquainted with those examples which the prime authors of eloquence have written in any learned tongue; yet true eloquence I find to be none but the serious and hearty love of truth; and that whose mind soever is fully possessed with a fervent desire to know good things, and with the dearest charity to infuse the knowledge of them into others, when such a man would speak, his words (by what I can express) like so many nimble and airy servitors trip about him at command, and in well-ordered files, as he would wish, fall aptly into their own places.[1]

[1] *Prose Works* 3. 165.

From *The Reason of Church-Government* (1641).

[On the Uses and Abuses of Poetry.]

These abilities, wheresoever they be found, are the inspired gift of God, rarely bestowed, but yet to some (though most abuse) in every nation; and are of power, beside the office of a pulpit, to imbreed and cherish in a great people the seeds of virtue and public civility, to allay the perturbations of the mind, and set the affections in right tune; to celebrate in glorious and lofty hymns the throne and equipage of God's almightiness, and what He works, and what He suffers to be wrought with high providence in His Church; to sing victorious agonies of martyrs and saints, the deeds and triumphs of just and pious nations doing valiantly through faith against the enemies of Christ; to deplore the general relapses of kingdoms and states from justice and God's true worship; lastly, whatsoever in religion is holy and sublime, in virtue amiable or grave, whatsoever hath passion or admiration in all the changes of that which is called fortune from without, or the wily subtleties and refluxes of man's thoughts from within; all these things with a solid and treatable smoothness to paint out and describe; teaching over the whole book of sanctity and virtue, through all the instances of example, with such delight to those especially of soft and delicious temper—who will not so much as look upon truth herself unless they see her elegantly dressed—that, whereas the paths of honesty and good life appear now rugged and difficult, though they be indeed easy and pleasant, they will then appear to all men both easy and pleasant, though they were rugged and difficult indeed. And what a benefit this would be to our youth and gentry may be soon guessed by what we know of the corruption and bane which they suck in daily from the writings and interludes of libidinous and ignorant poetasters, who, having scarce ever heard of that which is the main consistence of a true poem—the choice of such persons as they ought to introduce, and what is moral and decent to each one—do for the most part lay up vicious principles in sweet pills to be swallowed down, and make the taste of virtuous documents harsh and sour.[1]

From *Samson Agonistes* (1671).

[Milton's Preface.]

Tragedy, as it was anciently composed, hath been ever held the gravest, moralest, and most profitable of all other poems: therefore said by Aristotle to be of power, by raising pity, and fear or terror, to purge the mind of those and such-like passions; that is, to temper and reduce them to just measure with a kind of delight, stirred up by reading or seeing those passions well imitated. Nor is Nature wanting in her own effects to make good his assertion; for so in physic things of melancholic hue and quality are used against melancholy, sour against sour, salt to remove salt humors. Hence philosophers and other gravest writers, as Cicero, Plutarch, and others, frequently cite out of tragic poets, both to adorn and illustrate their discourse. The Apostle Paul himself thought it not unworthy to insert a verse of Euripides into the text of Holy Scripture (1 Cor. 15.33); and Paræus, commenting on the Revelation, divides the whole book, as a tragedy, into acts, distinguished each by a Chorus of heavenly harpings and song between. Heretofore men in highest dignity have labored not a little to be thought able to compose a tragedy. . . .

This is mentioned to vindicate Tragedy from the small esteem, or rather infamy, which in the account of many it undergoes at this day, with other common interludes; happening through the poet's error of intermixing comic stuff with tragic sadness and gravity, or introducing trivial and vulgar persons, which by all judicious hath been counted absurd, and brought in without discretion, corruptly to gratify the people. . . . In the modeling therefore of this poem, with good reason, the ancients and Italians are rather followed, as of much more authority and fame. . . .

[1] *Prose Works* 2. 479–80.

It suffices if the whole drama be found not produced beyond the fifth act. Of the style and uniformity, and that commonly called the plot, whether intricate or explicit—which is nothing indeed but such economy, or disposition of the fable, as may stand best with verisimilitude and decorum—they only will best judge who are not unacquainted with Æschylus, Sophocles, and Euripides, the three tragic poets unequaled yet by any, and the best rule to all who endeavor to write Tragedy. . . .

From *The Second Defence of the People of England* (1654).

True poets are the objects of my reverence and my love, and the constant sources of my delight. I know that the most of them, from the earliest times to those of Buchanan, have been the strenuous enemies of despotism; but these pedlars and milliners of verse who can bear? They applaud, and they revile, as it may happen—as gain, or passion, or the bottle may incite, without choice, discrimination, judgment, or moderation—princes and plebeians, the literate and illiterate, honest men and knaves. They heap together such a motley, indigested, and putrid mass of adulation that it would be better to be prosecuted with contempt than loaded with such praise. . . .

The poet must have been a miserable drudge, and without any feeling of propriety, to lavish such a prodigality of praise on a grammarian; a race of men who have been always thought to act as a sort of subordinate and menial part to the bard.[1]

Men in general entertained the highest opinion of his [Salmasius'] erudition, the celebrity of which he had been accumulating for many years, by many voluminous and massy publications, not indeed of any practical utility, but relating to the most abstruse discussions and crammed with quotations from the most illustrious authors. Nothing is so apt as this to excite the astonishment of the literary vulgar.[2]

[1] *Ibid.* I. 241–2.
[2] *Ibid.* I. 248.

[More was] a worthless scribbler who, quite ignorant of propriety, lavished the appellation of 'great' without any fitness or discrimination. To grammarians and critics, who are principally occupied in editing the works of others, or in correcting the errors of copyists, we willingly concede the palm of industry and erudition; but we never bestow on them the surname of 'great.' He alone is worthy of the appellation who either does great things, or teaches how they may be done, or describes them with a suitable majesty when they have been done; but those only are great things which tend to render life more happy, which increase the innocent enjoyments and comforts of existence, or which pave the way to a state of future bliss more permanent and more pure.[1]

From *Areopagitica* (1644).

[On the Reading of Supposedly 'Dangerous' Literature.]

Not to insist upon the examples of Moses, Daniel, and Paul, who were skilful in all the learning of the Egyptians, Chaldeans, and Greeks, which could not probably be without reading their books of all sorts, in Paul especially, who thought it no defilement to insert into Holy Scripture the sentences of three Greek poets, and one of them a tragedian; the question was notwithstanding sometimes controverted among the primitive doctors, but with great odds on that side which affirmed it both lawful and profitable, as was then evidently perceived when Julian the Apostate, and subtlest enemy to our faith, made a decree forbidding Christians the study of heathen learning; for, said he, they wound us with our own weapons, and with our own arts and sciences they overcome us. And, indeed, the Christians were put so to their shifts by this crafty means, and so much in danger to decline into all ignorance, that the two Appollinarii were fain, as a man may say, to coin all the seven liberal sciences out of the Bible, reducing it into divers forms of orations, poems, dialogues, even to the calculating of a new Christian grammar.

[1] *Prose Works* I. 246.

But, saith the historian Socrates, the Providence of God provided better than the industry of Appollinarius and his son, by taking away that illiterate law with the life of him who devised it. So great an injury they then held it to be deprived of Hellenic learning, and thought it a persecution more undermining and secretly decaying the Church than the open cruelty of Decius or Diocletian. . . . Basil teaches how some good use may be made of *Margites*, a sportful poem, not now extant, writ by Homer. . . . Dionysius Alexandrinus was, about the year 240, a person of great name in the Church for piety and learning, who had wont to avail himself much against heretics by being conversant with their books, until a certain presbyter laid it scrupulously to his conscience how he durst venture himself among those defiling volumes. The worthy man, loath to give offence, fell into a new debate with himself what was to be thought; when suddenly a vision sent from God (it is his own epistle that so avers it) confirmed him in these words: 'Read any books whatever come to thy hands, for thou art sufficient both to judge aright, and to examine each matter.' To this revelation he assented the sooner, as he confesses, because it was answerable to that of the Apostle to the Thessalonians: 'Prove all things; hold fast that which is good.'

And he might have added another remarkable saying of the same author: 'To the pure, all things are pure'—not only meats and drinks, but all kind of knowledge, whether of good or evil. The knowledge cannot defile, nor consequently the books, if the will and conscience be not defiled; for books are as meats and viands are, some of good, some of evil substance; and yet God in that unapocryphal vision said without exception: 'Rise, Peter, kill and eat'—leaving the choice to each man's discretion. Wholesome meats to a vitiated stomach differ little or nothing from unwholesome; and best books to a naughty mind are not unapplicable to occasions of evil. Bad meats will scarce breed good nourishment in the healthiest concoction; but herein the difference is of bad books—that they to a discreet and judicious reader serve in many respects to discover, to confute, to forewarn, and to illustrate. Whereof what better witness can ye expect I should produce than one of your own now sitting in Parliament, the chief of learned men reputed in this land, Mr. Selden; whose volume of natural and national laws proves, not only by great authorities brought together, but by exquisite reasons and theorems almost mathematically demonstrative, that all opinions, yea, errors, known, read, and collated, are of main service and assistance toward the speedy attainment of what is truest?

I conceive, therefore, that, when God did enlarge the universal diet of man's body (saving ever the rules of temperance), He then also, as before, left arbitrary the dieting and repasting of our minds, as wherein every mature man might have to exercise his own leading capacity. How great a virtue is temperance, how much of moment through the whole life of man! Yet God commits the managing so great a trust, without particular law or prescription, wholly to the demeanor of every grown man. And therefore when He Himself tabled the Jews from Heaven, that omer, which was every man's daily portion of manna, is computed to have been more than might have well sufficed the heartiest feeder thrice as many meals. For those actions which enter into a man rather than issue out of him, and therefore defile not, God uses not to captivate under a perpetual childhood of prescription, but trusts him with the gift of reason to be his own chooser: there were but little work left for preaching, if law and compulsion should grow so fast upon those things which heretofore were governed only by exhortation. Solomon informs us that much reading is a weariness to the flesh; but neither he, nor other inspired author, tells us that such or such reading is unlawful; yet, certainly, had God thought good to limit us herein, it had been much more expedient to have told us what was unlawful than what was wearisome. . . .

Good and evil we know in the field of this world grow up together almost inseparably; and the knowledge of good is so involved and interwoven with the knowledge of evil, and in so many cunning resemblances hardly to be discerned, that those confused seeds which were imposed upon Psyche as an incessant labor to cull out and sort asunder were not more intermixed. It was from out the rind of one apple tasted that the knowledge of good and evil, as two twins cleaving together, leaped forth into the world. And perhaps this is that doom which Adam fell into, of knowing good and evil—that is to say, of knowing good by evil.

As therefore the state of man now is, what wisdom can there be to choose, what continence to forbear, without the knowledge of evil? He that can apprehend and consider vice with all her baits and seeming pleasures, and yet abstain, and yet distinguish, and yet prefer that which is truly better, he is the true warfaring Christian. I cannot praise a fugitive and cloistered virtue, unexercised and unbreathed, that never sallies out and seeks her adversary, but slinks out of the race where that immortal garland is to be run for, not without dust and heat.

Assuredly we bring not innocence into the world; we bring impurity much rather; that which purifies us is trial, and trial is by what is contrary. That virtue therefore which is but a youngling in the contemplation of evil, and knows not the utmost that vice promises to her followers, and rejects it, is but a blank virtue, not a pure. Her whiteness is but an excremental whiteness; which was the reason why our sage and serious poet Spenser (whom I dare be known to think a better teacher than Scotus or Aquinas), describing true temperance under the person of Guyon, brings him in with his Palmer through the cave of Mammon and the bower of earthly bliss, that he might see and know, and yet abstain.

Since, therefore, the knowledge and survey of vice is in this world so necessary to the constituting of human virtue, and the scanning of error to the confirmation of truth, how can we more safely, and with less danger, scout into the regions of sin and falsity than by reading all manner of tractates, and hearing all manner of reason? And this is the benefit which may be had of books promiscuously read. But, of the harm that may result hence, three kinds are usually reckoned. First is feared the infection that may spread; but then all human learning and controversy in religious points must remove out of the world, yea, the Bible itself; for that oft-times relates blasphemy not nicely, it describes the carnal sense of wicked men not unelegantly, it brings in holiest men passionately murmuring against Providence through all the arguments of Epicurus. In other great disputes it answers dubiously and darkly to the common reader; and ask a Talmudist what ails the modesty of his marginal *Keri* that Moses and all the prophets cannot persuade him to pronounce the textual *Chetiv*. For these causes we all know the Bible itself put by the Papist into the first rank of prohibited books. The ancientest Fathers must be next removed, as Clement of Alexandria, and that Eusebian book of evangelic preparation, transmitting our ears through a hoard of heathenish obscenities to receive the Gospel. Who finds not that Irenæus, Epiphanius, Jerome, and others discover more heresies than they well confute, and that oft for heresy which is the truer opinion?

Nor boots it to say, for these, and all the heathen writers of greatest infection (if it must be thought so), with whom is bound up the life of human learning, that they wrote in an unknown tongue, so long as we are sure those languages are known as well to the worst of men, who are both most able and most diligent to instil the poison they suck, first into the courts of princes, acquainting them with the choicest delights and criticisms of sin; . . . . by which compendious way all the contagion that foreign books can infuse will find a passage to the people far easier and shorter than an Indian voyage, though it could be sailed either by the north of Cataio eastward, or of Canada westward, while our Spanish licensing gags the English press never so severely.

But, on the other side, that infection which is from books of controversy in religion is more doubtful and dangerous to the learned than to the ignorant; and yet those books must be permitted, untouched by the licenser. It will be hard to instance where any ignorant man hath been ever seduced by any papistical book in English, unless it were commended and expounded to him by some of that clergy; and indeed all such tractates, whether false or true, are as the prophecy of Isaiah was to the eunuch, not to be 'understood without a guide.' But of our priests and doctors how many have been corrupted by studying the comments of Jesuits and Sorbonists, and how fast they could transfuse that corruption into the people, our experience is both late and sad. . . .

Seeing, therefore, that those books, and those in great abundance, which are likeliest to taint both life and doctrine, cannot be suppressed without the fall of learning and of all ability in disputation, and that these books of either sort are most and soonest catching to the learned (from whom to the common people whatever is heretical or dissolute may quickly be conveyed), and that evil manners are as perfectly learnt without books a thousand other ways which cannot be stopped, and evil doctrine not with books can propagate except a teacher guide, which he might also do without writing, and so beyond prohibiting; I am not able to unfold how this cautelous enterprise of licensing can be exempted from the number of vain and impossible attempts. . . .

And again, if it be true that a wise man, like a good refiner, can gather gold out of the drossiest volume, and that a fool will be a fool with the best book, yea, or without book, there is no reason that we should deprive a wise man of any advantage to his wisdom while we seek to restrain from a fool that which, being restrained, will be no hindrance to his folly. For, if there should be so much exactness always used to keep that from him which is unfit for his reading, we should in the judgment of Aristotle not only, but of Solomon and of our Saviour, not vouchsafe him good precepts, and by consequence not willingly admit him to good books; as being certain that a wise man will make better use of an idle pamphlet than a fool will do of sacred Scripture.

It is next alleged we must not expose ourselves to temptations without necessity, and, next to that, not employ our time in vain things. To both these objections one answer will serve, out of the grounds already laid: that to all men such books are not temptations, nor vanities, but useful drugs and materials wherewith to temper and compose effective and strong medicines which man's life cannot want. The rest, as children and childish men, who have not the art to qualify and prepare these working minerals, well may be exhorted to forbear; but hindered forcibly they cannot be by all the licensing that sainted Inquisition could ever yet contrive. Which is what I promised to deliver next: that this order of licensing conduces nothing to the end for which it was framed; and hath almost prevented me by being clear already while thus much hath been explaining. See the ingenuity of truth, who, when she gets a free and willing hand, opens herself faster than the pace of method and discourse can overtake her.[1]

From *Eikonoklastes* (1649).

[A Moral Lesson from Shakespeare.]

And this is the substance of his first section till we come to the devout of it, modeled into the form of a private psalter. . . . But he who, from such a kind of psalmistry, or any other verbal devotion without the pledge and earnest of suitable deeds, can be persuaded of a zeal and true righteousness in the person, hath much yet to learn; and knows not that the deepest policy of a tyrant hath been ever to counterfeit religious. And Aristotle, in his *Politics*, hath mentioned that special craft among twelve other tyrannical sophisms. Neither want we examples: Andronicus Comnenus, the Byzantine Emperor, though a most cruel tyrant,

[1] *Prose Works* 2. 63–71.

is reported by Nicetas to have been a constant reader of St. Paul's Epistles; and by continual study had so incorporated the phrase and style of that transcendent apostle into all his familiar letters that the imitation seemed to vie with the original. Yet this availed not to deceive the people of that empire, who, notwithstanding his saint's vizard, tore him to pieces for his tyranny.

From stories of this nature both ancient and modern which abound, the poets also, and some English, have been in this point so mindful of decorum as to put never more pious words in the mouth of any person than of a tyrant. . . . I shall not instance an abstruse author, wherein the King might be less conversant, but one who, we well know, was the closet-companion of these his solitudes—William Shakespeare; who introduces the person of Richard the Third speaking in as high a strain of piety and mortification as is uttered in any passage of this book, and sometimes to the same sense and purpose with some words in this place. . . . Other stuff of this sort may be read throughout the whole tragedy, wherein the poet used not much licence in departing from the truth of history, which delivers him [Richard] a deep dissembler, not of his affections only, but of religion.[1]

[The Wrong Use of a Good Book.]

Who would have imagined so little fear in him of the true all-seeing Deity, so little reverence of the Holy Ghost, Whose office is to dictate and present our Christian prayers, so little care of truth in his last words, or honor to himself or to his friends, or sense of his afflictions or of that sad hour which was upon him, as immediately before his death to pop into the hand of that grave bishop who attended him, for a special relique of his saintly exercises, a prayer stolen word for word from the mouth of a heathen woman praying to a heathen god; and that in no serious book, but the vain amatorious poem of Sir Philip Sidney's *Arcadia*; a book in that kind full of worth and wit, but among

[1] *Ibid.* I. 325-7.

religious thoughts and duties not worthy to be named; nor to be read at any time without good caution, much less in time of trouble and affliction to be a Christian's prayer-book?[1]

From *The History of Britain* (1670).

[Milton's Opinion of Old English Verse.]

They entered England by Humber, and fought with Athelstan at a place called . . . Brunanburg . . . the bloodiest fight, say authors, that ever this island saw; to describe which the Saxon annalist, wont to be sober and succinct, whether the same or another writer, now laboring under the weight of his argument, and overcharged, runs on a sudden into such extravagant fancies and metaphors as bear him quite beside the scope of being understood. Huntingdon, though himself peccant enough in this kind, transcribes him word for word as a pastime to his readers. I shall only sum up what of him I can attain, in usual language.[2]

From *Paradise Lost* (1667).

[Modern Epic Verse: a Lesson from the Classics.]

The measure is English heroic verse without rime, as that of Homer in Greek, and of Virgil in Latin—rime being no necessary adjunct or true ornament of poem or good verse, in longer works especially, but the invention of a barbarous age, to set off wretched matter and lame metre; graced indeed since by the use of some famous modern poets, carried away by custom—but much to their own vexation, hindrance, and constraint—to express many things otherwise, and for the most part worse, than else they would have expressed them. Not without cause therefore some both Italian and Spanish poets of prime note have rejected rime both in longer and shorter works, as have also long since our best English tragedies, as a thing of itself, to all judici-

[1] *Prose Works* 1. 327–8.
[2] *Ibid.* 5. 334.

ous ears, trivial and of no true musical delight; which consists only in apt numbers, fit quantity of syllables, and the sense variously drawn out from one verse into another, not in the jingling sound of like endings—a fault avoided by the learned ancients both in poetry and all good oratory. This neglect, then, of rime so little is to be taken for a defect, though it may seem so perhaps to vulgar readers, that it rather is to be esteemed an example set, the first in English, of ancient liberty recovered to heroic poem from the troublesome and modern bondage of riming.

8. HOW MILTON USED HIS LEARNING IN CONTROVERSY

His Reasons for Engaging in Disputed Causes, and the Spirit in which he Wrote

From *The Doctrine and Discipline of Divorce* (1643).

If it were seriously asked—and it would be no untimely question, renowned Parliament, select Assembly!—who, of all teachers and masters that have ever taught, hath drawn the most disciples after him, both in religion and in manners, it might not be untruly answered, 'Custom'. Though virtue be commended for the most persuasive in her theory, and conscience in the plain demonstration of the spirit finds most evincing; yet whether it be the secret of divine will, or the original blindness we are born in, so it happens for the most part that custom still is silently received for the best instructor; except it be because her method is so glib and easy, in some manner like to that vision of Ezekiel, rolling up her sudden book of implicit knowledge, for him that will to take and swallow down at pleasure; which, proving but of bad nourishment in the concoction, as it was heedless in the devouring, puffs up unhealthily a certain big face of pretended learning, mistaken among credulous men for the wholesome habit of soundness and good constitution; but is indeed no other than that swollen visage of counterfeit knowledge and literature, which not only in private mars our education, but also in public is the common climber into every chair where either religion is preached or law reported; filling each estate of life and profession with abject and servile principles, depressing the high and Heaven-born spirit of man far beneath the condition wherein either God created him or sin hath sunk him. To pursue the allegory: custom, being but a mere face, as echo is a mere voice, rests not in her unaccomplishment until by secret inclination she accorporate herself with error, who, being a blind and serpentine body without a head, willingly accepts what he wants, and supplies what her incompleteness went seeking.

Hence it is that error supports custom, custom countenances error; and these two between them would persecute and chase away all truth and solid wisdom out of human life, were it not that God, rather than man, once in many ages calls together the prudent and religious councils of men, deputed to repress the encroachments, and to work off the inveterate blots and obscurities, wrought upon our minds by the subtle insinuating of error and custom; who, with the numerous and vulgar train of their followers, make it their chief design to envy and cry down the industry of free reasoning, under the terms of humor and innovation; as if the womb of teeming truth were to be closed up if she presume to bring forth aught that sorts not with their unchewed notions and suppositions.

Against which notorious injury and abuse of man's free soul to testify and oppose the utmost that study and true labor can attain, heretofore the incitement of men reputed grave hath led me among others; and now the duty and the right of an instructed Christian calls me, through the chance of good or evil report, to be the sole advocate of a discountenanced truth. A high enterprise, Lords and Commons! a high enterprise and a hard, and such as every seventh son of a seventh son does not venture on. Nor have I, amidst the clamor of so much envy and impertinence, whither to appeal but to the concourse of so much piety and wisdom here assembled.[1]

From *Areopagitica* (1644).

And lest some should persuade ye, Lords and Commons, that these arguments of learned men's discouragement at this your order are mere flourishes, and not real, I could recount what I have seen and heard in other countries where this kind of inquisition tyrannizes; when I have sat among their learned men

[1] *Prose Works* 3. 171-2.

(for that honor I had) and been counted happy to be born in such a place of philosophic freedom as they supposed England was, while themselves did nothing but bemoan the servile condition into which learning amongst them was brought: that this was it which had damped the glory of Italian wits; that nothing had been there written now these many years but flattery and fustian. There it was that I found and visited the famous Galileo, grown old, a prisoner to the Inquisition for thinking in astronomy otherwise than the Franciscan and Dominican licensers thought. And though I knew that England then was groaning loudest under the prelatical yoke, nevertheless I took it as a pledge of future happiness that other nations were so persuaded of her liberty. . . .

He whom an honest quæstorship had endeared to the Sicilians was not more by them importuned against Verres than the favorable opinion which I had among many who honor ye, and are known and respected by ye, loaded me with entreaties and persuasions that I would not despair to lay together that which just reason should bring into my mind towards the removal of an undeserved thraldom upon learning. That this is not therefore the disburdening of a particular fancy, but the common grievance of all those who had prepared their minds and studies above the vulgar pitch to advance truth in others, and from others to entertain it, thus much may satisfy.[1]

From *The Reason of Church-Government* (1642).

How happy were it for this frail, and, as it may be called, mortal, life of man (since all earthly things which have the name of good and convenient in our daily use are withal so cumbersome and full of trouble) if knowledge, yet which is the best and lightsomest possession of the mind, were, as the common saying is, no burden; and that what it wanted of being a load to any part of the body it did not with a heavy advantage overlay upon the spirit! For, not to speak of that knowledge that rests in the

[1] *Prose Works* 2. 82–3.

contemplation of natural causes and dimensions (which must needs be a lower wisdom, as the object is low), certain it is that he who hath obtained in more than the scantiest measure to know anything distinctly of God, and of His true worship, and what is infallibly good and happy in the state of man's life, what in itself evil and miserable, though vulgarly not so esteemed; he that hath obtained to know this, the only high valuable wisdom indeed—remembering also that God, even to a strictness, requires the improvement of these His entrusted gifts—cannot but sustain a sorer burden of mind, and more pressing, than any supportable toil or weight which the body can labor under, how and in what manner he shall dispose and employ those sums of knowledge and illumination which God hath sent him into this world to trade with.

And that which aggravates the burden more is that, having received amongst his allotted parcels certain precious truths of such an orient lustre as no diamond can equal, which nevertheless he has in charge to put off at any cheap rate—yea, for nothing to them that will—the great merchants of this world, fearing that this course would soon discover and disgrace the false glitter of their deceitful wares wherewith they abuse the people, like poor Indians, with beads and glasses, practise by all means how they may suppress the vending of such rarities, and at such a cheapness as would undo them and turn their trash upon their hands. Therefore, by gratifying the corrupt desires of men in fleshly doctrines, they stir them up to persecute with hatred and contempt all those that seek to bear themselves uprightly in this their spiritual factory; which they foreseeing, though they cannot but testify of truth, and the excellency of that heavenly traffic which they bring, against what opposition or danger soever, yet needs must it sit heavily upon their spirits that, being, in God's prime intention and their own, selected heralds of peace and dispensers of treasure inestimable, without price, to them that have no peace, they find, in the discharge of their commission, that they are made the greatest variance and offence, a very sword and fire both in house and city over the whole earth.

This is that which the sad prophet Jeremiah laments: 'Woe is me, my mother, that thou hast borne me, a man of strife and contention!' And, although divine inspiration must certainly have been sweet to those ancient prophets, yet the irksomeness of that truth which they brought was so unpleasant unto them that everywhere they call it a burden. Yea, that mysterious book of revelation which the great evangelist was bid to eat, as it had been some eye-brightening electuary of knowledge and foresight, though it were sweet in his mouth, and in the learning, it was bitter in his belly, bitter in the denouncing. Nor was this hid from the wise poet Sophocles, who, in that place of his tragedy where Tiresias is called to resolve King Œdipus in a matter which he knew would be grievous, brings him in bemoaning his lot—that he knew more than other men.

For surely to every good and peaceable man it must in nature needs be a hateful thing to be the displeaser and molester of thousands; much better would it like him, doubtless, to be the messenger of gladness and contentment, which is his chief intended business to all mankind, but that they resist and oppose their own true happiness. But, when God commands to take the trumpet and blow a dolorous or a jarring blast, it lies not in man's will what he shall say, or what he shall conceal. If he shall think to be silent, as Jeremiah did, because of the reproach and derision he met with daily—'And all his familiar friends watched for his halting,' to be revenged on him for speaking the truth—he would be forced to confess as *he* confessed: 'His word was in my heart as a burning fire shut up in my bones; I was weary with forbearing, and could not stay.' Which might teach these times not suddenly to condemn all things that are sharply spoken or vehemently written, as proceeding out of stomach, virulence, or ill-nature; but to consider rather that, if the prelates have leave to say the worst that can be said, or do the worst that can be done, while they strive to keep to themselves, to their great pleasure and commodity, those things which they ought to render up, no man can be justly offended with him that shall endeavor to impart and bestow, without any gain to himself, those sharp but saving words which would be a terror and a torment in him to keep back.

For me, I have determined to lay up as the best treasure and solace of a good old age, if God vouchsafe it me, the honest liberty of free speech from my youth, where I shall think it available in so dear a concernment as the Church's good. . . .

But this I foresee: that, should the Church be brought under heavy oppression, and God have given me ability the while to reason against that man that should be the author of so foul a deed; or, should she, by blessing from above on the industry and courage of faithful men, change this her distracted estate into better days, without the least furtherance or contribution of those few talents which God at that present had lent me; I foresee what stories I should hear within myself, all my life after, of discourage and reproach: 'Timorous and ungrateful, the Church of God is now again at the foot of her insulting enemies, and thou bewailest. What matters it for thee, or thy bewailing? When time was, thou couldst not find a syllable of all that thou hast read or studied to utter in her behalf. Yet ease and leisure was given thee for thy retired thoughts, out of the sweat of other men. Thou hast the diligence, the parts, the language of a man, if a vain subject were to be adorned or beautified; but when the cause of God and His Church was to be pleaded, for which purpose that tongue was given thee which thou hast, God listened if He could hear thy voice among His zealous servants, but thou wert dumb as a beast; from henceforward be that which thine own brutish silence hath made thee.'[1]

Lest it should be still imputed to me, as I have found it hath been, that some self-pleasing humor of vainglory hath incited me to contest with men of high estimation, now while green years are

[1] *Prose Works* 2. 472–5.

upon my head; from this needless surmisal I shall hope to dissuade the intelligent and equal auditor if I can but say successfully that which in this exigent behoves me; although I would be heard only, if it might be, by the elegant and learned reader, to whom principally for a while I shall beg leave I may address myself.

To him it will be no new thing though I tell him that, if I hunted after praise by the ostentation of wit and learning, I should not write thus out of mine own season when I have neither yet completed to my mind the full circle of my private studies— although I complain not of any insufficiency to the matter in hand; or, were I ready to my wishes, it were a folly to commit anything elaborately composed to the careless and interrupted listening of these tumultuous times. Next, if I were wise only to my own ends, I would certainly take such a subject as of itself might catch applause—whereas this hath all the disadvantages on the contrary; and such a subject as the publishing whereof might be delayed at pleasure, and time enough to pencil it over with all the curious touches of art, even to the perfection of a faultless picture; whenas in this argument the not deferring is of great moment to the good speeding, that, if solidity have leisure to do her office, art cannot have much. Lastly, I should not choose this manner of writing, wherein, knowing myself inferior to myself, led by the genial power of nature to another task, I have the use, as I may account, but of my left hand. . . . For although a poet, soaring in the high region of his fancies, with his garland and singing-robes about him, might without apology speak more of himself than I mean to do; yet for me, sitting here below in the cool element of prose, a mortal thing among many readers of no empyreal conceit, to venture and divulge unusual things of myself, I shall petition, to the gentler sort, it may not be envy to me.[1]

Although it nothing content me to have disclosed thus much beforehand, but that I trust hereby to make it manifest with what small willingness I endure to interrupt the pursuit of no

[1] *Prose Works* 2. 476–7.

less hopes than these, and leave a calm and pleasing solitariness, fed with cheerful and confident thoughts, to embark in a troubled sea of noises and hoarse disputes; put from beholding the bright countenance of truth in the quiet and still air of delightful studies, to come into the dim reflection of hollow antiquities sold by the seeming bulk, and there be fain to club quotations with men whose learning and belief lies in marginal stuffings; who, when they have like good sumpters laid ye down their horse-loads of citations and Fathers at your door, with a rhapsody of who and who were bishops here or there, ye may take off their pack-saddles—their day's work is done, and episcopacy, as they think, stoutly vindicated. Let any gentle apprehension, that can distinguish learned pains from unlearned drudgery, imagine what pleasure or profoundness can be in this, or what honor to deal against such adversaries.

But, were it the meanest under-service, if God by His secretary Conscience enjoin it, it were sad for me if I should draw back; for me especially, now when all men offer their aid to help, ease, and lighten the difficult labors of the Church, to whose service, by the intentions of my parents and friends, I was destined of a child, and in mine own resolutions; till, coming to some maturity of years, and perceiving what tyranny had invaded the Church— that he who would take orders must subscribe slave and take an oath withal, which, unless he took with a conscience that would retch, he must either straight perjure, or split his faith—I thought it better to prefer a blameless silence before the sacred office of speaking, bought and begun with servitude and for-swearing. Howsoever, thus church-outed by the prelates, hence may appear the right I have to meddle in these matters, as before the necessity and constraint appeared.[1]

From *An Apology for Smectymnuus* (1642).

If, readers, to that same great difficulty of well-doing what we certainly know were not added in most men as great a careless-

---

[1] *Ibid.* 2. 481-2.

ness of knowing what they and others ought to do, we had been long ere this, no doubt but all of us, much further on our way to some degree of peace and happiness in this kingdom. But, since our sinful neglect of practising that which we know to be undoubtedly true and good hath brought forth among us, through God's just anger, so great a difficulty now to know that which otherwise might be soon learnt, and hath divided us by a controversy of great importance indeed, but of no hard solution— which is the more our punishment; I resolved (of what small moment soever I might be thought) to stand on that side where I saw both the plain authority of Scripture leading, and the reason of justice and equity persuading; with this opinion, which esteems it more unlike a Christian to be a cold neuter in the cause of the Church than the law of Solon made it punishable after a sedition in the State.

And because I observe that fear and dull disposition, lukewarmness and sloth, are not seldomer wont to cloak themselves under the affected name of moderation than true and lively zeal is customably disparaged with the term of indiscretion, bitterness, and choler, I could not, to my thinking, honor a good cause more from the heart than by defending it earnestly, as oft as I could judge it to behove me, notwithstanding any false name that could be invented to wrong or undervalue an honest meaning. Wherein—although I have not doubted to single forth more than once such of them as were thought the chief and most nominated opposers on the other side, whom no man else undertook—if I have done well either to be confident of the truth, whose force is best seen against the ablest resistance, or to be jealous and tender of the hurt that might be done among the weaker by the entrapping authority of great names titled to false opinions; or, that it be lawful to attribute somewhat to gifts of God's imparting, which I boast not, but thankfully acknowledge, and fear also lest at my certain account they be reckoned to me rather many than few; or, if, lastly, it be but justice not to defraud of due esteem the wearisome labors and studious watchings wherein I have spent and tired out almost a whole youth; I shall not distrust to be acquitted of presumption.[1]

From *The Doctrine and Discipline of Divorce* (1643).

For me, as far as my part leads me, I have already my greatest gain—assurance and inward satisfaction to have done in this nothing unworthy of an honest life, and studies well employed. . . .

I seek not to seduce the simple and illiterate; my errand is to find out the choicest and the learnedest, who have this high gift of wisdom—to answer solidly, or to be convinced. I crave it from the piety, the learning, and the prudence which is housed in this place. It might perhaps more fitly have been written in another tongue; and I had done so, but that the esteem I have of my country's judgment, and the love I bear to my native language to serve it first with what I endeavor, make me speak it thus ere I essay the verdict of outlandish readers. And perhaps also here I might have ended nameless, but that the address of these lines chiefly to the Parliament of England might have seemed ingrateful not to acknowledge by whose religious care, unwearied watchfulness, courageous and heroic resolutions, I enjoy the peace and studious leisure to remain

The Honorer and Attendant of their
   noble Worth and Virtues,
      John Milton.[2]

From *The Judgment of Martin Bucer concerning Divorce* (1644).

Certainly if it be in man's discerning to sever Providence from chance, I could allege many instances wherein there would appear cause to esteem of me no other than a passive instrument

[1] *Prose Works* 3. 94–6.
[2] *Ibid.* 3. 178–9.

under some Power and counsel, higher and better than can be human, working to a general good in the whole course of this matter; for that I owe no light or leading received from any man in the discovery of this truth, what time I first undertook it in *The Doctrine and Discipline of Divorce*, and had only the infallible grounds of Scripture to be my guide, He who tries the inmost heart, and saw with what severe industry and examination of myself I set down every period, will be my witness.

When I had almost finished the first edition, I chanced to read in the notes of Hugo Grotius upon the Fifth of Matthew (whom I straight understood inclining to reasonable terms in this controversy), and something he whispered rather than disputed about the law of charity and the true end of wedlock. Glad, therefore, of such an able assistant, however at much distance, I resolved at length to put off into this wild and calumnious world; for God, it seems, intended to prove me, whether I durst alone take up a rightful cause against a world of disesteem, and found I durst. My name I did not publish, as not willing it should sway the reader either for me or against me. But when I was told that the style, which what it ails to be so soon distinguishable I cannot tell, was known by most men, and that some of the clergy began to inveigh and exclaim on what I was credibly informed they had not read, I took it then for my proper season both to show them a name that could easily contemn such an indiscreet kind of censure, and to reinforce the question with a more accurate diligence; that, if any of them would be so good as to leave railing, and to let us hear so much of his learning and Christian wisdom as will be strictly demanded of him in his answering to this problem, care was had he should not spend his preparations against a nameless pamphlet.

By this time I had learned that Paulus Fagius, one of the chief divines in Germany, sent for by Frederic the Palatine to reform his dominion, and after that invited hither in King Edward's days to be a professor of divinity in Cambridge, was of the same opinion touching divorce which these men so lavishly traduced in me. What I found I inserted where fittest place was, thinking sure they would respect so grave an author, at least to the moderating of their odious inferences. And having now perfected a second edition, I referred the judging thereof to your high and impartial sentence, honored Lords and Commons! for I was confident, if anything generous, anything noble and above the multitude, were left yet in the spirit of England, it could be nowhere sooner found, and nowhere sooner understood, than in that house of justice and true liberty where ye sit in council. Nor doth the event hitherto, for some reasons which I shall not here deliver, fail me of what I conceived so highly. Nevertheless, being far otherwise dealt with by some, of whose profession and supposed knowledge I had better hope, and esteemed the deviser of a new and pernicious paradox, I felt no difference within me from that peace and firmness of mind which is of nearest kin to patience and contentment; both for that I knew I had divulged a truth linked inseparably with the most fundamental rules of Christianity, to stand or fall together, and was not uninformed that divers learned and judicious men testified their daily approbation of the book.

Yet at length it hath pleased God, who had already given me satisfaction in myself, to afford me now a means whereby I may be fully justified also in the eyes of men. When the book had been now the second time set forth well-nigh three months, as I best remember, I then first came to hear that Martin Bucer had written much concerning divorce; whom earnestly turning over, I soon perceived, but not without amazement, in the same opinion, confirmed with the same reasons which in that published book, without the help or imitation of any precedent writer, I had labored out and laid together—not but that there is some difference in the handling, in the order, and the number of arguments—but still agreeing in the same conclusion. So as I may justly gratulate mine own mind with due acknowledgment of assistance from above, which led me, not as a learner but as a collateral teacher, to a sympathy of judgment with no less a man than Martin Bucer.[1]

From *Eikonoklastes* (1649).

And, further, since it appears manifestly the cunning drift of a factious and defeated party to make the same advantage of his [the King's] book which they did before of his regal name and authority, and intend it not so much the defence of his former actions, as the promoting of their own future designs . . . now the third time to corrupt and disorder the minds of weaker men, by new suggestions and narrations, either falsely or fallaciously representing the state of things to the dishonor of this present government, and the retarding of a general peace, so needful to this afflicted nation, and so nigh obtained; I suppose it no injury to the dead, but a good deed rather to the living, if by better information given them, or, which is enough, by only remembering them the truth of what they themselves know to be here[2] misaffirmed, they may be kept from entering the third time unadvisedly into war and bloodshed.

For, as to any moment of solidity in the book itself, save only that a king is said to be the author (a name than which there needs no more, among the blockish vulgar, to make it wise, and excellent, and admired, nay, to set it next the Bible, though otherwise containing little else but the common grounds of tyranny and Popery dressed up, the better to deceive, in a new Protestant guise trimly garnished over), or as to any need of answering in respect of staid and well-principled men, I take it on me as a work assigned, rather than by me chosen or affected; which was the cause both of beginning it so late and finishing it so leisurely, in the midst of other employments and diversions.

And though well it might have seemed in vain to write at all, considering the envy and almost infinite prejudice likely to be

---

[1] *Prose Works* 3. 280–2.
[2] That is, in the *Eikon Basilike.*

stirred up, among the common sort, against whatever can be written or gainsaid to the King's book, so advantageous to a book is it only to be a king's; and though it be an irksome labor to write, with industry and judicious pains, that which, neither weighed nor well read, shall be judged, without industry or the pains of well-judging, by faction and the easy literature of custom and opinion; it shall be ventured yet, and the truth not smothered, but sent abroad in the native confidence of her single self, to earn, how she can, her entertainment in the world, and to find out her own readers; few, perhaps, but those few of such value and substantial worth as truth and wisdom, not respecting numbers and big names, have been ever wont in all ages to be contented with.[1]

From *A Defence of the People of England* (1651).

What style can be august and magnificent enough, what man has ability sufficient, to undertake so great a task? Since we find by experience that, in so many ages as are gone over the world, there has been but here and there a man found who has been able worthily to recount the actions of great heroes and potent states, can any man have so good an opinion of his own talents as to think himself capable of reaching these glorious and wonderful works of Almighty God, by any language, by any style, of his? Which enterprise though some of the most eminent persons in our Commonwealth have prevailed upon me by their authority to undertake, and would have it be my business to vindicate with my pen against envy and calumny (which are proof against arms) those glorious performances of theirs; whose opinion of me I take as a very great honor, that they should pitch upon me before others to be serviceable in this kind to those most valiant deliverers of my native country; and true it is that from my very youth I have been bent extremely upon such sort of studies as inclined me, if not to do great things myself, at least to celebrate

[1] *Prose Works* i. 308–10.

those that did; yet, as having no confidence in any such advantages, I have recourse to the Divine asistance.[1]

From *The Second Defence of the People of England* (1654).

But God Himself is truth; in propagating which, as men display a greater integrity and zeal, they approach nearer to the similitude of God, and possess a greater portion of His love. We cannot suppose the Deity envious of truth, or unwilling that it should be freely communicated to mankind. The loss of sight, therefore, which this inspired sage, who was so eager in promoting knowledge among men, sustained, cannot be considered as a judicial punishment. . . . But, since my enemies boast that this affliction is only a retribution for the transgressions of my pen, I again invoke the Almighty to witness that I never at any time wrote anything which I did not think agreeable to truth, to justice, and to piety. This was my persuasion then, and I feel the same persuasion now. Nor was I ever prompted to such exertions by the influence of ambition, by the lust of lucre or of praise; it was only by the conviction of duty and the feeling of patriotism, a disinterested passion for the extension of civil and religious liberty.[2]

OBSERVATIONS ON THE USE OF AUTHORITIES

From *Animadversions upon the Remonstrant's Defence against Smectymnuus* (1641).

He bids ask of the old paths, or for the old ways, where or which is the good way; which implies that all old ways are not good, but that the good way is to be searched with diligence among the old ways; which is a thing that we do in the oldest records we have—the Gospel. And, if others may chance to spend more time with you in canvassing later antiquity, I suppose it is not for that they ground themselves thereon, but that they endeavor, by showing the corruptions, uncertainties, and dis-

---

[1] *Prose Works* I. 4–5.
[2] *Ibid.* I. 236-8.

agreements of those volumes and the easiness of erring or over-
slipping in such a boundless and vast search, if they may not
convince those that are so strongly persuaded thereof; yet to
free ingenuous minds from an over-awful esteem of those more
ancient than trusty Fathers, whom custom and fond opinion,
weak principles, and the neglect of sounder and superior knowledge hath exalted so high as to have gained them a blind reverence; whose books, in bigness and number so endless and im-
measurable, I cannot think that either God or nature, either
divine or human wisdom, did ever mean should be a rule or re-
liance to us in the decision of any weighty and postive doctrine;
for certainly every rule and instrument of necessary knowledge
that God hath given us ought to be so in proportion as may be
wielded and managed by the life of man, without penning him up
from the duties of human society; and such a rule and instrument
of knowledge perfectly is the Holy Bible. But he that shall bind
himself to make antiquity his rule, if he read but part (besides the
difficulty of choice), his rule is deficient and utterly unsatisfying,
for there may be other writers of another mind which he hath not
seen; and, if he undertake all, the length of man's life cannot extend to give him a full and requisite knowledge of what was done
in antiquity.[1]

From *An Apology for Smectymnuus* (1642).

I have not, . . . I confess, read more of the councils, save here and
there; I should be sorry to have been such a prodigal of my time;
but, that which is better, I can assure this confuter, I have read
into them all. And, if I want anything yet, I shall reply something
toward that which in the defence of Murena was answered by
Cicero to Sulpitius the lawyer: 'If ye provoke me (for at no hand
else will I undertake such a frivolous labor) I will in three months
be an expert councilist.' For be not deceived, readers, by men
that would overawe your ears with big names and huge tomes
that contradict and repeal one another, because they can cram a

[1] *Ibid.* 3. 66.

margin with citations. Do but winnow their chaff from their wheat; ye shall see their great heap shrink and wax thin past belief.[1]

From *The Judgment of Martin Bucer concerning Divorce* (1644).

Thus far Martin Bucer, whom, where I might without injury to either part of the cause, I deny not to have epitomized; in the rest, observing a well-warranted rule not to give an inventory of so many words, but to weigh their force. I could have added that eloquent and right Christian discourse written by Erasmus on this argument, not disagreeing in effect from Bucer. But this, I hope, will be enough to excuse me, with the mere Englishman, to be no forger of new and loose opinions. Others may read him in his own phrase on the First to the Corinthians, and ease me, who never could delight in long citations, much less in whole traductions; whether it be natural disposition or education in me, or that my mother bore me a speaker of what God made mine own, and not a translator.[2]

From *Tetrachordon* (1645).

Thus having inquired the institution how it was in the beginning, . . . and having attended each clause and word necessary with a diligence not drowsy, we shall now fix with some advantage, and, by a short view backward, gather up the ground we have gone, and sum up the strength we have into one argumentative head with that organic force that logic proffers us. All arts acknowledge that then only we know certainly when we can define; for definition is that which refines the pure essence of things from the circumstance. . . . But to proceed in the pursuit of an accurate definition, it will avail us something, and whet our thoughts, to examine what fabric hereof others have already reared.[3]

[1] *Prose Works* 3. 162–3.
[2] *Ibid.* 3. 313–4.
[3] *Ibid.* 3. 341–2.

Seeing most men from their youth so accustom as not to scan
reason nor clearly to apprehend it, but to trust for that the names
and numbers of such as have got, and many times undeservedly,
the reputation among them to know much; and because there is
a vulgar also of teachers, who are as blindly by whom they fancy
led as they lead the people, it will not be amiss for them who had
rather list themselves under this weaker sort, and follow authorities, to take notice that this opinion which I bring hath been
favored and by some of those affirmed who in their time were
able to carry what they taught, had they urged it, through all
Christendom. . . . But since, by His appointment on Whom
the times and seasons wait, every point of doctrine is not fatal to
be thoroughly sifted out in every age, it will be enough for me to
find that the thoughts of wisest heads heretofore, and hearts no
less reverenced for devotion, have tended this way and contributed their lot in some good measure towards this which hath
been here attained.[1]

These authorities without long search I had to produce, all
excellent men, some of them such as many ages had brought
forth none greater; almost the meanest of them might deserve to
obtain credit in a singularity; what might not then all of them,
joined in an opinion so consonant to reason? . . . Nor could
I have wanted more testimonies, had the cause needed a more
solicitous inquiry. But herein the satisfaction of others hath been
studied, not the gaining of more assurance to mine own persuasion, although authorities contributing reason withal be a good
confirmation and a welcome. But God (I solemnly attest Him!)
withheld from my knowledge the consenting judgment of these
men so late until they could not be my instructors, but only my
unexpected witnesses to partial men that in this work I had not
given the worst experiment of an industry joined with integrity,
and the free utterance, though of an unpopular truth. Which
yet to the people of England may, if God so please, prove a

[1] *Ibid.* 3. 414–5.

memorable informing; certainly a benefit which was intended them long since by men of highest repute for wisdom and piety, Bucer and Erasmus.

Only this one authority more, whether in place or out of place, I am not to omit; which if any can think a small one, I must be patient. It is no smaller than the whole assembled authority of England, both Church and State, and in those times which are on record for the purest and sincerest that ever shone yet on the reformation of this island—the time of Edward the Sixth. That worthy Prince, having utterly abolished the canon law out of his dominions, as his father did before him, appointed by full vote of Parliament a committee of two-and-thirty chosen men, divines and lawyers, of whom Cranmer the Archbishop, Peter Martyr, and Walter Haddon (not without the assistance of Sir John Cheke, the King's tutor, a man at that time counted the learnedest of Englishmen, and for piety not inferior) were the chief, to frame anew some ecclesiastical laws that might be instead of what was abrogated. The work with great diligence was finished, and with as great approbation of that reforming age was received; and had been doubtless, as the learned Preface thereof testifies, established by act of Parliament, had not the good King's death, so soon ensuing, arrested the further growth of religion also, from that season to this. . . .

Whereby the wariness and deliberation from which that discourse proceeded will appear, and that God hath aided us to make no bad conclusion of this point; seeing the opinion which of late hath undergone ill censures among the vulgar hath now proved to have done no violence to Scripture, unless all these famous authors alleged have done the like; nor hath affirmed aught more than what indeed the most nominated Fathers of the Church, both ancient and modern, are unexpectedly found affirming, the laws of God's peculiar people, and of primitive Christendom found to have practised, reformed churches and states to have imitated, and especially the most pious church-

times of this kingdom to have framed and published, and, but
for sad hindrances in the sudden change of religion, had enacted
by the Parliament. Henceforth let them who condemn the assertion of this book for new and licentious be sorry; lest, while
they think to be of the graver sort and take on them to be
teachers, they expose themselves rather to be pledged up and
down by men who intimately know them, to the discovery and
contempt of their ignorance and presumption.[1]

From *Colasterion* (1645).

As ignorantly, and too ignorantly to deceive any reader but an
unlearned, he talks of Justin Martyr's *Apology*, not telling us
which of the twain; for that passage, in the beginning of his first,
which I have cited elsewhere, plainly makes against him. So doth
Tertullian, cited next, and next Erasmus; the one against Marcion,
the other in his annotations on Matthew and To the Corinthians.
And thus ye have the list of his choice antiquities, as pleasantly
chosen as ye would wish from a man of his handy vocation,
puffed up with no luck at all above the stint of his capacity.[2]

From *Eikonoklastes* (1649).

Thus far the occasion of this discourse against tumults; now to
the discourse itself, voluble enough, and full of sentence, but that
for the most part either specious rather than solid, or to his
cause nothing pertinent.[3]

But what needed written acts, whenas anciently it was esteemed
part of his crown oath not to dissolve parliaments till all grievances were considered? Whereupon the old 'Modi of Parliament'
calls it flat perjury if he dissolve them before; as I find cited in
a book mentioned at the beginning of this chapter, to which
and other law-tractates I refer the more lawyerly mooting of this
point, which is neither my element nor my proper work here;
since the book which I have to answer pretends reason, not

---

[1] *Prose Works* 3. 431–3.
[2] *Ibid.* 3. 445.
[3] *Ibid.* 1. 345.

authorities and quotations, and I hold reason to be the best arbitrator, and the law of law itself.[1]

It being therefore most unlike a law to ordain a remedy so slender and unlawlike to be the utmost means of all public safety—or prevention, as advice is—which may at any time be rejected by the sole judgment of one man, the King, and so unlike the law of England, which lawyers say is the quintessence of reason and mature wisdom; we may conclude that the king's . . . voice was never any law. . . . Thus much to the law of it, by a better evidence than rolls and records—reason.[2]

From *A Defence of the People of England* (1651).

You were never yet able to stain the renown and everlasting glory of the English nation, that, with so great a resolution as we hardly find the like recorded in any history, having struggled with and overcome not only their enemies in the field but the superstitious persuasions of the common people, have purchased to themselves in general amongst all posterity the name of deliverers; the body of the people having undertook and performed an enterprise which in other nations is thought to proceed only from a magnanimity that is peculiar to heroes. . . .

And what if it has pleased God to choose such men to execute His vengeance upon the greatest potentates on earth, as He chose to be made partakers of the benefit of the Gospel? 'Not many wise, not many learned, not many powerful, not many noble; that by those that are not He might bring to nought those that are, and that no flesh might glory in His sight.' And who are you that babble to the contrary? Dare you affect the reputation of a learned man? I confess you are pretty well versed in phrase-books and lexicons and glossaries, insomuch that you seem to have spent your time in nothing else. But you do not make appear that you have read any good authors with so much judgment as to have benefited by them. Other copies, and various readings, and words

[1] *Prose Works* I. 355.
[2] *Ibid.* I. 359-60.

omitted, and corruptions of texts, and the like—these you are full of; but no footstep of any solid learning appears in all you have writ. Or do ye think yourself a wise man, that quarrel and contend about the meanest trifles that may be? that, being altogether ignorant in astronomy and physic, yet are always railing at the professors of both, whom all men credit in what things belong to their own sciences? that would be ready to curse them to the pit of hell that should offer to deprive you of the vainglory of having corrected or supplied the least word or letter in any copy you have criticized upon? And yet you are mad to hear yourself called a grammarian. . . .

Whosoever, therefore, he be, though from among the dregs of that common people that you are so keen upon, . . . has but sucked in this principle—that he was not born for his Prince, but for God and his country—he deserves the reputation of a learned, and an honest, and a wise man more, and is of greater use in the world, than yourself. For such a one is learned without letters; you have letters, but no learning, that understand so many languages, turn over so many volumes, and yet are but asleep when all is done.[1]

If you had consulted Tully, you would have understood both Sallust and Samuel better. . . . Many passages to this purpose he quotes out of poets, and calls them not the right, but the custom or manner of kings; and, he says, we ought to read and consider them, not only for curiosity' sake, but that we may learn to beware of them and avoid them.[2]

Though I am of opinion, . . . and always was, that the law of God does exactly agree with the law of nature, . . . I do not purpose to frame a long discourse of nature in general, and the original of civil societies; that argument has been largely handled by many learned men, both Greek and Latin.[3]

[1] *Ibid.* 1. 28–30.
[2] *Ibid.* 1. 39–40.
[3] *Ibid.* 1. 108–9.

From the philosophers you appeal to the poets; and I am very willing to follow you thither. . . . But you must know . . . that one is not to regard what the poet says, but what person in the play speaks, and what that person says; for different persons are introduced, sometimes good, sometimes bad; sometimes wise men, sometimes fools; and such words are put into their mouths as it is most proper for them to speak; not such as the poet would speak if he were to speak in his own person.[1]

'But Tacitus,' say you, . . . 'writes thus:'. . . but you tell us not where Tacitus has these words, for you were conscious to yourself that you imposed upon your readers in quoting them— which I presently smelt out, though I could not find the place of a sudden; for that expression is not Tacitus' own, who is an approved writer, and of all others the greatest enemy to tyrants; but Tacitus relates that of M. Terentius, a gentleman of Rome, [who,] being accused for a capital crime, amongst other things that he said to save his life, flattered Tiberius on this manner. . . . And you cite this passage as if Tacitus had said it himself. . . . If you had read Tacitus himself, and not transcribed some loose quotations out of him by other authors, he would have taught you whence that imperial right had its original. . . . The same thing you might have learned out of Dio, if your natural levity and unsettledness of judgment would have suffered you to apprehend anything that is solid.[2]

Now, since so many and so great authors assert that a kingly government both in name and thing may very well subsist even where the people, though they do not ordinarily exercise the supreme power, yet have it actually residing in them, and exercise it upon occasion; be not you of so mean a soul as to fear the downfall of grammar, and the confusion of the signification of words, to that degree as to betray the liberty of mankind and the State, rather

[1] *Prose Works* i. 126.
[2] *Ibid.* i. 128–9.

than your glossary should not hold water. And know, for the future, that words must be conformable to things, not things to words.[1]

From *The Second Defence of the People of England* (1654).

I wrote nothing more than what Bucer on the Kingdom of Christ, Fagius on Deuteronomy, and Erasmus on the First Epistle to the Corinthians (which was more particularly designed for the instruction of the English) had written before me, for the most useful purposes and with the most disinterested views; . . . though I regret that I published this work in English, for then it would not have been exposed to the view of those common readers who are wont to be as ignorant of their own blessings as they are insensible to others' sufferings.[2]

From *The Christian Doctrine.*

Though all this be so self-evident as to require no explanation, . . . it is wonderful with what futile subtleties, or rather with what juggling artifices, certain individuals have endeavored to elude or obscure the plain meaning of these passages; leaving no stone unturned, recurring to every shift, attempting every means, as if their object were not to preach the pure and unadulterated truth of the Gospel to the poor and simple, but rather by dint of vehemence and obstinacy to sustain some absurd paradox from falling, by the treacherous aid of sophisms and verbal distinctions borrowed from the barbarous ignorance of the Schools.[3]

And surely what is proposed to us as an object of belief, especially in a matter involving a primary article of faith, ought not to be an inference forced and extorted from passages relating to an entirely different subject, in which the readings are sometimes various, and the sense doubtful—nor hunted out by careful research from among articles and particles—nor elicited by dint of ingenuity, like the answers of an oracle, from sentences of dark

[1] *Ibid.* 1. 141.
[2] *Ibid.* 1. 252-3.
[3] *Ibid.* 4. 92.

or equivocal meaning— but should be susceptible of abundant proof from the clearest sources. For it is in this that the superiority of the Gospel to the law consists; this, and this alone, is consistent with its open simplicity; this is that true light and perspicuity which we had been taught to expect would be its characteristic.[1]

It seems exceedingly unreasonable—not to say dangerous— that, in a matter of so much difficulty, believers should be required to receive a doctrine, represented by its advocates as of primary importance and of undoubted certainty, on anything less than the clearest testimony of Scripture; and that a point which is confessedly contrary to human reason should nevertheless be considered as susceptible of proof from human reason only, or rather from doubtful and obscure disputations.[2]

Since, then, this mystery is so great, we are admonished by that very consideration not to assert anything respecting it rashly or presumptuously, on mere grounds of philosophical reasoning; not to add to it anything of our own; not even to adduce in its behalf any passage of Scripture of which the purport may be doubtful, but to be contented with the clearest texts, however few in number. If we listen to such passages, and are willing to acquiesce in the simple truth of Scripture unencumbered by metaphysical comments, to how many prolix and preposterous arguments shall we put an end! How much occasion of heresy shall we remove! How many ponderous volumes of dabblers in theology shall we cast out, purging the temple of God from the contamination of their rubbish! Nothing would be more plain and agreeable to reason, nothing more suitable to the understanding even of the meanest individual, than such parts of the Christian faith as are declared in Scripture to be necessary for salvation, if teachers, even of the reformed Church, were as yet sufficiently impressed with the propriety of insisting on nothing

1 *Prose Works* 4. 116.
2 *Ibid.* 4. 159.

but divine authority in matters relating to God, and of limiting themselves to the contents of the sacred volume. What is essential would easily appear, when freed from the perplexities of controversy; what is mysterious would be suffered to remain inviolate, and we should be fearful of overstepping the bounds of propriety in its investigation.[1]

He [Zanchius] proves his point with sufficient accuracy, but neglects to follow up his conclusions; losing himself in a multitude of minute exceptions, and apparently fluctuating between the two opinions, so as to leave the reader (if not extremely attentive) in a state of uncertainty.[2]

MILTON'S USE OF RIDICULE AND INVECTIVE, AND HIS DEMEANOR IN THE WARMER KIND OF CONTROVERSY

From *An Apology for Smectymnuus* (1642).

And, whereas this confuter taxes the whole discourse of levity, I shall show ye, readers, wheresoever it shall be objected in particular, that I have answered with as little lightness as the Remonstrant hath given example. I have not been so light as the palm of a bishop, which is the lightest thing in the world when he brings out his book of ordination; for then, contrary to that which is wont in releasing out of prison, any one that will pay his fees is laid hands on.

Another reason it would not be amiss though the Remonstrant were told wherefore he was in that unusual manner beleagured, and this was it: to pluck out of the heads of his admirers the conceit that all who are not prelatical are gross-headed, thick-witted, illiterate, shallow. Can nothing, then, but episcopacy teach men to speak good English, to pick and order a set of words judiciously? Must we learn from canons and quaint sermonings, interlined with barbarous Latin, to illumine a period, to wreathe an enthymema with masterous dexterity? I rather incline, as I

[1] *Ibid.* 4. 289–90.
[2] *Ibid.* 4. 395–6.

have heard it observed that a Jesuit's Italian, when he writes, is ever naught, though he be born and bred a Florentine, so to think that from like causes we may go near to observe the same in the style of a prelate. For doubtless that indeed according to art is most eloquent which turns and approaches nearest to nature, from whence it came; and they express nature best who in their lives least wander from her safe leading, which may be called regenerate reason; so that how he should be truly eloquent who is not withal a good man, I see not. . . .

For, as in teaching doubtless the spirit of meekness is most powerful, so are the meek only fit persons to be taught. As for the proud, the obstinate, and false doctors of men's devices, be taught they will not, but discovered and laid open they must be. For how can they admit of teaching who have the condemnation of God already upon them for refusing divine instruction?—that is, to be filled with their own devices, as in the Proverbs we may read. Therefore we may safely imitate the method that God uses: 'with the froward to be froward, and to throw scorn upon the scorner'—whom, if anything, nothing else will heal.[1]

And thus, readers, by the example which he hath set me, I have given ye two or three notes of him out of his title-page; by which his firstlings, fear not to guess boldly at his whole lump, for that guess will not fail ye; and, although I tell him keen truth, yet he may bear with me, since I am like to chase him into some good sound knowledge; and others, I trust, shall not misspend their leisure.[2]

If . . . the question were in oratory, whether a vehement vein, throwing out indignation or scorn upon an object that merits it, were among the aptest *ideas* of speech to be allowed, it were my work, and that an easy one, to make it clear both by the rules of best rhetoricians and the famousest examples of the Greek and

[1] *Prose Works* 3. 100–1.
[2] *Ibid.* 3. 105.

Roman orations. But, since the religion of it is disputed, and not the art, I shall make use only of such reasons and authorities as religion cannot except against.

It will be harder to gainsay than for me to evince that, in the teaching of men diversely tempered, different ways are to be tried. The Baptist, we know, was a strict man, remarkable for austerity and set order of life. Our Saviour, who had all gifts in Him, was Lord to express His indoctrinating power in what sort Him best seemed: sometimes by a mild and familiar converse; sometimes with plain and impartial home-speaking, regardless of those whom the auditors might think He should have had in more respect; otherwhile with bitter and ireful rebukes, if not teaching, yet leaving excuseless, those His wilful impugners. What was all in Him was divided among many others the teachers of His Church; some to be severe and ever of a sad gravity, that they may win such, and check sometimes those who be of nature over-confident and jocund; others were sent more cheerful, free, and still as it were at large, in the midst of an untrespassing honesty; that they who are so tempered may have by whom they might be drawn to salvation, and they who are too scrupulous, and dejected of spirit, might be often strengthened with wise consolations, and revivings; no man being forced wholly to dissolve that groundwork of nature which God created in him—the sanguine to empty out all his sociable liveliness, the choleric to expel quite the unsinning predominance of his anger—but that each radical humor and passion, wrought upon and corrected as it ought, might be made the proper mould and foundation of every man's peculiar gifts and virtues. Some also were indued with a staid moderation and soundness of argument, to teach and convince the rational and sober-minded; yet not therefore that to be thought the only expedient course of teaching, for, in times of opposition, when either against new heresies arising or old corruptions to be reformed, this cool, unpassionate mildness of positive wisdom is not enough to damp and astonish the proud resistance of carnal and false doctors; then, (that I may have leave to soar awhile as the poets use) Zeal, whose substance is ethereal, arming in complete diamond, ascends his fiery chariot, drawn with two blazing meteors figured like beasts (but of a higher breed than any the zodiac yields), resembling two of those four which Ezekiel and St. John saw: the one visaged like a lion, to express power, high authority, and indignation; the other of countenance like a man, to cast derision and scorn upon perverse and fraudulent seducers. With these the invincible warrior, Zeal, shaking loosely the slack reins, drives over the heads of scarlet prelates, and such as are insolent to maintain traditions, bruising their stiff necks under his flaming wheels.[1]

Now that the confutant may also know, as he desires, what force of teaching there is sometimes in laughter, I shall return him, in short, that laughter, being one way of answering 'a fool according to his folly,' teaches two sorts of persons: first, the fool himself, 'not to be wise in his own conceit,' as Solomon affirms; which is certainly a great document to make an unwise man know himself. Next, it teacheth the hearers, inasmuch as scorn is one of those punishments which belong to men carnally wise, which is oft in Scripture declared; for, when such are punished, 'the simple are thereby made wise,' if Solomon's rule be true. And I would ask to what end Elijah mocked the false prophets? . . . Doubtless we cannot imagine that great servant of God had any other end, in all which he there did, but to teach and instruct the poor misled people.[2]

But lest some may haply think or thus expostulate with me after this debatement: 'Who made you the busy almoner to deal about this dole of laughter and reprehension, which no man thanks your bounty for?'—to the urbanity of that man I should answer much after this sort: That I, friend objector, having read

[1] *Prose Works* 3. 128–9.
[2] *Ibid.* 3. 131–2.

of heathen philosophers, some to have taught that whosoever would but use his ear to listen might hear the voice of his guiding genius ever before him, calling, and as it were pointing, to that way which is his part to follow; others, as the Stoics, to account reason, which they call the Hegemonicon, to be the common Mercury conducting without error those that give themselves obediently to be led accordingly: having read this, I could not esteem so poorly of the faith which I profess, that God had left nothing, to those who had forsaken all other doctrines for His, to be an inward witness and warrant of what they have to do, as that they should need to measure themselves by other men's measures, how to give scope or limit to their proper actions.[1]

One thing I beg of ye, readers: as ye bear any zeal to learning, to elegance, and that which is called *decorum* in the writing of praise, especially on such a noble argument, ye would not be offended though I rate this cloistered lubber according to his deserts. . . .

Which of those worthy deeds whereof we and our posterity must confess this parliament to have done so many and so noble—which of those memorable acts comes first into his praises? None of all; not one. What will he then praise them for? Not for anything doing, but for deferring to do; for deferring to chastise his lewd and insolent compriests—not that they have deferred all, but that he hopes they will remit what is yet behind. For the rest of his oratory that follows, so just is it in the language of stall-epistle nonsense that, if he who made it can understand it, I deny not but that he may deserve for his pains a cast doublet. When a man would look he should vent something of his own, as ever in a set speech the manner is with him that knows anything, he, lest we should not take notice enough of his barren stupidity, declares it by alphabet, and refers us to odd remnants in his topics. Nor yet content with the wonted room of his margin, but he must cut out large docks and creeks into his text, to

---

[1] *Ibid*. 3. 132–3.

unlade the foolish frigate of his unseasonable authorities; not therewith to praise the Parliament, but to tell them what he would have them do. What else there is, he jumbles together in such a lost construction as no man, either lettered or unlettered, will be able to piece up. I shall spare to transcribe him, but if I do him wrong let me be so dealt with.[1]

From *The Judgment of Martin Bucer concerning Divorce* (1644).

The truth is, there will be due to them for this their unadvised rashness the best donative that can be given them—I mean, a round reproof; now that where they thought to be most magisterial they have displayed their own want both of reading and of judgment: first, to be so unacquainted in the writings of Bucer, which are so obvious, and so useful in their own faculty; next, to be so caught in a prejudicating weakness as to condemn that for lewd which (whether they knew or not) these elect servants of Christ commended for lawful; and for new, that which was taught by these almost the first and greatest authors of reformation, who were never taxed for so teaching. . . . This is also another fault which I must tell them: that they have stood now almost this whole year clamoring afar off, while the book hath been twice printed, twice brought up, and never once vouchsafed a friendly conference with the author, who would be glad and thankful to be shown an error either by private dispute or public answer, and could retract as well as wise men before him; might also be worth the gaining, as one who heretofore hath done good service to the Church, by their own confession.[2]

If this be not enough to qualify my traducers, and that they think it more for the wisdom of their virulence not to recant the injuries they have bespoke me, I shall not, for much more disturbance than they can bring me, intermit the prosecution of those thoughts which may render me best serviceable either to this age or, if it so happen, to posterity.[3]

[1] *Prose Works* 3. 144-5.
[2] *Ibid.* 3. 283.
[3] *Ibid.* 3. 286-7.

From *Tetrachordon* (1645).

The former book, as pleased some to think who were thought judicious, had of reason in it to a sufficiency; what they required was that the Scriptures there alleged might be discussed more fully. To their desires thus much further hath been labored in the Scriptures. Another sort, also, who wanted more authorities and citations, have not been here unthought of. If all this attain not to satisfy them, as I am confident that none of those our great controversies at this day hath had a more demonstrative explaining, I must confess to admire what it is; for doubtless it is not reason nowadays that satisfies or suborns the common credence of men to yield so easily, and grow so vehement, in matters much more disputable, and far less conducing to the daily good and peace of life.

Some whose necessary shifts have long inured them to cloak the defects of their unstudied years, and hatred now to learn, under the appearance of a grave solidity (which estimation they have gained among weak perceivers) find the case of slighting what they cannot refute, and are determined, as I hear, to hold it not worth the answering. . . . Others, which is their courtesy, confess that wit and parts may do much to make that seem true which is not; as was objected to Socrates, by them who could not resist his efficacy, that he ever made the worse cause seem the better; and thus thinking themselves discharged of the difficulty, love not to wade further into the fear of a convincement. These will be their excuses to decline the full examining of this serious point.

So much the more I press it and repeat it, Lords and Commons! that ye beware, while time is, ere this grand secret and only art of ignorance, affecting tyranny, grow powerful and rule among us. For, if sound argument and reason shall be thus put off either by an undervaluing silence or the masterly censure of a railing word or two in the pulpit, or by rejecting the force of truth as the mere cunning of eloquence and sophistry, what can be the end of this but that all good learning and knowledge will suddenly decay?

Ignorance, and illiterate presumption, which is yet but our disease, will turn at length into our very constitution, and prove the hectic evil of the age; worse to be feared, if it get once to reign over us, than any 'Fifth Monarchy.' If this shall be the course, that what was wont to be a chief commendation, and the ground of other men's confidence in an author—his diligence, his learning, his elocution, whether by right or by ill meaning granted him—shall be turned now to a disadvantage and suspicion against him; that what he writes, though unconfuted, must therefore be mistrusted, therefore not received, for the industry, the exactness, the labor, in it confessed to be more than ordinary—as if wisdom had now forsaken the thirsty and laborious inquirer, to dwell against her nature with the arrogant and shallow babbler; to what purpose all those pains and that continual searching required of us by Solomon to the attainment of understanding? Why are men bred up with such care and expense to a life of perpetual studies? Why do yourselves with such endeavor seek to wipe off the imputation of intending to discourage the progress and advance of learning?[1]

The manner of these men coming to our Saviour, not to learn, but to tempt Him, may give us to expect that their answer will be such as is fittest for them—not so much a teaching as an entangling. No man, though never so willing or so well enabled to instruct, but, if he discern his willingness and candor made use of to entrap him, will suddenly draw in himself, and, laying aside the facile vein of perspicuity, will know his time to utter clouds and riddles. . . . Our Saviour at no time expressed any great desire to teach the obstinate and unteachable Pharisees; but when they came to tempt Him, then least of all. . . . Besides, it is a general precept not only of Christ, but of all other sages, not to instruct the unworthy and the conceited, who love tradition more than truth, but to perplex and stumble them purposely with contrived obscurities.[2]

[1] *Prose Works* 3. 319–21.
[2] *Ibid.* 3. 370.

This also may be thought not improbably—that Christ, stirred up in His spirit against these tempting Pharisees, answered them in a certain form of indignation usual among good authors; whereby the question or the truth is not directly answered, but something which is fitter for them who ask to hear. So, in the ecclesiastical stories, one demanding how God employed Himself before the world was made, had answer that He was making hell for curious questioners.[1]

From *Colasterion* (1645).

At length a book was brought to my hands, entitled *An Answer to the Doctrine and Discipline of Divorce*. Gladly I received it, and very attentively composed myself to read, hoping that now some good man had vouchsafed the pains to instruct me better than I could yet learn out of all the volumes which for this purpose I had visited. Only this I marveled, and other men have since —whenas I, in a subject so new to this age and so hazardous to please, concealed not my name, why this author, defending that part which is so creeded by the people, would conceal his. But ere I could enter three leaves into the pamphlet (for I defer the peasantly rudeness which, by the licenser's leave, I met with afterwards), my satisfaction came in abundantly that it could be nothing why he durst not name himself but the guilt of his own wretchedness.

For, first, not to speak of his abrupt and bald beginning, his very first page notoriously bewrays him an illiterate and arrogant presumer in that which he understands not: bearing us in hand as if he knew both Greek and Hebrew, and is not able to spell it; which had he been, it had been either written as it ought or scored upon the printer. If it be excused as the carelessness of his deputy, be it known the learned author himself is inventoried and summed up to the utmost value of his livery-cloak. Whoever he be, though this to some may seem a slight contest, I shall yet continue to think that man full of other secret injustice and

[1] *Ibid.* 3. 388.

deceitful pride who shall offer in public to assume the skill though it be but of a tongue which he hath not, and would catch his readers to believe of his ability that which is not in him. The licenser, indeed, as his authority now stands, may license much; but, if these Greek orthographies were of his licensing, the boys at school might reckon with him at his grammar.

Nor did I find this his want of the pretended languages alone, but accompanied with such a low and homespun expression of his mother-English all along, without joint or frame, as made me, ere I knew further of him, often stop and conclude that this author could for certain be no other than some mechanic. Nor was the style flat and rude, and the matter grave and solid—for then there had been pardon; but so shallow and so unwary was that also as gave sufficiently the character of a gross and sluggish, yet a contentious and overweening, pretender. . . .

So that, whether his meaning were to inform his own party or to confute his adversary, instead of showing us the true doctrine and discipline of divorce, he shows us nothing but his own contemptible ignorance. . . . But one thing more I observed, a singular note of his stupidity, and that his trade is not to meddle with books, much less with confutations: whenas the *Doctrine of Divorce* had now a whole year been published the second time, with many arguments added, and the former ones bettered and confirmed, this idle pamphlet comes reeling forth against the first edition only; as may appear to any by the pages quoted.[1]

Then he stumbles that I should say 'the gentlest ends of marriage,' confessing that he understands it not. And I believe him heartily; for how should he, a serving-man both by nature and by function, an idiot by breeding, and a solicitor by presumption, ever come to know or feel within himself what the meaning is of 'gentle?'[2]

[1] *Prose Works* 3. 435–7.
[2] *Ibid.* 3. 449.

His explanation done, he charges me with a wicked gloss, and almost blasphemy, for saying that Christ in teaching meant not always to be taken word for word, but, like a wise physician administering one excess against another, to reduce us to a perfect mean. Certainly to teach thus were no dishonest method. Christ himself hath often used hyperboles in his teaching; and gravest authors, both Aristotle, in the second of his *Ethics to Nicomachus*, and Seneca, in his seventh *De Beneficiis*, advise us to stretch out the line of precept oft-times beyond measure, that, while we tend further, the mean might be the easier attained.[1]

I[2] have now done that which for many causes I might have thought could not likely have been my fortune to be put to—this underwork of scouring and unrubbishing the low and sordid ignorance of such a presumptuous losel. Yet Hercules had the labor once imposed upon him to carry dung out of the Augean stable. At any hand I would be rid of him; for I had rather, since the life of man is likened to a scene, that all my entrances and exits might mix with such persons only whose worth erects them and their actions to a grave and tragic deportment, and not to have to do with clowns and vices. But, if a man cannot peaceably walk into the world, but must be infested, sometimes at his face with dors and horseflies, sometimes beneath with bawling whippets and shin-barkers, and these to be set on by plot and consultation with a junto of clergymen and licensers, commended also and rejoiced in by those whose partiality cannot yet forego old papistical principles; have I not cause to be in such a manner defensive as may procure me freedom to pass more unmolested hereafter by those encumbrances, not so much regarded for themselves as for those who incite them? And what defence can properly be used in such a despicable encounter

[1] *Ibid.* 3. 452.
[2] *Colasterion* contains some of the most bitter invective that Milton ever wrote. In these words at the close of the treatise, he apologizes to his readers for his severity.

as this, but either the slap or the spurn? If they can afford me none but a ridiculous adversary, the blame belongs not to me, though the whole dispute be strewed and scattered with ridiculous. And, if he have such an ambition to know no better who are his mates, but among those needy thoughts which, though his two faculties of serving-man and solicitor should compound into one mongrel, would be but thin and meagre; if in this penury of soul he can be possible to have the lustiness to think of fame; let him but send me how he calls himself, and I may chance not fail to indorse him on the backside of posterity, not a golden, but a brazen—ass. Since my fate extorts from me a talent of sport, which I had thought to hide in a napkin, he shall be my Batrachomyomachia, my Bavius, my Calandrino, the common adagy of ignorance and overweening: nay, perhaps, as the provocation may be, I may be driven to curl up this gliding prose into a rough Sotadic that shall rime him into such a condition as, instead of judging good books to be burnt by the executioner, he shall be readier to be his own hangman. Thus much to this nuisance.

But as for the subject itself, which I have writ and now defend according as the opposition bears—if any man equal to the matter shall think it appertains him to take in hand this controversy, either excepting against aught written, or persuaded he can show better how this question, of such moment to be thoroughly known, may receive a true determination, not leaning on the old and rotten suggestions whereon it yet leans; if his intents be sincere to the public, and shall carry him on without bitterness to the opinion, or to the person, dissenting; let him not, I entreat him, guess, by the handling which meritoriously hath been bestowed on this object of contempt and laughter, that I account it any displeasure done me to be contradicted in print, but, as it leads to the attainment of anything more true, shall esteem it a benefit; and shall know how to return his civility and fair argument in such a sort as he shall confess that to do so is my choice, and to have done thus was my chance.[1]

[1] *Prose Works* 3. 460-1.

From *A Defence of the People of England* (1651).

I had neither words nor arguments long to seek for the defence of so good a cause, if I had enjoyed such a measure of health as would have endured the fatigue of writing. And being but weak in body, I am forced to write by piecemeal, and break off almost every hour, though the subject be such as requires an unintermitted study and intenseness of mind. But though this bodily indisposition may be a hindrance to me in setting forth the just praises of my most worthy countrymen, who have been the saviors of their native country, and whose exploits, worthy of immortality, are already famous all the world over; yet I hope it will be no difficult matter for me to defend them from the insolence of this silly little scholar, and from that saucy tongue of his, at least. Nature and laws would be in an ill case if slavery should find what to say for itself, and liberty be mute; and if tyrants should find men to plead for them, and they that can master and vanquish tyrants should not be able to find advocates. And it were a deplorable thing, indeed, if the reason mankind is endued withal, and which is the gift of God, should not furnish more arguments for men's preservation, for their deliverance, and, as much as the nature of the thing will bear, for making them equal to one another, than for their oppression.[1]

From *A Treatise of Civil Power in Ecclesiastical Causes* (1659).

Pomp and ostentation of reading is admired among the vulgar, but doubtless in matters of religion he is learnedest who is plainest. The brevity I use, not exceeding a small manual, will not, therefore, I suppose, be thought the less considerable, unless with them, perhaps, who think that great books only can determine great matters. I rather choose the common rule—not to make much ado where less may serve; which in controversies, and those especially of religion, would make them less tedious, and by consequence read oftener, by many more, and with more benefit.[2]

[1] *Ibid*. 1. 6.
[2] *Ibid*. 2. 548.

From *Of True Religion* (1673).

It cannot be denied that the authors or late revivers of all these sects or opinions were learned, worthy, zealous, and religious men, as appears by their lives written; and the same of their many eminent and learned followers; perfect and powerful in the Scriptures, holy and unblameable in their lives; and it cannot be imagined that God would desert such painful and zealous laborers in His Church, and oft-times great sufferers for their conscience, to damnable errors and a reprobate sense, who had so often implored the assistance of His Spirit; but rather, having made no man infallible, that He hath pardoned their errors, and accepts their pious endeavors sincerely searching all things, according to the rule of Scripture, with such guidance and direction as they can obtain of God by prayer.[1]

Shall we condescend to dispute with them? The Scripture is our only principle in religion; and by that only they will not be judged, but will add other principles of their own, which, forbidden by the Word of God, we cannot assent to. And the common maxim also in logic is: 'Against them who deny principles we are not to dispute.' Let them bound their disputations on the Scripture only, and an ordinary Protestant, well-read in the Bible, may turn and wind their Doctors. They will not go about to prove their idolatries by the Word of God, but run to shifts and evasions and frivolous distinctions: idols, they say, are laymen's books, and a great means to stir up pious thoughts and devotion in the learnedest. I say they are no means of God's appointing, but plainly the contrary.[2]

How shall we prove all things—which includes all opinions, at least founded on Scripture—unless we not only tolerate them, but patiently hear them and seriously read them? If he who thinks himself in the truth professes to have learnt it, not by implicit faith, but by attentive study of the Scriptures and full persuasion

[1] *Prose Works* 2. 512.
[2] *Ibid.* 2. 515.

of heart, with what equity can he refuse to hear or read him who demonstrates to have gained his knowledge by the same way? Is it a fair course to assert truth by arrogating to himself the only freedom of speech, and stopping the mouths of others equally gifted? This is the direct way to bring in that papistical implicit faith which we all disclaim. They pretend it would unsettle the weaker sort; the same groundless fear is pretended by the Romish clergy in prohibiting the Scripture. At least, then, let them have leave to write in Latin, which the common people understand not, that what they hold may be discussed among the learned only. We suffer the idolatrous books of Papists, without this fear, to be sold and read as common as our own; why not much rather of Anabaptists, Arians, Arminians, and Socinians? There is no learned man but will confess he hath much profited by reading controversies—his senses awaked, his judgment sharpened, and the truth which he holds more firmly established. If then it be profitable for him to read, why should it not at least be tolerable and free for his adversary to write? In logic they teach that contraries laid together more evidently appear; it follows then that, all controversies being permitted, falsehood will appear more false, and truth the more true; which must needs conduce much, not only to the confounding of Popery, but to the general confirmation of unimplicit truth.[1]

From *The Christian Doctrine*.

If I communicate the result of my inquiries to the world at large—if, as God is my witness, it be with a friendly and benignant feeling towards mankind that I readily give as wide a circulation as possible to what I esteem my best and richest possession, I hope to meet with a candid reception from all parties, and that none at least will take unjust offense, even though many things should be brought to light which will at once be seen to differ from certain received opinions. I earnestly beseech all lovers of truth not to cry out that the Church is thrown into

[1] *Ibid.* 2. 517–8.

confusion by that freedom of discussion and inquiry which is granted to the schools, and ought certainly to be refused to no believer, since we are ordered 'to prove all things,' and since the daily progress of the light of truth is productive far less of disturbance to the Church than of illumination and edification.

Nor do I see how the Church can be more disturbed by the investigation of truth than were the Gentiles by the first promulgation of the Gospel; since, so far from recommending or imposing anything on my own authority, it is my particular advice that every one should suspend his opinion, on whatever points he may not feel himself fully satisfied, till the evidence of Scripture prevail, and persuade his reason into assent and faith. Concealment is not my object. It is to the learned that I address myself, or, if it be thought that the learned are not the best umpires and judges of such things, I should at least wish to submit my opinions to men of a mature and manly understanding, possessing a thorough knowledge of the doctrines of the Gospel; on whose judgments I should rely with far more confidence than on those of novices in these matters.[1]

I cannot enter upon subjects of so much difficulty as the Son of God and the Holy Spirit without again premising a few introductory remarks.

If, indeed, I were a member of the Church of Rome, which requires implicit obedience to its creed on all points of faith, I should have acquiesced from education or habit in its simple decree and authority. . . . But since I enrol myself among the number of those who acknowledge the Word of God alone as the rule of faith, and freely advance what appears to me much more clearly deducible from the Holy Scriptures than the commonly received opinion, I see no reason why any one who belongs to the same Protestant, or reformed, Church, and professes to acknowledge the same rule of faith as myself, should take offence at my freedom, particularly as I impose my authority

[1] *Prose Works* 4. 4–5.

on no one, but merely propose what I think more worthy of be-lief than the creed in general acceptation. I only entreat that my readers will ponder and examine my statements in a spirit which desires to discover nothing but the truth, and with a mind free from prejudice. For, without intending to oppose the authority of Scripture, which I consider inviolably sacred, I only take upon myself to refute human interpretations, as often as the occasion requires, conformably to my right, or rather to my duty, as a man. If, indeed, those with whom I have to contend were able to produce direct attestation from Heaven to the truth of the doctrine which they espouse, it would be nothing less than impiety to venture to raise, I do not say a clamor, but so much as a murmur, against it. But inasmuch as they can lay claim to nothing more than human powers, assisted by that spiritual illumination which is common to all, it is not unreasonable that they should on their part allow the privileges of diligent research and free discussion to another inquirer, who is seeking truth through the same means and in the same way as themselves, and whose desire of benefiting mankind is equal to their own.[1]

Considering, however, that all the Greek writers, sacred as well as profane, use the word *blasphemy* in a general sense, as implying any kind of reproach against any person whatever, which is also the received usage of the corresponding word in Hebrew; . . . considering, I say, that such is the meaning invariably attached to the Greek word even by the sacred writers, I am of opinion that those who introduced this foreign term into the Latin language did wrong in restricting it to the single sense of speaking evil of God; especially since, at the same time that they narrowed its meaning in one direction, they expanded it in another to an almost indefinite vagueness; insomuch that, pre-suming on the general ignorance as to the true signification of the word, they have not scrupled to brand as blasphemy every opinion differing from their own on the subject of God or religion.

[1] *Ibid.* 4. 78–9.

. . . This sin therefore is not to be imputed to those who, in sincerity of heart, and with no contentious purpose, promulgate or defend their conscientious persuasions respecting God, founded, as appears to them, on the Scriptures.[1]

From *A Treatise of Civil Power in Ecclesiastical Causes* (1659).

But some are ready to cry out, 'What shall then be done to blasphemy?' Them I would first exhort not thus to terrify and pose the people with a Greek word; but to teach them better what it is, being a most usual and common word in that language to signify any slander, any malicious or evil speaking, whether against God or man, or anything to good belonging; blasphemy, or evil speaking against God maliciously, is far from conscience in religion, according to that of Mark 9. 39: 'There is none who doth a powerful work in My name, and can lightly speak evil of Me.' If this suffice not, I refer them to that prudent and well-deliberated Act (August 9, 1650) where the Parliament defines blasphemy against God, as far as it is a crime belonging to civil judicature, *plenius ac melius Chrysippo et Crantore*—in plain English, more warily, more judiciously, more orthodoxally than twice their number of divines have done in many a prolix volume; although in all likelihood they whose whole study and profession these things are should be most intelligent and authentic therein, as they are for the most part; yet neither they nor these unerring always, or infallible. But we shall not carry it thus; another Greek apparition stands in our way—*heresy*, and *heretic*; in like manner also railed at to the people as in a tongue unknown. They should first interpret to them that *heresy*, by what it signifies in that language, is no word of evil note, meaning only the choice or following of any opinion, good or bad, in religion or any other learning, and thus not only in heathen authors but in the New Testament itself without censure or blame; . . . though some, who write of heresy after their own heads, would make it far worse than schism; whenas on the

[1] *Prose Works* 5. 60–2.

contrary, *schism* signifies division, and in the worst sense; *heresy*, choice only of one opinion before another, which may be without discord.[1]

From *Areopagitica* (1644).

Well knows he who uses to consider, that our faith and knowledge thrives by exercise, as well as our limbs and complexion. Truth is compared in Scripture to a streaming fountain: if her waters flow not in a perpetual progression, they sicken into a muddy pool of conformity and tradition. A man may be a heretic in the truth; and, if he believe things only because his pastor says so, or the Assembly so determines, without knowing other reason, though his belief be true, yet the very truth he holds becomes his heresy.[2]

From *The Second Defence of the People of England* (1654).

Those who speak the truth acknowledge that our army excels all others, not only in courage, but in virtue and in piety. Other camps are the scenes of gambling, swearing, riot, and debauchery; in ours, the troops employ what leisure they have in searching the Scriptures and hearing the Word, nor is there one who thinks it more honorable to vanquish the enemy than to propagate the truth; and they not only carry on a military warfare against their enemies, but an evangelical one against themselves.

And, indeed, if we consider the proper objects of war, what employment can be more becoming soldiers who are raised to defend the laws, to be the support of our political and religious institutions? Ought they not then to be less conspicuous for ferocity than for the civil and the softer virtues, and to consider it as their true and proper destination, not merely to sow the seeds of strife and reap the harvest of destruction, but to procure peace and security for the whole human race? If there be any who, either from the mistakes of others, or the infirmities

[1] *Ibid*. 2. 526-7.
[2] *Ibid*. 2. 85.

of their own minds, deviate from these noble ends, we ought not to punish them with the sword, but rather labor to reform them by reason, by admonition, by pious supplications to God, to Whom alone it belongs to dispel all the errors of the mind, and to impart to whom He will the celestial light of truth. We approve no heresies which are truly such; we do not even tolerate some; we wish them extirpated, but by those means which are best suited to the purpose—by reason and instruction, the only safe remedies for disorders of the mind; and not by the knife or the scourge, as if they were seated in the body.[1]

[1] *Prose Works* I. 274-5.

9. THE EDUCATION OF THE CLERGY

From a Letter to Alexander Gill. Cambridge, July 2, 1628.

Among us, so far as I know, there are only two or three who, without any acquaintance with criticism or philosophy, do not instantly engage with raw and untutored judgments in the study of theology; and of this they acquire only a slender smattering, not more than sufficient to enable them to patch together a sermon with scraps pilfered, with little discrimination, from this author and from that. Hence I fear lest our clergy should relapse into the sacerdotal ignorance of a former age.[1]

From *The Reason of Church-Government* (1642).

If . . . it appear so hard and so little known how to govern a house well, which is thought of so easy discharge and for every man's undertaking, what skill of man, what wisdom, what parts can be sufficient to give laws and ordinances to the elect household of God![2]

From *Animadversions upon the Remonstrant's Defence against Smectymnuus* (1641).

As for your young scholars that petition for bishoprics and deaneries to encourage them in their studies, and that many gentlemen else will not put their sons to learning—away with such young mercenary striplings, and their simoniacal fathers! . . . How can it be but ever unhappy to the Church of England, while she shall think to entice men to the pure service of God by the same means that were used to tempt our Saviour to the service of the devil—by laying before Him honor and preferment? Fit professors indeed are they like to be, to teach others that godliness with content is great gain, whenas their godliness of teaching had not been but for worldly gain. The

[1] *Familiar Letters*, No. 3. *Prose Works* 3. 489–90.
[2] *Prose Works* 2. 443.

heathen philosophers thought that virtue was for its own sake inestimable, and the greatest gain of a teacher to make a soul virtuous; so Xenophon writes of Socrates, who never bargained with any for teaching them; he feared not lest those who had received so high a benefit from him would not of their own free will return him all possible thanks. Was moral virtue so lovely and so alluring, and heathen men so enamoured of her, as to teach and study her with greatest neglect and contempt of worldly profit and advancement? And is Christian piety so homely and so unpleasant, and Christian men so cloyed with her, as that none will study and teach her but for lucre and preferment? . . .

But they will grant, perhaps, piety may thrive, but learning will decay. I would fain ask these men at whose hands they seek inferior things, as wealth, honor, their dainty fare, their lofty houses? No doubt but they will soon answer that all these things they seek at God's hands. Do they think, then, that all these meaner and superfluous things come from God, and the divine gift of learning from the den of Plutus, or the cave of Mammon? Certainly never any clear spirit, nursed up from brighter influences, with a soul enlarged to the dimensions of spacious art and high knowledge, ever entered there but with scorn, and thought it ever foul disdain to make pelf or ambition the reward of his studies; it being the greatest honor, the greatest fruit and proficiency, of learned studies to despise these things. Not liberal science, but illiberal, must that needs be that mounts in contemplation merely for money.

And what would it avail us to have a hireling clergy, though never so learned? For such can have neither true wisdom nor grace, and then in vain do men trust in learning where these be wanting. If, in less noble and almost mechanic arts, according to the definitions of those authors, he is not esteemed to deserve the name of a complete architect, an excellent painter, or the like, that bears not a generous mind above the peasantly regard of wages and hire; much more must we think him a most imperfect and incomplete divine who is so far from being a contemner of filthy lucre that his whole divinity is moulded and bred up in the beggarly and brutish hopes of a fat prebendary, deanery, or bishopric; which poor and low-pitched desires, if they do but mix with those other heavenly intentions that draw a man to this study, it is justly expected that they should bring forth a base-born issue of divinity. . . .

And, in matters of religion, there is not anything more intoler-able than a learned fool, or a learned hypocrite. The one is ever cooped up at his empty speculations—a sot, an idiot, for any use that mankind can make of him, or else sowing the world with nice and idle questions, and with much toil and difficulty wad-ing to his auditors up to the eyebrows in deep shallows that wet not the instep; a plain unlearned man that lives well by that light which he has is better and wiser, and edifies others more towards a godly and happy life, than he. The other is still using his sophisticated arts, and bending all his studies, how to make his insatiate avarice and ambition seem pious and ortho-doxal by painting his lewd and deceitful principles with a smooth and glossy varnish in a doctrinal way, to bring about his wicked-est purposes. . . . But a true pastor of Christ's sending hath this especial mark, that for greatest labors and greatest merits in the Church he requires either nothing, if he could so subsist, or a very common and reasonable supply of human necessaries.

We cannot therefore do better than to leave this care of ours to God. He can easily send laborers into His harvest that shall not cry 'Give, give,' but be contented with a moderate and beseeming allowance. Nor will He suffer true learning to be wanting where true grace and our obedience to Him abounds; for, if He give us to know Him aright, and to practise this our knowledge in right-established discipline, how much more will He replenish us with all abilities in tongues and arts that may conduce to His glory and our good! He can stir up rich fathers to bestow exquisite edu-cation upon their children, and so dedicate them to the service of the Gospel; . . . for certainly there is no employment more honorable, more worthy to take up a great spirit, more requiring a generous and free nurture, than to be the messenger and herald of heavenly truth from God to man, and, by the faithful work of holy doctrine, to procreate a number of faithful men, making a kind of creation like to God's by infusing His spirit and likeness into them to their salvation, as God did into him; arising to what climate soever he turn him, like that Sun of Righteousness that sent him, with healing in his wings, and new light to break in upon the chill and gloomy hearts of his hearers, raising out of darksome barrenness a delicious and fragrant spring of saving knowledge and good works.

Can a man thus employed find himself discontented, . . . or be discouraged though men call him not 'lord', whenas the due performance of his office would gain him, even from lords and princes, the voluntary title of Father? Would he tug for a barony to sit and vote in Parliament, knowing that no man can take from him the gift of wisdom and sound doctrine, which leaves him free, though not to be a member, yet a teacher and persuader of the Parliament? And in all wise apprehensions the persuasive power in man to win others to goodness by instruction is greater, and more divine, than the compulsive power to restrain men from being evil by terror of the law; and therefore Christ left Moses to be the lawgiver, but Himself came down amongst us to be a teacher, with which office His heavenly wisdom was so well pleased as that He was angry with those that would have put a piece of temporal judicature into His hands, disclaiming that He had any commission from above for such matters.[1]

In the meanwhile let no man carry in his head either such narrow or such evil eyes as not to look upon the churches of Belgia and Helvetia and that envied city Geneva. Where in the Christian world doth learning more flourish than in these places? Not among your beloved Jesuits, nor their favorers, though you

[1] *Prose Works* 3. 80–3.

take all the prelates into the number, and instance in what kind of learning you please. And how in England all noble sciences attending upon the train of Christian doctrine may flourish more than ever; and how the able professors of every art may with ample stipends be honestly provided; and, finally, how there may be better care had that their hearers may benefit by them, and all this without the prelates; the courses are so many and so easy that I shall pass them over.[1]

From *The Reason of Church-Government* (1642).

First, therefore, if, to do the work of the Gospel, Christ our Lord took upon Him the form of a servant, how can His servant in this ministry take upon him the form of a lord? I know Bilson hath deciphered us all the gallantries of *Signore* and *Monsignore*, and *Monsieur*, as circumstantially as any punctualist of Castile, Naples, or Fontainebleau could have done; but this must not so compliment us out of our right minds as to be to learn that the form of a servant was a mean, laborious, and vulgar life, aptest to teach; which form Christ thought fittest, that He might bring about His will according to His own principles, choosing the meaner things of this world, that He might put under the high.[2]

From *An Apology for Smectymnuus* (1642).

But, since there is such necessity to the hearsay of a tire, a periwig, or a vizard that plays must have been seen, what difficulty was there in that, when in the colleges so many of the young divines and those in next aptitude to divinity have been seen so often upon the stage, writhing and unboning their clergy limbs to all the antic and dishonest gestures of Trinculoes, buffoons, and bawds, prostituting the shame of that ministry which either they had, or were nigh having, to the eyes of courtiers and court ladies, with their grooms and mademoiselles?

[1] *Ibid.* 3. 85.
[2] *Ibid.* 2. 483.

There, while they acted and over-acted, among other young scholars, I was a spectator; they thought themselves gallant men, and I thought them fools; they made sport, and I laughed; they mispronounced, and I misliked; and, to make up the Atticism, they were out, and I hissed. Judge now whether so many good text-men were not sufficient to instruct me of false beards and vizards, without more expositors; and how can this confuter take the face to object to me the seeing of that which his reverend prelates allow, and incite their young disciples to act? For if it be unlawful to sit and behold a mercenary comedian personating that which is least unseemly for a hireling to do, how much more blameful is it to endure the sight of as vile things acted by persons either entered, or presently to enter, into the ministry; and how much more foul and ignominious for them to be the actors![1]

From *The Tenure of Kings and Magistrates* (1649).

I have something also to the divines, though brief to what were needful: not to be disturbers of the civil affairs, being in hands better able and more belonging to manage them, but to study harder and to attend the office of good pastors, knowing that he whose flock is least among them hath a dreadful charge, not performed by mounting twice into the chair with a formal preachment huddled up at the odd hours of a whole lazy week, but by incessant pains and watching in season and out of season, from house to house, over the souls of whom they have to feed. Which if they ever well considered, how little leisure would they find to be the most pragmatical sidesmen of every popular tumult and sedition! and all this while are to learn what the true end and reason is of the Gospel which they teach, and what a world it differs from the censorious and supercilious lording over conscience.[2]

[1] *Prose Works* 3. 114–5.
[2] *Ibid.* 2. 36.

From *Areopagitica* (1644).

It is no new thing, never heard of before, for a parochial minister who has his reward and is at his Hercules' Pillars in a warm benefice, to be easily inclinable, if he have nothing else that may rouse up his studies, to finish his circuit in an English Concordance and a Topic Folio—the gatherings and savings of a sober graduateship—a Harmony, and a Catena, treading the constant round of certain common doctrinal heads, attended with their uses, motives, marks, and means; out of which, as out of an alphabet or *sol-fa*, by forming and transforming, joining and disjoining variously, a little bookcraft and two hours' meditation might furnish him unspeakably to the performance of more than a weekly charge of sermoning; not to reckon up the infinite helps of interlinearies, breviaries, synopses, and other loitering gear. [1]

From *Considerations Touching the Likeliest Means to Remove Hirelings out of the Church* (1659).

I offer it to the reason of any man whether he think the knowledge of Christian religion harder than any other art or science to attain. I suppose he will grant that it is far easier, both of itself, and in regard of God's assisting Spirit, not particularly promised us to the attainment of any other knowledge but of this only; since it was preached as well to the shepherds of Bethlehem by angels as to the Eastern wise men by that star; and our Saviour declares Himself anointed to preach the Gospel to the poor (Luke 4. 18); then surely to their capacity. They who after Him first taught it were otherwise unlearned men; they who before Hus and Luther first reformed it were for the meanness of their condition called 'the poor men of Lyons,' and in Flanders at this day *le Gueus*, which is to say, beggars. Therefore are the Scriptures translated into every vulgar tongue, as being held, in main matters of belief and salvation, plain and easy to the poorest; and such no less than their teachers have the Spirit to guide them in all truth (John 14. 26, and 16.13).

[1] *Ibid.* 2. 86–7.

Hence we may conclude, if men be not all their lifetime under a teacher to learn logic, natural philosophy, ethics, or mathematics, which are more difficult, that certainly it is not necessary to the attainment of Christian knowledge that men should sit all their life long at the feet of a pulpited divine; while he, a *Lollard* indeed over his elbow-cushion, in almost the seventh part of forty or fifty years teaches them scarce half the principles of religion; and his sheep oft-times sit the while to as little purpose of benefiting as the sheep in their pews at Smithfield; and, for the most part, by some simony or other, bought and sold like them; or, if this comparison be too low, like those women, (2 Tim. 3. 7) 'Ever learning and never attaining,' yet not so much through their own fault as through the unskilful and immethodical teaching of their pastor, teaching here and there, at random, out of this or that text, as his ease or fancy, and oft-times as his stealth, guides him. Seeing, then, that Christian religion may be so easily attained, and by meanest capacities, it cannot be much difficult to find ways both how the poor, yea, all men, may be soon taught what is to be known of Christianity, and they who teach them recompensed. . . . To these I might add other helps which we enjoy now, to make more easy the attainment of Christian religion by the meanest: the entire Scripture translated into English with plenty of notes; and, somewhere or other, I trust, may be found some wholesome body of divinity, as they call it, without school-terms and metaphysical notions, which have obscured rather than explained our religion, and made it seem difficult without cause. . . .

Be the expense less or more, if it be found burdensome to the churches, they have in this land an easy remedy in their recourse to the civil magistrate; who hath in his hands the disposal of no small revenues, left perhaps anciently to superstitious, but meant undoubtedly to good and best, uses; and, therefore, once made public, appliable by the present magistrate to such uses as the Church, or solid reason from whomsoever, shall convince him to think best. And those uses may be, no doubt, much rather than as glebes and augmentations are now bestowed, to grant such requests as these of the churches; or, to erect in greater number, all over the land, schools, and competent libraries to those schools, where languages and arts may be taught free together, without the needless, unprofitable, and inconvenient removing to another place. So all the land would be soon better civilized, and they who are taught freely at the public cost might have their education given them on this condition: that, therewith content, they should not gad for preferment out of their own country, but continue there thankful for what they received freely, bestowing it as freely on their own country, without soaring above the meanness wherein they were born.

But how they shall live, when they are thus bred and dismissed, will be still the sluggish objection. To which is answered that those public foundations may be so instituted as the youth therein may be at once brought up to a competence of learning and to an honest trade; and the hours of teaching so ordered as their study may be no hindrance to their labor or other calling. This was the breeding of St. Paul, though born of no mean parents, a free citizen of the Roman Empire; so little did his trade debase him that it rather enabled him to use that magnanimity of preaching the Gospel through Asia and Europe at his own charges. Thus those preachers among the poor Waldenses, the ancient stock of our Reformation, without these helps which I speak of, bred up themselves in trades, and especially in physic and surgery, as well as in the study of Scripture (which is the only true theology), that they might be no burden to the Church, and, by the example of Christ, might cure both soul and body; through industry joining that to their ministry which He joined to His by gift of the Spirit. Thus relates Peter Gilles in his *History of the Waldenses in Piedmont*. But our ministers think scorn to use a trade, and count it the reproach of this age that tradesmen preach the Gospel.[1]

[1] *Prose Works* 3. 23–8.

They pretend that their education, either at school or university, hath been very chargeable, and therefore ought to be repaired in future by a plentiful maintenance; whenas it is well-known that the better half of them (and oft-times poor and pitiful boys, of no merit or promising hopes that might entitle them to the public provision but their poverty and the unjust favor of friends) have had the most of their breeding, both at school and university, by scholarships, exhibitions, and fellowships, at the public cost—which might engage them the rather to give freely as they have freely received. Or, if they have missed of these helps at the latter place, they have, after two or three years, left the course of their studies there, if they ever well began them, and undertaken, though furnished with little else but ignorance, boldness, and ambition, if with no worse vices, a chaplainship in some gentleman's house, to the frequent embasing of his sons with illiterate and narrow principles. Or, if they have lived there upon their own, who knows not that seven years' charge of living there, to them who fly not from the government of their parents to the licence of a university, but come seriously to study, is no more than may be well defrayed and reimbursed by one year's revenue of an ordinary good benefice? If they had then means of breeding from their parents, it is likely they have more now; and, if they have, it needs must be mechanic and uningenuous in them to bring a bill of charges for the learning of those liberal arts and sciences which they have learned (if they have indeed learned them, as they seldom have) to their own benefit and accomplishment. . . .

Next, it is a fond error, though too much believed among us, to think that the university makes a minister of the Gospel. What it may conduce to other arts and sciences I dispute not now; but that which makes fit a minister, the Scripture can best inform us to be only from above, whence also we are bid to seek them. . . .

All this is granted, you will say, but yet that it is also requisite he should be trained in other learning, which can be nowhere better had than at universities. I answer that what learning, either human or divine, can be necessary to a minister, may as easily and less chargeably be had in any private house. How deficient else, and to how little purpose, are all those piles of sermons, notes, and comments on all parts of the Bible, bodies and marrows of divinity, besides all other sciences, in our English tongue; many of the same books which in Latin they read at the university! And the small necessity of going thither to learn divinity I prove first from the most part of themselves, who seldom continue there till they have well got through logic, their first rudiments; though, to say truth, logic also may much better be wanting in disputes of divinity than in the subtile debates of lawyers and statesmen, who yet seldom or never deal with syllogisms. And those theological disputations there held by professors and graduates are such as tend least of all to the edification or capacity of the people, but rather perplex and leaven pure doctrine with scholastical trash than enable any minister to the better preaching of the Gospel. Whence we may also compute, since they come to reckonings, the charges of his needful library; which, though some shame not to value at £600, may be competently furnished for £60. If any man for his own curiosity or delight be in books further expensive, that is not to be reckoned as necessary to his ministerial either breeding or function. 'But Papists and other adversaries cannot be confuted without Fathers and councils—immense volumes, and of vast charges.' I will show them therefore a shorter and a better way of confutation (Titus 1.9): 'Holding fast the faithful word, as he hath been taught, that he may be able by sound doctrine both to exhort, and to convince gainsayers'—who are confuted as soon as heard, bringing that which is either not in Scripture, or against it. To pursue them further through the obscure and entangled wood of antiquity—Fathers and councils fighting one against another—is needless, endless, not requisite in a minister, and refused by the first reformers of our religion. And yet we may be confident, if these things be thought needful—let the State but erect in public good store of libraries, and there will not want men in the Church who of their own inclinations will become able in this kind against Papist or any other adversary.

I have thus at large examined the usual pretences of hirelings, colored over most commonly with the cause of learning and universities; as if with divines learning stood and fell, wherein for the most part their pittance is so small. And, to speak freely, it were much better there were not one divine in the universities, no school-divinity known—the idle sophistry of monks, the canker of religion—and that they who intended to be ministers were trained up in the Church only by the Scripture, and in the original languages thereof at school, without fetching the compass of other arts and sciences more than what they can well learn at secondary leisure, and at home. Neither speak I this in contempt of learning or the ministry, but hating the common cheats of both; hating that they who have preached out bishops, prelates, and canonists should, in what serves their own ends, retain their false opinions, their pharisaical leaven, their avarice, and closely their ambition, their pluralities, their non-residences, their odious fees, and use their legal and Popish arguments for tithes. . . .

Doubtless, if God only be He who gives ministers to His Church till the world's end, and through the whole Gospel never sent us for ministers to the schools of philosophy, but rather bids us beware of such 'vain deceit,' . . . if all the faithful be now 'a holy and a royal priesthood,' . . . not excluded from the dispensation of things holiest, . . . there will not want ministers elected out of all sorts and orders of men; for the Gospel makes no difference from the magistrate himself to the meanest artificer, if God evidently favor him with spiritual gifts, as He can easily, and oft hath done, while those bachelor divines and doctors of the tippet have been passed by.[1]

---

[1] *Prose Works* 3. 35-40.

10. THE EDUCATION OF STATESMEN AND RULERS

From *Comus* (1637).

> And all this tract that fronts the falling sun
> A noble Peer of mickle trust and power
> Has in his charge, with tempered awe to guide
> An old and haughty Nation, proud in arms;
> Where his fair offspring, nursed in princely lore,
> Are coming to attend their father's state.[1]

From *An Apology for Smectymnuus* (1642).

Now, although it be a digression from the ensuing matter, yet, because it shall not be said I am apter to blame others than to make trial myself; and that I may after this harsh discord touch upon a smoother string, awhile to entertain myself, and him that list, with some more pleasing fit; and, not the least, to testify the gratitude which I owe to those public benefactors of their country for the share I enjoy in the common peace and good by their incessant labors; I shall be so troublesome to this disclaimer for once as to show him what he might have better said in their praise; wherein I must mention only some few things of many, for more than that to a digression may not be granted. Although certainly their actions are worthy not thus to be spoken of by the way, yet, if hereafter it befall me to attempt something more answerable to their great merits, I perceive how hopeless it will be to reach the height of their praises at the accomplishment of that expectation that waits upon their noble deeds, the unfinishing whereof already surpasses what others before them have left enacted with their utmost performance through many ages. And to the end we may be confident that what they do proceeds neither from uncertain opinion nor sudden counsels, but from mature wisdom, deliberate virtue, and dear affection to the

[1] *Comus* 30–6.

227

public good, I shall begin at that which made them likeliest in the eyes of good men to effect those things, for the recovery of decayed religion and the Commonwealth, which they who were best-minded had long wished for, but few, as the times then were desperate, had the courage to hope for.

First, therefore, the most of them being either of ancient and high nobility, or at least of known and well-reputed ancestry—which is a great advantage towards virtue one way, but in respect of wealth, ease, and flattery, which accompany a nice and tender education, is as much a hindrance another way—the good which lay before them they took, in imitating the worthiest of their progenitors; and the evil which assaulted their younger years by the temptation of riches, high birth, and that usual bringing up (perhaps too favorable and too remiss) through the strength of an inbred goodness and with the help of divine grace, that had marked them out for no mean purposes, they nobly overcame.

Yet had they a greater danger to cope with; for, being trained up in the knowledge of learning and sent to those places which were intended to be the seed-plots of piety and the liberal arts, but were become the nurseries of superstition and empty speculation, as they were prosperous against those vices which grow upon youth out of idleness and superfluity, so were they happy in working off the harms of their abused studies and labors, correcting by the clearness of their own judgment the errors of their misinstruction, and were, as David was, wiser than their teachers. And—although their lot fell into such times and to be bred in such places where, if they chanced to be taught anything good, or of their own accord had learnt it, they might see that presently untaught them by the custom and ill example of their elders—so far in all probability was their youth from being misled by the single power of example as their riper years were known to be unmoved with the baits of preferment and undaunted for any discouragement and terror, which appeared often to those that loved religion and their native liberty; which two things God hath inseparably knit together, and hath disclosed to us that they who seek to corrupt our religion are the same that would enthral our civil liberty.

Thus in the midst of all disadvantages and disrespects (some also at last not without imprisonment and open disgraces in the cause of their country) having given proof of themselves to be better made and framed by nature to the love and practice of virtue than others under the holiest precepts and best examples have been headstrong and prone to vice; and having, in all the trials of a firm ingrafted honesty, not oftener buckled in the conflict than given every opposition the foil; this moreover was added by favor from Heaven, as an ornament and happiness to their virtue— that it should be neither obscure in the opinion of men, nor eclipsed for want of matter equal to illustrate itself; God and man consenting in joint approbation to choose them out as worthiest above others to be both the great reformers of the Church, and the restorers of the Commonwealth.[1]

From *The Tenure of Kings and Magistrates* (1649).

Another sort[2] there is, who, coming in the course of these affairs to have their share in great actions above the form of law or custom—at least to give their voice and approbation—begin to swerve and almost shiver at the majesty and grandeur of some noble deed, as if they were newly entered into a great sin; disputing precedents, forms, and circumstances, when the Commonwealth nigh perishes for want of deeds in substance, done with just and faithful expedition. To these I wish better instruction, and virtue equal to their calling; the former of which, that is to say, instruction, I shall endeavor, as my duty is, to bestow on them; and exhort them not to startle from the just and pious resolution of adhering, with all their strength and assistance, to

[1] *Prose. Works* 3. 145-7.
[2] Milton here remarks upon the conduct of men who were untrained in the fundamental principles of statecraft.

the present Parliament and Army, in the glorious way wherein justice and victory hath set them—the only warrants through all ages, next under immediate revelation, to exercise supreme power—in those proceedings, which hitherto appear equal to what hath been done in any age or nation heretofore justly or magnanimously. . . .

Neither let mild and tender dispositions be foolishly softened from their duty and perseverance with the unmasculine rhetoric of any puling priest or chaplain, sent as a friendly letter of advice, for fashion's sake in private, and forthwith published—by the sender himself, that we may know how much of friend there was in it—to cast an odious envy upon them to whom it was pretended to be sent in charity. Nor let any man be deluded by either the ignorance or the notorious hypocrisy and self-repugnance of our dancing divines, who have the conscience and the boldness to come with Scripture in their mouths, glossed and fitted for their turns with a double contradictory sense, transforming the sacred verity of God to an idol with two faces, looking at once two several ways; and with the same quotations to charge others which in the same case they made serve to justify themselves.[1]

From *The History of Britain* (1670).

For a parliament being called—to address many things, as it was thought—the people with great courage, and expectation to be eased of what discontented them, chose their behoof in Parliament such as they thought best-affected to the public good, and some indeed men of wisdom and integrity; the rest (to be sure the greater part) whom wealth or ample possessions or bold and active ambition (rather than merit) had commended to the same place. . . . Some—who had been called from shops and warehouses, without other merit, to sit in supreme councils and committees—as their breeding was, fell to huckster the Commonwealth. Others did thereafter as men could soothe and humor

[1] *Prose Works* 2. 5–6.

them best; so, he who would give most, or, under covert of hypocritical zeal, insinuate basest, enjoyed unworthily the rewards of learning and fidelity, or escaped the punishment of his crimes and misdeeds.[1]

From *Eikonoklastes* (1649).

Kings most commonly, though strong in legions, are but weak at argument; as they who ever have accustomed from the cradle to use their will only as their right hand, their reason always as their left. Whence, unexpectedly constrained to that kind of combat, they prove but weak and puny adversaries. Nevertheless, for their sakes who through custom, simplicity, or want of better teaching have not more seriously considered kings than in the gaudy name of majesty, and admire them and their doings as if they breathed not the same breath with other mortal men, I shall make no scruple to take up . . . this gauntlet, though a king's, in the behalf of liberty and the Commonwealth.[2]

From *The Tenure of Kings and Magistrates* (1649).

And surely no Christian prince, not drunk with high mind and prouder than those pagan Cæsars that deified themselves, would arrogate so unreasonably above human condition, or derogate so basely from a whole nation of men his brethren, as if for him only subsisting and to serve his glory, valuing them in comparison of his own brute will and pleasure no more than so many beasts, or vermin under his feet—not to be reasoned with, but to be trod on; among whom there might be found so many thousand men, for wisdom, virtue, nobleness of mind, and all other respects but the fortune of his dignity, far above him.[3]

From *Eikonoklastes* (1649).

To know the will of God better than his whole kingdom—whence should he have it? Certainly his court-breeding and his perpetual conversation with flatterers was but a bad school.[4]

[1] *Ibid.* 5. 236–7.
[2] *Ibid.* 1. 308.
[3] *Ibid.* 2. 13.
[4] *Ibid.* 1. 360–1.

But, had his reason mastered him as it ought, and not been mastered long ago by his sense and humor (as the breeding of most kings hath been ever sensual and most humored), perhaps he would have made no difficulty. . . . His love of truth would have led him to the search of truth, and have taught him not to lean so much upon his own understanding.[1]

And if he, in the best maturity of his years and understanding, made no better use to himself or others of his so long and manifold afflictions, either looking up to God, or looking down upon the reason of his own affairs, there can be no probability that his son—bred up, not in the soft effeminacies of a court only, but in the rugged and more boisterous licence of undisciplined camps and garrisons, for years unable to reflect with judgment upon his own condition, and thus ill-instructed by his father—should give his mind to walk by any other rules than these, bequeathed him as on his father's death-bed, and as the choicest of all that experience which his most serious observation and retirement in good or evil days had taught him.[2]

From *The Second Defence of the People of England* (1654).

It was not in vain that you[3] made such large collections of books, and so many monuments of learning; not, indeed, that they could contribute much to your instruction, but because they so well teach your subjects to appreciate the merits of your reign and the rare excellence of your virtue and your wisdom. For the Divinity Himself seems to have inspired you with a love of wisdom, and a thirst for improvement, beyond what any books ever could have produced. It excites our astonishment to see a force of intellect so truly divine, a particle of celestial flame so resplendently pure, in a region so remote; of which an atmosphere so darkened with clouds and so chilled with frosts could not extinguish the light nor repress the operations. The rocky

---

[1] *Prose Works* 1. 399.
[2] *Ibid.* 1. 474.
[3] Christina, Queen of Sweden. See above, p. 123, note 1.

and barren soil, which is often as unfavorable to the growth of genius as of plants, has not impeded the maturation of your faculties; and that country, so rich in metallic ore, which appears like a cruel stepmother to others, seems to have been a fostering parent to you, and after the most strenuous attempts to have at last produced a progeny of pure gold.[1]

From Milton's *Commonplace Book*.

Nobilitas

Our English herald Guillim, though his office consist chiefly about titular dignity and gentry by birth, yet confesses, speaking of those whose first ancestors were raised for their worth, that, if they vaunt of their lineage or titular dignity and want their virtues, they are but like base serving-men who carry on their sleeves the badge of some noble family, yet are themselves but ignoble persons.[2]

From *The Second Defence of the People of England* (1654).

John Bradshaw, a name which will be repeated with applause wherever liberty is cherished or is known, was sprung from a noble family. All his early life he sedulously employed in making himself acquainted with the laws of his country; he then practised with singular success and reputation at the bar; he showed himself an intrepid and unwearied advocate for the liberties of the people; he took an active part in the most momentous affairs of the State, and occasionally discharged the functions of a judge with the most inviolable integrity.

At last, when he was entreated by the Parliament to preside in the trial of the King, he did not refuse the dangerous office. To a profound knowledge of the law, he added the most comprehensive views, the most generous sentiments, manners the most obliging and the most pure. Hence he discharged that office with a propriety almost without a parallel; he inspired both respect

[1] *Prose Works* I. 250.
[2] *Commonplace Book*, p. 191.

and awe; and, though menaced by the daggers of so many as-
sassins, he conducted himself with so much consistency and gravity, with so much presence of mind and so much dignity of demeanor, that he seems to have been purposely destined by Providence for that part which he so nobly acted on the theatre of
the world. . . . In other respects there was no forbidding
austerity, no moroseness in his manner; he was courteous and
benign; but the great character which he then sustained he with
perfect consistency still sustains, so that you would suppose that
not only then, but in every future period of his life, he was sitting in judgment upon the King.

In the public business his activity is unwearied, and he alone is
equal to a host. At home his hospitality is as splendid as his fortune will permit; in his friendships there is the most inflexible
fidelity; and no one more readily discerns merit, or more liberally
rewards it. Men of piety and learning, ingenious persons in all
professions, those who have been distinguished by their courage
or their misfortunes, are free to participate his bounty; and, if
they want not his bounty, they are sure to share his friendship
and esteem. He never ceases to extol the merits of others, or to
conceal his own; and no one was ever more ready to accept the
excuses, or to pardon the hostility, of his political opponents. If
he undertake to plead the cause of the oppressed, to solicit the
favor or deprecate the resentment of the powerful, to reprove the
public ingratitude towards any particular indivdual, his address
and his perseverance are beyond all praise. On such occasions no
one could desire a patron or a friend more able, more zealous, or
more eloquent. No menace could divert him from his purpose; no
intimidation on the one hand, and no promise of emolument or
promotion on the other, could alter the serenity of his countenance, or shake the firmness of his soul.[1]

Oliver Cromwell was sprung from a line of illustrious ancestors, who were distinguished for the civil functions which they

---

[1] *Prose Works* 1. 266–8.

sustained under the monarchy, and still more for the part which they took in restoring and establishing true religion in this country. In the vigor and maturity of his life, which he passed in retirement, he was conspicuous for nothing more than for the strictness of his religious habits and the innocence of his life; and he had tacitly cherished in his breast that flame of piety which was afterwards to stand him in so much stead on the greatest occasions and in the most critical exigencies. In the last parliament which was called by the King, he was elected to represent his native town, when he soon became distinguished by the justness of his opinions and the vigor and decision of his counsels.

When the sword was drawn, he offered his services, and was appointed to a troop of horse, whose numbers were soon increased by the pious and the good who flocked from all quarters to his standard; and in a short time he almost surpassed the greatest generals in the magnitude and the rapidity of his achievements. Nor is this surprising, for he was a soldier disciplined to perfection in the knowledge of himself. He had either extinguished, or by habit had learned to subdue, the whole host of vain hopes, fears, and passions which infest the soul. He first acquired the government of himself, and over himself acquired the most signal victories; so that, on the first day he took the field against the external enemy, he was a veteran in arms, consummately practised in the toils and exigencies of war. . . .

This alone seems to be a sufficient proof of his extraordinary and almost supernatural virtue: that by the vigor of his genius, or the excellence of his discipline, adapted, not more to the necessities of war than to the precepts of Christianity, the good and the brave were from all quarters attracted to his camp, not only as to the best school of military talents, but of piety and virtue; and that, during the whole war, and the occasional intervals of peace, amid so many vicissitudes of faction and of events, he retained and still retains the obedience of his troops, not by largesses or indulgence, but by his sole authority and the regularity of his pay. In this instance his fame may rival that of Cyrus, of Epaminondas, or any of the great generals of antiquity. Hence he collected an army as numerous and as well-equipped as any one ever did in so short a time; which was uniformly obedient to his orders, and dear to the affections of the citizens; which was formidable to the enemy in the field, but never cruel to those who laid down their arms; which committed no lawless ravages on the persons or the property of the inhabitants, who, when they compared their conduct with the turbulence, the intemperance, the impiety, and the debauchery of the Royalists, were wont to salute them as friends and to consider them as guests. They were a stay to the good, a terror to the evil, and the warmest advocates for every exertion of piety and virtue.[1]

In this state of desolation to which we were reduced, you, O Cromwell! alone remained to conduct the government and to save the country. We all willingly yield the palm of sovereignty to your unrivaled ability and virtue, except the few among us who, either ambitious of honors which they have not the capacity to sustain, or who envy those which are conferred on one more worthy than themselves, or else who do not know that nothing in the world is more pleasing to God, more agreeable to reason, more politically just, or more generally useful, than that the supreme power should be vested in the best and wisest of men.[2]

From *The History of Britain* (1670).

The year eight hundred made way for a great alteration in England, uniting her seven kingdoms into one, by Ecbert the famous West-Saxon. Him Birthric, dying childless, left next to reign, the only survivor of that lineage, descending from Inegild the brother of King Ina. And according to his birth liberally bred, he began early from his youth to give signal hopes of more than ordinary worth growing up in him. . . .

[1] *Prose Works* 1. 285–6.
[2] *Ibid.* 1. 288.

He [Ecbert] again put to his shifts, escaped thence into France; but, after three years' banishment there, which perhaps contributed much to his education, Charles the Great then reigning, he was called over by the public voice, . . . and with general applause created King of West-Saxons.[1]

This done, Ethelwolf sent his son Alfred, a child of five years, well accompanied, to Rome, whom Leo the Pope both consecrated to be king afterwards, and adopted to be his son.[2]

After which troublesome time, Alfred enjoyed three years' peace—by him spent, as his manner was, not idly or voluptuously, but in all virtuous employments, both of mind and body, becoming a prince of his renown—ended his days in the year nine hundred, the fifty-first of his age, the thirtieth of his reign, and was buried regally at Winchester.

He was born at a place called Wanading in Berkshire; his mother Osburga, the daughter of Oslac the King's cupbearer, a Goth by nation, and of noble descent. He was of person comlier than all his brethren, of pleasing tongue and graceful behavior, ready wit and memory; yet, through the fondness of his parents towards him, had not been taught to read till the twelfth year of his age. But the great desire of learning which was in him soon appeared by his conning of Saxon poems day and night, which with great attention he heard by others repeated. He was, besides, excellent at hunting, and the new art, then, of hawking, but more exemplary at devotion, having collected into a book certain prayers and psalms, which he carried ever with him in his bosom to use on all occasions.

He thirsted after all liberal knowledge, and oft complained that in his youth he had no teachers, in his middle age so little vacancy from wars and the cares of his kingdom; yet leisure he found, sometimes, not only to learn much himself, but to communicate thereof what he could to his people by translating books out of

[1] *Ibid.* 5. 303-4.
[2] *Ibid.* 5. 311.

Latin into English—Orosius, Boethius, Bede's *History*, and others;
permitted none unlearned to bear office, either in Court or Commonwealth. . . .

The extremities which befell him in the sixth of his reign,
Neothan Abbot told him were justly come upon him for neglect-
ing in his younger days the complaint of such as, injured and oppressed, repaired to him, as then second person in the kingdom,
for redress; which neglect, were it such indeed, were yet excusable
in a youth, through jollity of mind unwilling, perhaps, to be de-
tained long with sad and sorrowful narrations; but, from the time
of his undertaking regal charge, no man more patient in hearing
causes, more inquisitive in examining, more exact in doing justice
and providing good laws—which are yet extant—more severe in
punishing unjust judges or obstinate offenders; . . . so that
justice seemed in his days not to flourish only, but to triumph.

No man than he more frugal of two precious things in man's life
—his time, and his revenue; no man wiser in the disposal of both.
His time, the day and night, he distributed, by the burning of certain tapers, into three equal portions: the one was for devotion,
the other for public or private affairs, the third for bodily refreshment; how each hour passed, he was put in mind by one who
had that office. His whole annual revenue, which his first care
was should be justly his own, he divided into two equal parts.
The first he employed to secular uses, and subdivided those into
three: the first to pay his soldiers, household servants, and guard,
of which, divided into three bands, one attended monthly by turn;
the second was to pay his architects and workmen, whom he had
got together of several nations—for he was also an elegant builder,
above the custom and conceit of Englishmen in those days; the
third he had in readiness to relieve or honor strangers, according
to their worth, who came from all parts to see him and to live
under him. The other equal part of his yearly wealth he dedicated
to religious uses, those of four sorts: the first to relieve the poor,
the second to the building and maintenance of two monasteries,

the third of a school, where he persuaded the sons of many noblemen to study sacred knowledge and liberal arts—some say at Oxford; the fourth was for the relief of foreign churches, as far as India to the shrine of St. Thomas, sending thither Sigelm, Bishop of Sherburn, who both returned safe and brought with him many rich gems and spices; gifts also and a letter he received from the Patriarch at Jerusalem, sent many to Rome, and from them received relics. Thus far and much more might be said of his noble mind, which rendered him the mirror of princes. His body was diseased in his youth with a great soreness in the siege, and, that ceasing of itself, with another inward pain of unknown cause, which held him by frequent fits to his dying day; yet not disenabled to sustain those many glorious labors of his life both in peace and war.[1]

But King Edward thus nobly doing, and thus honored, the year following [925] died at Farendon; a builder and restorer even in war, not a destroyer of his land. . . . His laws are yet to be seen.[2]

[Athelstan] was thirty years old at his coming to the crown, mature in wisdom from his childhood, comely of person and behavior; so that Alfred his grandfather, in blessing him, was wont to pray he might live to have the kingdom, and put him yet a child into soldier's habit. He had his breeding in the court of Elfled his aunt, of whose virtues more than female we have related. . . .

This famous Athelstan [was] a bounteous, just, and affable king. . . . His laws are extant among the laws of other Saxon kings to this day.[3]

These only are [Edgar's] faults upon record, rather to be wondered how they were so few and so soon left, he coming at

[1] *Prose Works* 5. 325–6.
[2] *Ibid.* 5. 332.
[3] *Ibid.* 5. 336–7.

sixteen to the licence of a sceptre; and that his virtues were so many and mature, he dying before the age wherein wisdom can in others attain to any ripeness.[1]

About this time also [1043] King Edward [the Confessor], according to promise, took to wife Edith or Egith, Earl Godwin's daughter, commended much for beauty, modesty, and—beyond what is requisite in a woman—learning. Ingulf, then a youth lodging in the Court with his father, saw her oft and, coming from the school, was sometimes met by her and posed, not in grammar only, but in logic.[2]

From *Paradise Regained* (1671).

[Pride of Learning Rebuked by True Wisdom.]

'And thou thyself seem'st otherwise inclined
Than to a worldly crown, addicted more
To contemplation and profound dispute;
As by that early action may be judged,
When, slipping from thy mother's eye, thou went'st
Alone into the temple; there wast found
Among the gravest Rabbis, disputant
On points and questions fitting Moses' chair,
Teaching, not taught. The childhood shows the man,
As morning shows the day. Be famous then
By wisdom; as thy empire must extend,
So let extend thy mind o'er all the world
In knowledge, all things in it comprehend.
All knowledge is not couched in Moses' law,
The Pentateuch, or what the Prophets wrote;
The Gentiles also know, and write, and teach
To admiration, led by Nature's light;
And with the Gentiles much thou must converse,
Ruling them by persuasion, as thou mean'st.
Without their learning, how wilt thou with them,
Or they with thee, hold conversation meet?
How wilt thou reason with them, how refute
Their idolisms, traditions, paradoxes?

[1] *Prose Works* 5. 344.
[2] *Ibid.* 5. 373.

Error by his own arms is best evinced.
  Look once more, ere we leave this specular mount,
Westward, much nearer by south-west; behold
Where on the Ægean shore a city stands,
Built nobly, pure the air and light the soil—
Athens, the eye of Greece, mother of arts
And eloquence, native to famous wits
Or hospitable, in her sweet recess,
City or suburban, studious walks and shades.
See there the olive-grove of Academe,
Plato's retirement, where the Attic bird
Trills her thick-warbled notes the summer long;
There flowery hill Hymettus with the sound
Of bees' industrious murmur oft invites
To studious musing; there Ilissus rolls
His whispering stream. Within the walls then view
The schools of ancient sages; his who bred
Great Alexander to subdue the world,
Lyceum there, and painted Stoa next.
There thou shalt hear and learn the secret power
Of harmony, in tones and numbers hit
By voice or hand, and various-measured verse,
Æolian charms, and Dorian lyric odes,
And his who gave them breath, but higher sung,
Blind Melesigenes, thence Homer called,
Whose poem Phœbus challenged for his own.
Thence what the lofty grave tragedians taught
In chorus or iambic, teachers best
Of moral prudence, with delight received
In brief sententious precepts, while they treat
Of fate, and chance, and change in human life,
High actions and high passions best describing.
Thence to the famous orators repair,
Those ancient, whose resistless eloquence
Wielded at will that fierce democraty,
Shook the Arsenal, and fulmined over Greece
To Macedon and Artaxerxes' throne.
To sage Philosophy next lend thine ear,
From Heaven descended to the low-roofed house
Of Socrates—see there his tenement—

Whom, well inspired, the oracle pronounced
Wisest of men; from whose mouth issued forth
Mellifluous streams, that watered all the schools
Of Academics old and new, with those
Surnamed Peripatetics, and the sect
Epicurean and the Stoic severe.
These here revolve, or, as thou likest, at home,
Till time mature thee to a kingdom's weight;
These rules will render thee a king complete,
Within thyself, much more with empire joined.'
 To whom our Saviour sagely thus replied:
'Think not but that I know these things, or think
I know them not; not therefore am I short
Of knowing what I ought. He who receives
Light from above, from the Fountain of Light,
No other doctrine needs, though granted true;
But these are false, or little else but dreams,
Conjectures, fancies, built on nothing firm.
The first and wisest of them all professed
To know this only, that he nothing knew;
The next to fabling fell and smooth conceits;
A third sort doubted all things, though plain sense;
Others in virtue placed felicity,
But virtue joined with riches and long life;
In corporal pleasure he, and careless ease;
The Stoic last in philosophic pride,
By him called virtue, and his virtuous man,
Wise, perfect in himself, and all possessing,
Equal to God, oft shames not to prefer,
As fearing God nor man, contemning all
Wealth, pleasure, pain or torment, death and life—
Which when he lists he leaves, or boasts he can;
For all his tedious talk is but vain boast
Or subtle shifts conviction to evade.
Alas! what can they teach, and not mislead,
Ignorant of themselves, of God much more,
And how the world began, and how Man fell
Degraded by himself, on grace depending?
Much of the soul they talk, but all awry,
And in themselves seek virtue; and to themselves

All glory arrogate, to God give none;
Rather accuse Him under usual names,
Fortune and Fate, as one regardless quite
Of mortal things.
Who therefore seeks in these
True wisdom finds her not; or, by delusion
Far worse, her false resemblance only meets,
An empty cloud. However, many books,
Wise men have said, are wearisome; who reads
Incessantly, and to his reading brings not
A spirit and judgment equal or superior,
(And what he brings what need he elsewhere seek?),
Uncertain and unsettled still remains,
Deep-versed in books and shallow in himself,
Crude, or intoxicate, collecting toys
And trifles for choice matters—worth a sponge—
As children gathering pebbles on the shore.
Or if I would delight my private hours
With music or with poem, where so soon
As in our native language can I find
That solace? All our Law and Story strewed
With hymns, our Psalms with artful terms inscribed,
Our Hebrew songs and harps, in Babylon
That pleased so well our victors' ear, declare
That rather Greece from us these arts derived—
Ill imitated, while they loudest sing
The vices of their deities, and their own,
In fable, hymn, or song, so personating
Their gods ridiculous, and themselves past shame.
Remove their swelling epithets, thick-laid
As varnish on a harlot's cheek, the rest,
Thin-sown with aught of profit or delight,
Will far be found unworthy to compare
With Sion's songs, to all true tastes excelling,
Where God is praised aright, and godlike men,
The Holiest of Holies, and His Saints
(Such are from God inspired, not such from thee);
Unless where moral virtue is expressed
By light of Nature not in all quite lost.

Their orators thou then extoll'st, as those
The top of eloquence—statists indeed,
And lovers of their country, as may seem;
But herein to our prophets far beneath,
As men divinely taught, and better teaching
The solid rules of civil government
In their majestic unaffected style,
Than all the oratory of Greece and Rome.
In them is plainest taught and easiest learnt
What makes a nation happy, and keeps it so,
What ruins kingdoms, and lays cities flat;
These only, with our Law, best form a king.'[1]

[1] *Paradise Regained* 4. 212–364.

11. INTELLIGENCE AND LIBERTY

From *Comus* (1637).

> He that has light within his own clear breast
> May sit i' the centre, and enjoy bright day:
> But he that hides a dark soul and foul thoughts,
> Benighted walks under the midday sun;
> Himself is his own dungeon.[1]

From *Samson Agonistes* (1671).

> *Samson.* Oh, wherefore was my birth from Heaven foretold
> Twice by an Angel, who at last, in sight
> Of both my parents, all in flames ascended
> From off the altar where an offering burned,
> As in a fiery column charioting
> His godlike presence, and from some great act
> Or benefit revealed to Abraham's race?
> Why was my breeding ordered and prescribed
> As of a person separate to God,
> Designed for great exploits, if I must die
> Betrayed, captived, and both my eyes put out,
> Made of my enemies the scorn and gaze,
> To grind in brazen fetters under task
> With this heaven-gifted strength? . . .
>
> But what is strength without a double share
> Of wisdom? Vast, unwieldy, burdensome,
> Proudly secure, yet liable to fall
> By weakest subtleties; not made to rule,
> But to subserve where wisdom bears command.[2]
>
> *Samson.* His pardon I implore; but, as for life,
> To what end should I seek it? When in strength
> All mortals I excelled, and great in hopes,
> With youthful courage, and magnanimous thoughts
> Of birth from Heaven foretold and high exploits,

---

[1] *Comus* 381–5.
[2] *Samson Agonistes* 23–36; 53–7.

Full of divine instinct, after some proof
Of acts indeed heroic, far beyond
The sons of Anak, famous now and blazed,
Fearless of danger, like a petty god
I walked about, admired of all, and dreaded
On hostile ground, none daring my affront;
Then, swollen with pride, into the snare I fell
Of fair fallacious looks, venereal trains,
Softened with pleasure and voluptuous life,
At length to lay my head and hallowed pledge
Of all my strength in the lascivious lap
Of a deceitful concubine, who shore me,
Like a tame wether, all my precious fleece,
Then turned me out ridiculous, despoiled,
Shaven, and disarmed among my enemies.
   Chorus. Desire of wine and all delicious drinks,
Which many a famous warrior overturns,
Thou couldst repress; nor did the dancing ruby,
Sparkling out-poured, the flavor, or the smell,
Or taste that cheers the heart of gods and men,
Allure thee from the cool crystalline stream.
   Samson. Wherever fountain or fresh current flowed
Against the eastern ray, translucent, pure
With touch ethereal of Heaven's fiery rod,
I drank, from the clear milky juice allaying
Thirst, and refreshed; nor envied them the grape
Whose heads that turbulent liquor fills with fumes.
   Chorus. O madness! to think use of strongest wines
And strongest drinks our chief support of health,
When God with these forbidden made choice to rear
His mighty champion, strong above compare,
Whose drink was only from the liquid brook!
   Samson. But what availed this temperance, not complete
Against another object more enticing?
What boots it at one gate to make defence,
And at another to let in the foe,
Effeminately vanquished? By which means,
Now blind, disheartened, shamed, dishonored, quelled,
To what can I be useful? wherein serve
My nation, and the work from Heaven imposed?

But to sit idle on the household hearth,
A burdenous drone; to visitants a gaze,
Or pitied object; these redundant locks,
Robustious to no purpose, clustering down,
Vain monument of strength; till length of years
And sedentary numbness craze my limbs
To a contemptible old age obscure.[1]

From Milton's *Commonplace Book.*

De Fortitudine

The cause of valor a good conscience; for an evil conscience, as an English author noteth well, will otherwise gnaw at the roots of valor like a worm, and undermine all resolutions.[2]

From *Paradise Lost* (1667).

'At first I thought that liberty and Heaven
To heavenly souls had been all one; but now
I see that most through sloth had rather serve,
Ministering Spirits, trained up in feast and song:
Such hast thou armed, the minstrelsy of Heaven,
Servility with freedom to contend,
As both their deeds compared this day shall prove.'
    To whom in brief thus Abdiel stern replied:
'Apostate! still thou err'st, nor end wilt find
Of erring, from the path of truth remote.
Unjustly thou deprav'st it with the name
Of servitude, to serve whom God ordains,
Or Nature: God and Nature bid the same,
When he who rules is worthiest, and excels
Them whom he governs. This is servitude—
To serve the unwise, or him who hath rebelled
Against his worthier, as thine now serve thee,
Thyself not free, but to thyself enthralled.'[3]

From *Eikonoklastes* (1649).

For me, though neither asked, nor in a nation that gives such rewards to wisdom, I shall pronounce my sentence somewhat different from Zorobabel; and shall defend that either truth and

---

[1] *Samson Agonistes* 521–72.
[2] *Commonplace Book*, p. 18.
[3] *Paradise Lost* 6. 164–81.

justice are all one (for truth is but justice in our knowledge, and justice is but truth in our practice—and he indeed so explains himself, in saying that with truth is no accepting of persons, which is the property of justice), or else, if there be any odds, that justice, though not stronger than truth, yet, by her office, is to put forth and exhibit more strength in the affairs of mankind. For truth is properly no more than contemplation, and her utmost efficiency is but teaching; but justice in her very essence is all strength and activity, and hath a sword put into her hand to use against all violence and oppression on the earth. . . .

We may conclude, therefore, that justice, above all other things, is and ought to be the strongest; she is the strength, the kingdom, the power and majesty of all ages. Truth herself would subscribe to this, though Darius and all the monarchs of the world should deny.[1]

From *Areopagitica* (1644).

If I should thus far presume upon the meek demeanor of your civil and gentle greatness, Lords and Commons! as what your published order hath directly said, that to gainsay, I might defend myself with ease if any should accuse me of being new or insolent, did they but know how much better I find ye esteem it to imitate the old and elegant humanity of Greece than the barbaric pride of a Hunnish and Norwegian stateliness. And, out of those ages to whose polite wisdom and letters we owe that we are not yet Goths and Jutlanders, I could name him who from his private house wrote that discourse to the Parliament of Athens that persuades them to change the form of democraty which was then established. Such honor was done in those days to men who professed the study of wisdom and eloquence, not only in their own country, but in other lands, that cities and seignories heard them gladly and with great respect, if they had aught in public to admonish the State. Thus did Dion Prusæus, a stranger and a private orator, counsel the Rhodians against a

[1] *Prose Works* I. 484–5.

former edict; and I abound with other like examples, which to set here would be superfluous. But if from the industry of a life wholly dedicated to studious labors, and those natural endowments haply not the worst for two-and-fifty degrees of northern latitude, so much must be derogated as to count me not equal to any of those who had this privilege, I would obtain to be thought not so inferior, as yourselves are superior to the most of them who received their counsel. And how far you excel them, be assured, Lords and Commons! there can no greater testimony appear than when your prudent spirit acknowledges and obeys the voice of reason, from what quarter soever it be heard speaking.[1]

I deny not but that it is of greatest concernment in the Church and Commonwealth to have a vigilant eye how books demean themselves, as well as men; and thereafter to confine, imprison, and do sharpest justice on them as malefactors; for books are not absolutely dead things, but do contain a potency of life in them to be as active as that soul was whose progeny they are; nay, they do preserve as in a vial the purest efficacy and extraction of that living intellect that bred them. I know they are as lively and as vigorously productive as those fabulous dragon's teeth, and, being sown up and down, may chance to spring up armed men. And yet, on the other hand, unless wariness be used, as good almost kill a man as kill a good book. Who kills a man kills a reasonable creature, God's image; but he who destroys a good book kills reason itself, kills the image of God, as it were, in the eye. Many a man lives a burden to the earth, but a good book is the precious life-blood of a master-spirit, embalmed and treasured up on purpose to a life beyond life. 'Tis true, no age can restore a life, whereof perhaps there is no great loss; and revolutions of ages do not oft recover the loss of a rejected truth, for the want of which whole nations fare the worse. We should be wary, therefore, what persecution we raise against the living labors of public men, how we spill that seasoned life of man,

[1] *Ibid.* 2. 51–3.

preserved and stored up in books; since we see a kind of homi-
cide may be thus committed—sometimes a martyrdom; and, if it
extend to the whole impression, a kind of massacre, whereof
the execution ends not in the slaying of an elemental life, but
strikes at the ethereal and fifth essence, the breath of reason itself
—slays an immortality rather than a life. But, lest I should be
condemned of introducing licence while I oppose licensing, I refuse not the pains to be so much historical as will serve to show
what hath been done by ancient and famous commonwealths
against this disorder, till the very time that this project of
licensing crept out of the Inquisition, was catched up by our prelates, and hath caught some of our presbyters.

In Athens, where books and wits were ever busier than in any
other part of Greece, I find but only two sorts of writings which
the magistrate cared to take notice of—those either blasphemous
and atheistical, or libelous. Thus, the books of Protagoras were
by the judges of Areopagus commanded to be burnt, and himself
banished the territory, for a discourse begun with his confessing
not to know whether there were gods, or whether not. And,
against defaming, it was agreed that none should be traduced by
name (as was the manner of *Vetus Comœdia*), whereby we may
guess how they censured libeling; and this course was quick
enough, as Cicero writes, to quell both the desperate wits of
other atheists and the open way of defaming, as the event showed.
Of other sects and opinions, though tending to voluptuousness
and the denying of divine Providence, they took no heed. Therefore we do not read that either Epicurus, or that libertine school of
Cyrene, or what the Cynic impudence uttered, was ever questioned
by the laws. Neither is it recorded that the writings of those old
comedians were suppressed, though the acting of them were for-
bid; and that Plato commended the reading of Aristophanes, the
loosest of them all, to his royal scholar Dionysius is commonly
known, and may be excused, if holy Chrysostom, as is reported,

nightly studied so much the same author, and had the art to cleanse a scurrilous vehemence into the style of a rousing sermon.

That other leading city of Greece, Lacedæmon—considering that Lycurgus their lawgiver was so addicted to elegant learning as to have been the first that brought out of Ionia the scattered works of Homer, and sent the poet Thales from Crete to prepare and mollify the Spartan surliness with his smooth songs and odes, the better to plant among them law and civility—it is to be wondered how museless and unbookish they were, minding naught but the feats of war. . . .

The Romans also, for many ages trained up only to a military roughness resembling most the Lacedæmonian guise, knew of learning little but what their Twelve Tables, and the Pontific College with their augurs and flamens, taught them in religion and law; so unacquainted with other learning that, when Carneades and Critolaus, with the Stoic Diogenes, coming ambassadors to Rome, took thereby occasion to give the city a taste of their philosophy, they were suspected for seducers by no less a man than Cato the Censor, who moved it in the Senate to dismiss them speedily, and to banish all such Attic babblers out of Italy. But Scipio and others of the noblest senators withstood him and his old Sabine austerity; honored and admired the men; and the Censor himself at last, in his old age, fell to the study of that whereof before he was so scrupulous.[1]

Plato, a man of high authority indeed, but least of all for his *Commonwealth*, in the book of his *Laws* (which no city ever yet received) fed his fancy with making many edicts to his airy burgomasters, which they who otherwise admire him wish had been rather buried and excused in the genial cups of an academic night-sitting. By which laws he seems to tolerate no kind of learning but by unalterable decree, consisting most of practical traditions to the attainment whereof a library of smaller bulk than his own dialogues would be abundant; and there also enacts that no poet

[1] *Prose Works* 2. 51-8.

should so much as read to any private man what he had written until the judges and law-keepers had seen it and allowed it. But, that Plato meant this law peculiarly to that commonwealth which he had imagined, and to no other, is evident.   .   .   .

If we think to regulate printing, thereby to rectify manners, we must regulate all recreations and pastimes, all that is delightful to man. No music must be heard, no song be set or sung, but what is grave and Doric. There must be licensing dancers, that no gesture, motion, or deportment be taught our youth but what by their allowance shall be thought honest; for such Plato was provided of.   .   .   .

To sequester out of the world into Atlantic and Utopian polities which never can be drawn into use will not mend our condition; but to ordain wisely as in this world of evil in the midst whereof God hath placed us unavoidably. Nor is it Plato's licensing of books will do this, which necessarily pulls along with it so many other kinds of licensing as will make us all both ridiculous and weary, and yet frustrate; but those unwritten, or at least unconstraining, laws of virtuous education, religious and civil nurture, which Plato there mentions as the bonds and ligaments of the Commonwealth, the pillars and the sustainers of every written statute; these they be which will bear chief sway in such matters as these, when all licensing will be easily eluded.

Impunity and remissness, for certain, are the bane of a commonwealth; but here the great art lies—to discern in what the law is to bid restraint and punishment, and in what things persuasion only is to work. If every action which is good or evil in man at ripe years were to be under pittance, prescription, and compulsion, what were virtue but a name, what praise could be then due to well-doing, what gramercy to be sober, just, or continent? Many there be that complain of divine Providence for suffering Adam to transgress. Foolish tongues! when God gave him reason, He gave him freedom to choose, for reason is but choosing; he had been else a mere artificial Adam, such an Adam as he is in the motions.

We ourselves esteem not of that obedience, or love, or gift, which is of force. God therefore left him free, set before him a provoking object ever almost in his eyes; herein consisted his merit, herein the right of his reward, the praise of his abstinence. Wherefore did He create passions within us, pleasures round about us, but that these, rightly tempered, are the very ingredients of virtue? They are not skilful considerers of human things who imagine to remove sin by removing the matter of sin; for (besides that it is a huge heap increasing under the very act of diminishing), though some part of it may for a time be withdrawn from some persons, it cannot from all, in such a universal thing as books are; and, when this is done, yet the sin remains entire. Though ye take from a covetous man all his treasure, he has yet one jewel left—ye cannot bereave him of his covetousness. Banish all objects of lust, shut up all youth into the severest discipline that can be exercised in any hermitage: ye cannot make them chaste, that came not thither so. Such great care and wisdom is required to the right managing of this point.

Suppose we could expel sin by this means; look, how much we thus expel of sin, so much we expel of virtue, for the matter of them both is the same; remove that, and ye remove them both alike. This justifies the high providence of God, who, though He commands us temperance, justice, continence, yet pours out before us, even to a profuseness, all desirable things, and gives us minds that can wander beyond all limit and satiety. Why should we then affect a rigor contrary to the manner of God and of nature, by abridging or scanting those means which, books freely permitted, are both to the trial of virtue and the exercise of truth? . . .

God sure esteems the growth and completing of one virtuous person more than the restraint of ten vicious. And albeit whatever thing we hear or see, sitting, walking, traveling, or conversing, may be fitly called our book, and is of the same effect that writings are; yet, grant the thing to be prohibited were only books, it appears that this order hitherto is far insufficient to the end which it intends. . . .

Another reason whereby to make it plain that this order will miss the end it seeks, consider by the quality which ought to be in every licenser. It cannot be denied but that he who is made judge to sit upon the birth or death of books, whether they may be wafted into this world or not, had need to be a man above the common measure, both studious, learned, and judicious; there may be else no mean mistakes in the censure of what is passable or not; which is also no mean injury. If he be of such worth as behoves him, there cannot be a more tedious and unpleasing journey-work, a greater loss of time levied upon his head, than to be made the perpetual reader of unchosen books and pamphlets, oft-times huge volumes. There is no book that is acceptable unless at certain seasons; but to be enjoined the reading of that at all times, and in a hand scarce legible, whereof three pages would not down at any time in the fairest print, is an imposition I cannot believe how he that values time and his own studies, or is but of a sensible nostril, should be able to endure. . . .

I lastly proceed, from the no good it can do, to the manifest hurt it causes in being first the greatest discouragement and affront that can be offered to learning and to learned men. It was the complaint and lamentation of prelates, upon every least of a motion to remove pluralities and distribute more equally church-revenues, that then all learning would be for ever dashed and discouraged. But, as for that opinion, I never found cause to think that the tenth part of learning stood or fell with the clergy; nor could I ever but hold it for a sordid and unworthy speech of any Churchman who had a competency left him. If, therefore, ye be loath to dishearten utterly and discontent, not the mercenary crew of false pretenders to learning, but the free and ingenuous sort of such as evidently were born to study and love learning for itself, not for lucre or any other end but the service of God and of truth, and perhaps that lasting fame and perpetuity of praise which God and good men have consented shall be the reward of those whose published labors advance the good of mankind; then know that so far to distrust the judgment and the honesty of one who hath but a common repute in learning, and never yet offended, as not to count him fit to print his mind without a tutor and examiner, lest he should drop a schism or something of corruption, is the greatest displeasure and indignity to a free and knowing spirit that can be put upon him.

What advantage is it to be a man over it is to be a boy at school, if we have only escaped the ferula to come under the fescue of an *imprimatur?* if serious and elaborate writings, as if they were no more than the theme of a grammar-lad under his pedagogue, must not be uttered without the cursory eyes of a temporizing and extemporizing licenser? He who is not trusted with his own actions, his drift not being known to be evil, and standing to the hazard of law and penalty, has no great argument to think himself reputed in the commonwealth wherein he was born for other than a fool or a foreigner. When a man writes to the world, he summons up all his reason and deliberation to assist him; he searches, meditates, is industrious, and likely consults and confers with his judicious friends; after all which done, he takes himself to be informed in what he writes as well as any that wrote before him. If in this, the most consummate act of his fidelity and ripeness, no years, no industry, no former proof of his abilities, can bring him to that state of maturity as not to be still mistrusted and suspected, unless he carry all his considerate diligence, all his midnight watchings and expense of Palladian oil, to the hasty view of an unleisured licenser—perhaps much his younger, perhaps far his inferior in judgment, perhaps one who never knew the labor of book-writing—and, if he be not repulsed or slighted, must appear in print like a puny with his guardian, and his censor's hand on the back of his title to be his bail and surety that he is no idiot or seducer; it cannot be but a dishonor and derogation to the author, to the book, to the privilege and dignity of learning. . . .

And how can a man teach with authority—which is the life of teaching—how can he be a *doctor* in his book—as he ought to be, or else had better be silent—whenas all he teaches, all he delivers, is but under the tuition, under the correction of his patriarchal licenser, to blot or alter what precisely accords not with the hidebound humor which he calls his judgment? when every acute reader, upon the first sight of a pedantic licence, will be ready with these-like words to ding the book a quoit's distance from him: 'I hate a pupil-teacher! I endure not an instructor that comes to me under the wardship of an overseeing fist. I know nothing of the licenser but that I have his own hand here for his arrogance; who shall warrant me his judgment?' . . . And he might add, from Sir Francis Bacon, that such authorized books are but the language of the times. . . . Nay, which is more lamentable, if the work of any deceased author—though never so famous in his lifetime, and even to this day—comes to their hands for licence to be printed or reprinted; if there be found in his book one sentence of a venturous edge, uttered in the height of zeal (and who knows whether it might not be the dictate of a divine spirit?), yet, not suiting with every low decrepit humor of their own, though it were Knox himself, the reformer of a kingdom, that spake it, they will not pardon him their dash; the sense of that great man shall to all posterity be lost, for the fearfulness or the presumptuous rashness of a perfunctory licenser. . . .

Yet, if these things be not resented seriously and timely by them who have the remedy in their power, but that such iron-moulds as these shall have authority to gnaw out the choicest periods of exquisitest books and to commit such a treacherous fraud against the orphan remainders of worthiest men after death, the more sorrow will belong to that hapless race of men whose misfortune it is to have understanding. Henceforth let no man care to learn, or care to be more than worldly wise; for certainly in higher matters to be ignorant and slothful, to be a common steadfast dunce, will be the only pleasant life, and only in request.

And as it is a particular disesteem of every knowing person alive, and most injurious to the written labors and monuments of the dead, so to me it seems an undervaluing and vilifying of the whole nation. I cannot set so light by all the invention, the art, the wit, the grave and solid judgment which is in England as that it can be comprehended in any twenty capacities, how good soever; much less that it should not pass except their superintendence be over it, except it be sifted and strained with their strainers, that it should be uncurrent without their manual stamp. Truth and understanding are not such wares as to be monopolized and traded in by tickets and statutes and standards. We must not think to make a staple commodity of all the knowledge in the land, to mark and license it like our broadcloth and our wool-packs. What is it but a servitude like that imposed by the Philistines, not to be allowed the sharpening of our own axes and coulters, but we must repair from all quarters to twenty licensing forges?[1]

For if we be sure we are in the right, and do not hold the truth guiltily—which becomes not, if we ourselves condemn not our own weak and frivolous teaching, and the people for an untaught and irreligious gadding rout—what can be more fair than when a man judicious, learned, and of a conscience (for aught we know) as good as theirs that taught us what we know, shall, not privily from house to house (which is more dangerous) but openly by writing, publish to the world what his opinion is, what his reasons, and wherefore that which is now thought cannot be sound?[2]

What a collusion is this—whenas we are exhorted by the wise man to use diligence, 'to seek for wisdom as for hidden treasures,' early and late, that another order shall enjoin us to know nothing but by statute? When a man hath been laboring the hardest labor in the deep mines of knowledge, hath furnished out his findings in all their equipage, drawn forth his reasons as it were a battle ranged, scattered and defeated all objections in his way, calls out his adversary into the plain, offers him the advantage of wind and

[1] *Prose Works* 2. 71–81.
[2] *Ibid.* 2. 88.

sun, if he please, only that he may try the matter by dint of argument; for his opponents then to skulk, to lay ambushments, to keep a narrow bridge of licensing where the challenger should pass—though it be valor enough in soldiership—is but weakness and cowardice in the wars of truth. For who knows not that truth is strong, next to the Almighty? She needs no policies, nor stratagems, nor licensings, to make her victorious; those are the shifts and the defences that error uses against her power. Give her but room, and do not bind her when she sleeps, for then she speaks not true (as the old Proteus did, who spake oracles only when he was caught and bound); but then rather she turns herself into all shapes except her own, and perhaps tunes her voice according to the time (as Micaiah did before Ahab), until she be adjured into her own likeness.[1]

In the mean while if any one would write, and bring his helpful hand to the slow-moving reformation which we labor under— if truth have spoken to him before others, or but seemed at least to speak, who hath so be-Jesuited us that we should trouble that man with asking licence to do so worthy a deed, and not consider this—that, if it come to prohibiting, there is not aught more likely to be prohibited than truth itself, whose first appearance to our eyes, bleared and dimmed with prejudice and custom, is more unsightly and unplausible than many errors? . . . And what do they tell us vainly of new opinions, when this very opinion of theirs—that none must be heard but whom they like—is the worst and newest opinion of all others, and is the chief cause why sects and schisms do so much abound, and true knowledge is kept at distance from us? besides yet a greater danger which is in it: for, when God shakes a kingdom with strong and healthful commotions to a general reforming, it is not untrue that many sectaries and false teachers are then busiest in seducing; but yet more true it is that God then raises to His own work men of rare abilities and more than common industry, not only to look back

[1] *Prose Works* 2. 96.

and revive what hath been taught heretofore, but to gain further and to go on some new enlightened steps in the discovery of truth. For such is the order of God's enlightening His Church—to dispense and deal out by degrees His beam, so as our earthly eyes may best sustain it. . . .

And, if the men be erroneous who appear to be the leading schismatics, what withholds us but our sloth, our self-will, and distrust in the right cause, that we do not give them gentle meetings and gentle dismissions; that we debate not and examine the matter thoroughly with liberal and frequent audience—if not for their sakes, yet for our own? Seeing no man who hath tasted learning but will confess the many ways of profiting by those who, not contented with stale receipts, are able to manage and set forth new positions to the world. And were they but as the dust and cinders of our feet, so long as in that notion they may yet serve to polish and brighten the armory of truth, even for that respect they were not utterly to be cast away. But if they be of those whom God hath fitted for the special use of these times with eminent and ample gifts, and those perhaps neither among the priests, nor among the Pharisees, and we, in the haste of a precipitant zeal, shall make no distinction, but resolve to stop their mouths because we fear they come with new and dangerous opinions, as we commonly forejudge them ere we understand them; no less than woe to us, while, thinking thus to defend the Gospel, we are found the persecutors!

There have been not a few since the beginning of this Parliament, both of the Presbytery and others, who, by their unlicensed books to the contempt of an *imprimatur*, first broke that triple ice clung about our hearts, and taught the people to see day.[1]

From *A Defence of the People of England* (1651).

You inveigh against the common people, as being 'blind and brutish, ignorant of the art of governing'; you say there is 'nothing more empty, more vain, more inconstant, more uncertain

[1] *Ibid.* 2. 98–9.

than they.' All which is . . . true . . . of the rabble, but not of the middle sort, amongst whom the most prudent men and most skilful in affairs are generally found; others are most commonly diverted, either by luxury and plenty or by want and poverty, from virtue and the study of laws and government.[1]

From *The Second Defence of The People of England* (1654).

You everywhere concede that 'the Independents were superior, not in numbers, but in discipline and in courage.' Hence I contend that they well deserved the superiority which they acquired; for nothing is more agreeable to the order of nature, or more for the interest of mankind, than that the less should yield to the greater, not in numbers, but in wisdom and in virtue. Those who excel in prudence, in experience, in industry, and courage, however few they may be, will, in my opinion, finally constitute the majority, and everywhere have the ascendant.[2]

THE CHARACTER AND DESTINY OF THE ENGLISH PEOPLE

From *The Second Defence of the People of England* (1654).

I can easily repel any charge which may be adduced against me, either of want of courage or want of zeal; for, though I did not participate in the toils or dangers of the war, yet I was at the same time engaged in a service not less hazardous to myself, and more beneficial to my fellow-citizens. . . . Since from my youth I was devoted to the pursuits of literature, and my mind had always been stronger than my body, I did not court the labors of a camp, in which any common person would have been of more service than myself, but resorted to that employment in which my exertions were likely to be of most avail. Thus, with the better part of my frame I contributed as much as possible to the good of my country, and to the success of the glorious cause in which we were engaged. And I thought that, if God willed the success of such glorious achievements, it was equally agreeable to His will that there should be others by whom those achievements should be recorded with dignity and elegance; and that the truth, which had

[1] *Prose Works* I. 155.   [2] *Ibid.* I. 265.

been defended by arms, should also be defended by reason, which is the best and only legitimate means of defending it. Hence, while I applaud those who were victorious in the field, I will not complain of the province which was assigned me, but rather congratulate myself upon it, and thank the Author of all good for having placed me in a station which may be an object of envy to others rather than of regret to myself.

I am far from wishing to make any vain or arrogant comparisons, or to speak ostentatiously of myself; but, in a cause so great and glorious, and particularly on an occasion when I am called by the general suffrage to defend the very defenders of that cause, I can hardly refrain from assuming a more lofty and swelling tone than the simplicity of an exordium may seem to justify; and, much as I may be surpassed, in the powers of eloquence and copiousness of diction, by the illustrious orators of antiquity, yet the subject of which I treat was never surpassed, in any age, in dignity or in interest. It has excited such general and such ardent expectation that I imagine myself, not in the forum or on the rostra, surrounded only by the people of Athens or of Rome, but about to address in this, as I did in my former *Defence*, the whole collective body of people, cities, states, and councils of the wise and eminent, through the wide expanse of anxious and listening Europe. I seem to survey, as from a towering height, the far-extended tracts of sea and land, and innumerable crowds of spectators betraying in their looks the liveliest interest, and sensations the most congenial with my own. Here I behold the stout and manly prowess of the Germans disdaining servitude; there the generous and lively impetuosity of the French; on this side, the calm and stately valor of the Spaniard; on that, the composed and wary magnanimity of the Italian. Of all the lovers of liberty and virtue—the magnanimous and the wise, in whatever quarter they may be found—some secretly favor, others openly approve; some greet me with congratulations and applause; others, who had long been proof against conviction, at last yield themselves captive to the force of truth. Surrounded by congregated multitudes, I now imagine that, from the Columns of Hercules to the Indian Ocean, I behold the nations of the earth recovering that liberty which they so long had lost; and that the people of this island are transporting to other countries a plant of more beneficial qualities, and more noble growth, than that which Triptolemus is reported to have carried from region to region; that they are disseminating the blessings of civilization and freedom among cities, kingdoms, and nations.[1]

From *The Reason of Church-Government* (1642).

As for that which Barclay, in his *Image of Minds*, writes concerning the horrible and barbarous conceits of Englishmen in their religion—I deem it spoken like what he was, a fugitive Papist traducing the island whence he sprung. It may be more judiciously gathered from hence that the Englishman, of many other nations, is least atheistical, and bears a natural disposition of much reverence and awe towards the Deity; but, in his weakness and want of better instruction (which among us too frequently is neglected, especially by the meaner sort) turning the bent of his own wits with a scrupulous and ceaseless care what he might do to inform himself aright of God and His worship, he may fall not unlikely, sometimes, as any other landman, into an uncouth opinion. And, verily, if we look at his native towardliness in the rough-cast without breeding, some nation or other may haply be better composed to a natural civility and right judgment than he. But, if he get the benefit once of a wise and well-rectified nurture (which must first come in general from the godly vigilance of the Church), I suppose that, wherever mention is made of countries, manners, or men, the English people, among the first that shall be praised, may deserve to be accounted a right pious, right honest, and right hardy nation.[2]

[1] *Prose Works* 1. 218–20.
[2] *Ibid.* 2. 469–70.

INTELLIGENCE AND LIBERTY

From *Areopagitica* (1644).

Lords and Commons of England! consider what nation it is whereof ye are, and whereof ye are the governors—a nation not slow and dull, but of a quick, ingenious, and piercing spirit; acute to invent, subtile and sinewy to discourse, not beneath the reach of any point the highest that human capacity can soar to. Therefore the studies of learning in her deepest sciences have been so ancient and so eminent among us that writers of good antiquity and able judgment have been persuaded that even the school of Pythagoras, and the Persian wisdom, took beginning from the old philosophy of this island. And that wise and civil Roman, Julius Agricola, who governed once here for Cæsar, preferred the natural wits of Britain before the labored studies of the French. Nor is it for nothing that the grave and frugal Transylvanian sends out yearly from as far as the mountainous borders of Russia, and beyond the Hercynian wilderness, not their youth, but their staid men, to learn our language and our theological arts. Yet that which is above all this, the favor and the love of Heaven, we have great argument to think in a peculiar manner propitious and propending towards us. Why else was this nation chosen before any other, that out of her, as out of Sion, should be proclaimed and sounded forth the first tidings and trumpet of reformation to all Europe? And had it not been the obstinate perverseness of our prelates against the divine and admirable spirit of Wyclif, to supress him as a schismatic and innovator, perhaps neither the Bohemian Hus and Jerome, no, nor the name of Luther or of Calvin, had ever been known—the glory of reforming all our neighbors had been completely ours. But now, as our obdurate clergy have with violence demeaned the matter, we are become hitherto the latest and the backwardest scholars of whom God offered to have made us the teachers.

Now, once again, by all concurrence of signs and by the general instinct of holy and devout men, as they daily and solemnly express their thoughts, God is decreeing to begin some new and great period in His Church, even to the reforming of reformation itself. What does He, then, but reveal Himself to His servants, and, as His manner is, first to His Englishmen? I say, as His manner is, first to us, though we mark not the method of His counsels, and are unworthy. Behold now this vast city, a city of refuge, the mansion-house of liberty, encompassed and surrounded with His protection. The shop of war hath not there more anvils and hammers working, to fashion out the plates and instruments of armed justice in defence of beleaguered truth, than there be pens and heads there, sitting by their studious lamps, musing, searching, revolving new notions and ideas wherewith to present, as with their homage and their fealty, the approaching reformation; others as fast reading, trying all things, assenting to the force of reason and convincement.

What could a man require more from a nation so pliant and so prone to seek after knowledge? What wants there, to such a towardly and pregnant soil, but wise and faithful laborers, to make a knowing people, a nation of prophets, of sages, and of worthies? We reckon more than five months yet to harvest— there need not be five weeks; had we but eyes to lift up, the fields are white already. Where there is much desire to learn, there of necessity will be much arguing, much writing, many opinions; for opinion in good men is but knowledge in the making. Under these fantastic terrors of sect and schism we wrong the earnest and zealous thirst after knowledge and understanding which God hath stirred up in this city. What some lament of, we rather should rejoice at, should rather praise this pious forwardness among men to reassume the ill-deputed care of their religion into their own hands again. A little generous prudence, a little forbearance of one another, and some grain of charity, might win all these diligences to join and unite into one general and brotherly search after truth; could we but forego this prelatical tradition of crowding free consciences and Christian liberties into canons and precepts of men. I doubt not, if some great and worthy stranger should come among us, wise to discern the mould and temper of a people, and how to govern it, observing the high hopes and aims, the diligent alacrity of our extended thoughts and reasonings in the pursuance of truth and freedom, but that he would cry out as Pyrrhus did, admiring the Roman docility and courage: 'If such were my Epirots, I would not despair the greatest design that could be attempted to make a church or kingdom happy.'

Yet these are the men cried out against for schismatics and sectaries; as if, while the temple of the Lord was building, some cutting, some squaring the marble, others hewing the cedars, there should be a sort of irrational men who could not consider there must be many schisms and many dissections made in the quarry and in the timber ere the house of God can be built. And, when every stone is laid artfully together, it cannot be united into a continuity; it can but be contiguous, in this world; neither can every piece of the building be of one form; nay, rather, the perfection consists in this—that, out of many moderate varieties and brotherly dissimilitudes that are not vastly disproportional, arises the goodly and the graceful symmetry that commends the whole pile and structure.

Let us, therefore, be more considerate builders, more wise in spiritual architecture, when great reformation is expected. For now the time seems come wherein Moses, the great Prophet, may sit in Heaven rejoicing to see that memorable and glorious wish of his fulfilled—when not only our seventy elders, but all the Lord's people, are become prophets. No marvel, then, though some men—and some good men, too, perhaps, but young in goodness, as Joshua then was—envy them. They fret, and out of their own weakness are in agony, lest these divisions and subdivisions will undo us. The adversary again applauds, and waits the hour. 'When they have branched themselves out,' saith he, 'small enough into parties and partitions, then will be our time.' Fool! he sees not the firm root out of which we all grow, though into branches; nor will beware, until he see our small divided maniples cutting through at every angle of his ill-united and unwieldy brigade. And, that we are to hope better of all these supposed sects and schisms, and that we shall not need that solicitude, honest perhaps, though over-timorous, of them that vex in this behalf, but shall laugh in the end at those malicious applauders of our differences, I have these reasons to persuade me.

First, when a city shall be as it were besieged and blocked about, her navigable river infested, inroads and incursions round, defiance and battle oft rumored to be marching up, even to her walls and suburb trenches; that then the people, or the greater part, more than at other times, wholly taken up with the study of highest and most important matters to be reformed, should be disputing, reasoning, reading, inventing, discoursing, even to a rarity and admiration, things not before discoursed or written of, argues first a singular good will, contentedness, and confidence in your prudent foresight, and safe government, Lords and Commons! and from thence derives itself to a gallant bravery and well-grounded contempt of their enemies, as if there were no small number of as great spirits among us as his was who, when Rome was nigh besieged by Hannibal, being in the city, bought that piece of ground at no cheap rate whereon Hannibal himself encamped his own regiment. . . .

For as in a body, when the blood is fresh, the spirits pure and vigorous, not only to vital, but to rational faculties, and those in the acutest and pertest operations of wit and subtlety, it argues in what good plight and constitution the body is; so, when the cheerfulness of the people is so sprightly up as that it has not only wherewith to guard well its own freedom and safety, but to spare, and to bestow upon the solidest and sublimest points of controversy and new invention, it betokens us not degenerated, nor drooping to a fatal decay by casting off the old and wrinkled skin of corruption, to outlive these pangs and wax young again, entering the glorious ways of truth and prosperous virtue, destined to become great and honorable in these latter ages. Methinks I see in my mind a noble and puissant nation rousing herself like a strong man after sleep, and shaking her invincible locks. Methinks I see her as an eagle mewing her mighty youth and kindling her undazzled eyes at the full midday beam; purging and unscaling her long-abused sight at the fountain itself of heavenly radiance, while the whole noise of timorous and flocking birds, with those also that love the twilight, flutter about, amazed at what she means, and in their envious gabble would prognosticate a year of sects and schisms.[1]

From *The Doctrine and Discipline of Divorce* (1643).

Whatever else ye can enact will scarce concern a third part of the British name; but the benefit and good of this your magnanimous example will easily spread far beyond the banks of Tweed and the Norman isles. It would not be the first or second time since our ancient Druids, by whom this island was the cathedral of philosophy to France, left off their pagan rites, that England hath had this honor vouchsafed from Heaven, to give out reformation to the world. Who was it but our English Constantine that baptized the Roman Empire? Who but the Northumbrian Willibrord, and Winifrid of Devon, with their followers, were the first apostles of Germany? Who but Alcuin and Wyclif, our countrymen, opened the eyes of Europe, the one in arts, the other in religion? Let not England forget her precedence of teaching nations how to live.[2]

ADVICE AND WARNING ON THE PRESERVATION OF LIBERTY

From *The Doctrine and Discipline of Divorce* (1643).

Let not other men think their conscience bound to search continually after the truth, to pray for enlightening from above, to publish what they think they have so obtained, and debar me from conceiving myself tied by the same duties. Ye have now—

[1] *Prose Works* 2. 90–4.   [2] *Ibid.* 3. 178.

doubtless by the favor and appointment of God—ye have now in your hands a great and populous nation to reform; from what corruption, what blindness in religion, ye know well; in what a degenerate and fallen spirit from the apprehension of native liberty and true manliness, I am sure ye find; with what unbounded licence rushing to whoredoms and adulteries, needs not long inquiry; insomuch that the fears which men have of too strict a discipline perhaps exceed the hopes that can be in others of ever introducing it with any great success. What if I should tell ye now of dispensations and indulgences—to give a little the reins, to let them play and nibble with the bait a while, a people as hard of heart as that Egyptian colony that went to Canaan? . . .

'What middle way can be taken, then,' may some interrupt, 'if we must neither turn to the right nor to the left, and that the people hate to be reformed?' Mark, then, judges and lawgivers, and ye whose office it is to be our teachers, for I will utter now a doctrine—if ever any other—though neglected or not understood, yet of great and powerful importance to the governing of mankind.

He who wisely would restrain the reasonable soul of man within due bounds must first himself know perfectly how far the territory and dominion extends of just and honest liberty. As little must he offer to bind that which God hath loosened as to loosen that which He hath bound. The ignorance and mistake of this high point hath heaped up one huge half of all the misery that hath been since Adam. In the Gospel we shall read a supercilious crew of masters, whose holiness, or rather whose evil eye, grieving that God should be so facile to man, was to set straiter limits to obedience than God hath set, to enslave the dignity of man, to put a garrison upon his neck of empty and over-dignified precepts; and we shall read our Saviour never more grieved and troubled than to meet with such a peevish madness among men against their own freedom. How can we expect Him to be less offended with us, when much of the same folly shall be found yet remaining where it least ought, to the perishing of thousands? The greatest burden in the world is superstition, not only of ceremonies in the Church, but of imaginary and scarecrow sins at home. What greater weakening, what more subtle stratagem against our Christian warfare, when, besides the gross body of real transgressions to encounter, we shall be terrified by a vain and shadowy menacing of faults that are not? When things indifferent shall be set to overfront us under the banners of sin, what wonder if we be routed, and, by this art of our adversary, fall into the subjection of worst and deadliest offences? . . .

And farewell all hope of true reformation in the State, while such an evil as this lies undiscerned or unregarded in the house; on the redress whereof depends, not only the spiritful and orderly life of our grown men, but the willing and careful education of our children. Let this, therefore, be new examined, this tenure and freehold of mankind, this native and domestic charter given us by a greater Lord than that Saxon king, the Confessor. Let the statutes of God be turned over, be scanned anew, and considered not altogether by the narrow intellectuals of quotationists and commonplaces, but (as was the ancient right of councils) by men of what liberal profession soever, of eminent spirit and breeding, joined with a diffuse and various knowledge of divine and human things; able to balance and define good and evil, right and wrong, throughout every state of life; able to show us the ways of the Lord straight and faithful as they are—not full of cranks and contradictions and pitfalling dispenses, but with divine insight and benignity measured out to the proportion of each mind and spirit, each temper and disposition, created so different each from other, and yet, by the skill of wise conducting, all to become uniform in virtue.[1]

From *The Reason of Church-Government* (1642).

In the publishing of human laws (which for the most part aim not beyond the good of civil society) to set them barely forth to

[1] *Prose Works* 3. 174–7.

the people, without reason or preface, like a physical prescript, or only with threatenings, as it were a lordly command, in the judgment of Plato was thought to be done neither generously nor wisely. His advice was, seeing that persuasion certainly is a more winning and more manlike way to keep men in obedience than fear, that, to such laws as were of principal moment, there should be used as an induction some well-tempered discourse, showing how good, how gainful, how happy it must needs be to live according to honesty and justice; which, being uttered with those native colors and graces of speech as true eloquence, the daughter of virtue, can best bestow upon her mother's praises, would so incite, and, in a manner, charm, the multitude into the love of that which is really good as to embrace it ever after, not of custom and awe (which most men do), but of choice and purpose, with true and constant delight.

But this practice we may learn from a better and more ancient authority than any heathen writer hath to give us; and, indeed, being a point of so high wisdom and worth, how could it be but we should find it in that Book within whose sacred context all wisdom is unfolded? Moses, therefore, the only lawgiver that we can believe to have been visibly taught of God, knowing how vain it was to write laws to men whose hearts were not first seasoned with the knowledge of God and of His works, began from the Book of Genesis as a prologue to his laws; . . . that the nation of the Jews, reading therein the universal goodness of God to all creatures in the creation, . . . might be moved to obey sincerely by knowing so good a reason of their obedience.[1]

From *The Second Defence of the People of England* (1654).

Since there are often in a republic men who have the same itch for making a multiplicity of laws as some poetasters have for making many verses, and since laws are usually worse in pro-

[1] *Prose Works* 2. 439-40.

portion as they are more numerous, if you[1] shall not enact so many new laws as you abolish old which do not operate so much as warnings against evil as impediments in the way of good; and if you shall retain only those which are necessary, which do not confound the distinctions of good and evil, which, while they prevent the frauds of the wicked, do not prohibit the innocent freedoms of the good, which punish crimes without interdicting those things which are lawful, only on account of the abuses to which they may occasionally be exposed (for the intention of laws is to check the commission of vice, but liberty is the best school of virtue, and affords the strongest encouragements to the practice); then, if you make a better provision for the education of our youth than has hitherto been made; if you prevent the promiscuous instruction of the docile and the indocile, of the idle and the diligent, at the public cost, but reserve the rewards of learning for the learned, and of merit for the meritorious; if you permit the free discussion of truth without any hazard to the author, or any subjection to the caprice of an individual—which is the best way to make truth flourish and knowledge abound (the censure of the half-learned, the envy, the pusillanimity, or the prejudice which measures the discoveries of others, and, in short, every degree of wisdom, by the measure of its own capacity, will be prevented from doling out information to us according to their own arbitrary choice); lastly, if you shall not dread to hear any truth or any falsehood, whatever it may be, but if you shall least of all listen to those who think that they can never be free till the liberties of others depend on their caprice, and who attempt nothing with so much zeal and vehemence as to fetter not only the bodies but the minds of men, who labor to introduce into the State the worst of all tyrannies—the tyranny of their own depraved habits and pernicious opinions; you will always be dear to those who think not merely that their own sect or faction, but that all citizens of all descriptions should enjoy equal rights and equal laws. If there be any one who thinks that this is not liberty

[1] Cromwell.

enough, he appears to me to be rather inflamed with the lust of ambition or of anarchy than with the love of a genuine and well-regulated liberty. . . .

For it is of no little consequence, O citizens, by what principles you are governed either in acquiring liberty or in retaining it when acquired. And unless that liberty which is of such a kind as arms can neither procure nor take away, which alone is the fruit of piety, of justice, of temperance, and unadulterated virtue, shall have taken deep root in your minds and hearts, there will not long be wanting one who will snatch from you by treachery what you have acquired by arms. War has made many great whom peace makes small. If, after being released from the toils of war, you neglect the arts of peace, if your peace and your liberty be a state of warfare, if war be your only virtue, the summit of your praise, you will, believe me, soon find peace the most adverse to your interests. Your peace will be only a more distressing war, and that which you imagined liberty will prove the worst of slavery. Unless by the means of piety, not frothy and loquacious, but operative, unadulterated, and sincere, you clear the horizon of the mind from those mists of superstition which arise from the ignorance of true religion, you will always have those who will bend your necks to the yoke as if you were brutes; who, notwithstanding all your triumphs, will put you up to the highest bidder, as if you were mere booty made in war, and will find an exuberant source of wealth in your ignorance and superstition. Unless you will subjugate the propensity to avarice, to ambition and sensuality, and expel all luxury from yourselves and from your families, you will find that you have cherished a more stubborn and intractable despot at home than you ever encountered in the field. . . . Let these be the first enemies whom you subdue; this constitutes the campaign of peace; these are triumphs, difficult indeed, but bloodless, and far more honorable than those trophies which are purchased only by slaughter and by rapine.[1]

[1] *Prose Works* I. 293-5.

INTELLIGENCE AND LIBERTY

From *The Ready and Easy Way to Establish a Free Commonwealth* (1660).

To make the people fittest to choose, and the chosen fittest to govern, will be to mend our corrupt and faulty education—to teach the people faith not without virtue, temperance, modesty, sobriety, parsimony, justice; not to admire wealth or honor; to hate turbulence and ambition; to place every one his private welfare and happiness in the public peace, liberty, and safety. They shall not then need to be much mistrustful of their chosen patriots in the grand council, who will be then rightly called the true keepers of our liberty.[1]

The other part of our freedom consists in the civil rights and advancements of every person according to his merit; . . . both which, in my opinion, may be best and soonest obtained if every county in the land were made a kind of subordinate commonalty or commonwealth, and one chief town or more, according as the shire is in circuit, made cities (if they be not so called already) where the nobility and chief gentry, from a proportionable compass of territory annexed to each city, may build houses or palaces befitting their quality, may bear part in the government, make their own judicial laws, or use those that are, and execute them by their own elected judicatures and judges, without appeal, in all things of civil government between man and man. . . .

They should have here also schools and academies, at their own choice, wherein their children may be bred up in their own sight to all learning and noble education; not in grammar only, but in all liberal arts and exercises. This would soon spread much more knowledge and civility, yea, religion, through all parts of the land, by communicating the natural heat of government and culture more distributively to all extreme parts, which now lie numb and neglected; would soon make the whole nation more industrious, more ingenious at home, more potent, more honorable

[1] *Ibid.* 2. 126.

abroad. To this a free commonwealth will easily assent (nay, the Parliament hath had already some such thing in design), for, of all governments, a commonwealth aims most to make the people flourishing, virtuous, noble, and high-spirited.[1]

However, with all hazard I have ventured what I thought my duty, to speak in season, and to forewarn my country in time; wherein I doubt not but there be many wise men in all places and degrees, but am sorry the effects of wisdom are so little seen among us. Many circumstances and particulars I could have added in those things whereof I have spoken; but a few main matters, now put speedily in execution, will suffice to recover us, and set all right. And there will want at no time who are good at circumstances; but men who set their minds on main matters, and sufficiently urge them, in these most difficult times I find not many.[2]

FATAL DEFECTS
From *Tetrachordon* (1645).

In every commonwealth, when it decays, corruption makes two main steps: first, when men cease to do according to the inward and uncompelled actions of virtue, caring only to live by the outward constraint of law, and turn the simplicity of real good into the craft of seeming so by law. To this hypocritical honesty was Rome declined in that age wherein Horace lived and discovered it to Quintius:

> Whom do we count a good man, whom but he
> Who keeps the laws and statutes of the Senate,
> Who judges in great suits and controversies,
> Whose witness and opinion wins the cause?
> But his own house, and the whole neighborhood,
> Sees his foul inside through his whited skin.

The next declining is when law becomes now too strait for the secular manners, and those too loose for the cincture of law. This

---

[1] *Prose Works* 2. 135-6.
[2] *Ibid.* 2. 138.

brings in false and crooked interpretations to eke out law, and invents the subtle encroachments of obscure traditions hard to be disproved.[1]

From *Eikonoklastes* (1649).

Which low dejection and debasement of mind in the people, I must confess, I cannot willingly ascribe to the natural disposition of an Englishman, but rather to two other causes: first, to the prelates and their fellow-teachers, though of another name and sect, whose pulpit-stuff, both first and last, hath been the doctrine and perpetual infusion of servility and wretchedness to all their hearers, and whose lives the type of worldliness and hypocrisy, without the least true pattern of virtue, righteousness, or self-denial in their whole practice. I attribute it, next, to the factious inclination of most men divided from the public by several ends and humors of their own.[2]

Thus in a graceless age things of highest praise and imitation, under a right name, to make them infamous and hateful to the people are miscalled. Certainly, if ignorance and perverseness will needs be national and universal, then they who adhere to wisdom and to truth are not therefore to be blamed for being so few as to seem a sect or faction. But in my opinion it goes not ill with that people where these virtues grow so numerous and well joined together as to resist and make head against the rage and torrent of that boisterous folly and superstition that possesses and hurries on the vulgar sort.[3]

For by that means, 'having sole influence upon the clergy, and they upon the people, after long search and many disputes,' he could not possibly find a more compendious and politic way to uphold and settle tyranny than by subduing first the consciences of vulgar men with the insensible poison of their slavish doctrine; for then the body and besotted mind without much reluctancy was likeliest to admit the yoke.[4]

[1] *Ibid.* 3. 367.
[2] *Ibid.* 1. 313.
[3] *Ibid.* 1. 317.
[4] *Ibid.* 1. 480–1.

[*On the Detraction which Followed upon my Writing certain Treatises*]
(1645).

> I did but prompt the age to quit their clogs
>> By the known rules of ancient liberty,
>> When straight a barbarous noise environs me
>> Of owls and cuckoos, asses, apes, and dogs;
> As when those hinds that were transformed to frogs
>> Railed at Latona's twin-born progeny,
>> Which after held the sun and moon in fee.
> But this is got by casting pearl to hogs,
> That bawl for freedom in their senseless mood,
>> And still revolt when Truth would set them free.
> Licence they mean when they cry Liberty;
> For who loves that must first be wise and good:
>> But from that mark how far they rove we see,
>> For all this waste of wealth and loss of blood.[1]

RETROSPECT, ADMONITION, AND ULTIMATE HOPE

From *The History of Britain* (1670).

At Cæsar's coming hither, such likeliest were the Britons as the writers of those times, and their own actions, represent them—in courage and warlike readiness to take advantage by ambush or sudden onset, not inferior to the Romans, nor Cassibelan to Cæsar; in weapons, arms, and the skill of encamping, embattling, fortifying, overmatched. Their weapons were a short spear and light target, a sword also by their side, their fight sometimes in chariots fanged at the axle with iron scythes; their bodies most part naked, only painted with woad in sundry figures—to seem terrible, as they thought—but, pursued by enemies, not nice of their painting to run into bogs, worse than wild Irish, up to the neck, and there to stay many days holding a certain morsel in their mouths no bigger than a bean, to suffice hunger; but that receipt, and the temperance it taught, is long since unknown among us. Their towns and strongholds were spaces of ground fenced about with a ditch and great trees felled overthwart each other; their buildings within were thatched houses for themselves and their cattle.

[1] *Sonnet 12.*

In peace, the upland inhabitants, besides hunting, tended their flocks and herds, but with little skill of country affairs. . . . Clothing they had none but what the skins of beasts afforded them, and that not always; yet gallantry they had, painting their own skins with several portraitures of beast, bird, or flower—a vanity which hath not yet left us, removed only from the skin to the skirt behung now with as many colored ribands and gewgaws. Towards the seaside they tilled the ground, and lived much after the manner of Gauls, their neighbors, or first planters. Their money was brazen pieces or iron rings, their best merchandise tin, the rest trifles of glass, ivory, and such-like; yet gems and pearls they had, saith Mela, in some rivers. Their ships of light timber wickered with osier between, and covered over with leather, served not therefore to transport them far, and their commodities were fetched away by foreign merchants.

Their dealing, saith Diodorus, plain and simple without fraud; their civil government under many princes and states, not confederate or consulting in common, but mistrustful, and oft-times warring one with the other, which gave them up one by one an easy conquest to the Romans. Their religion was governed by a sort of priests or magicians called Druids—from the Greek name of an oak, which tree they had in great reverence, and the mistletoe, especially, growing thereon. Pliny writes them skilled in magic no less than those of Persia; by their abstaining from a hen, a hare, and a goose, from fish also, saith Dion, and their opinion of the soul's passing after death into other bodies, they may be thought to have studied Pythagoras; yet philosophers I cannot call them, reported men factious and ambitious, contending sometimes about the arch-priesthood not without civil war and slaughter; nor restrained they the people under them from a lewd, adulterous, and incestuous life. . . . But the Gospel, not long after preached here, abolished such impurities, and of the Romans we have cause not to say much worse than that they beat us into some civility.[1]

[1] *Prose Works* 5. 197–8.

The winter he [Agricola] spent all in worthy actions; teaching and promoting like a public father the institutes and customs of civil life. The inhabitants rude and scattered, and by that the proner to war, he so persuaded as to build houses, temples, and seats of justice; and by praising the forward, quickening the slow, assisting all, turned the name of necessity into an emulation. He caused, moreover, the noblemen's sons to be bred up in liberal arts, and, by preferring the wits of Britain before the studies of Gallia, brought them to affect the Latin eloquence who before hated the language. Then were the Roman fashions imitated, and the gown; after a while the incitements also and materials of vice and voluptuous life—proud buildings, baths, and the elegance of banqueting—which the foolisher sort called civility, but was indeed a secret art to prepare them for bondage.[1]

With the Empire fell also what before in this Western world was chiefly Roman: learning, valor, eloquence, history, civility, and even language itself; all these together, as it were, with equal pace diminishing and decaying.[2]

The Britons thus, as we heard, being left without protection from the Empire, and the land in a manner emptied of all her youth—consumed in wars abroad, or not caring to return home—themselves, through long subjection, servile in mind, slothful of body, and with the use of arms unacquainted, sustained but ill for many years the violence of those barbarous invaders who now daily grew upon them. For, although at first greedy of change, and to be thought the leading nation to freedom from the Empire, they seemed awhile to bestir them with a show of diligence in their new affairs, some secretly aspiring to rule, others adoring the name of liberty; yet, so soon as they felt by proof the weight of what it was to govern well themselves, and what was wantiing within them—not stomach or the love of licence, but the wisdom, the virtue, the labor, to use and maintain true liberty—they

---

[1] *Prose Works* 5. 214.
[2] *Ibid.* 5. 234-5.

soon remitted their heat, and shrunk more wretchedly under the burden of their own liberty than before under a foreign yoke.[1]

But they in the mean while, thus rid of their enemies, began afresh to till the ground, which after cessation yields her fruit in such abundance as had not formerly been known for many ages. But wantonness and luxury, the wonted companions of plenty, grew up as fast; and with them, if Gildas deserve belief, all other vices incident to human corruption. That which he notes especially to be the chief perverting of all good in the land, and so continued in his days, was the hatred of truth and all such as durst appear to vindicate and maintain it. Against them, as against the only disturbers, all the malice of the land was bent. Lies and falsities, and such as could best invent them, were only in request. Evil was embraced for good, wickedness honored and esteemed as virtue. And this quality their valor had—against a foreign enemy to be ever backward and heartless, to civil broils eager and prompt. In matters of government and the search of truth, weak and shallow; in falsehood and wicked deeds, pregnant and industrious. Pleasing to God, or not pleasing, with them weighed alike; and the worse most an end was the weightier. All things were done contrary to public welfare and safety, not only by secular men; for the clergy also, whose example should have guided others, were as vicious and corrupt—many of them besotted with continual drunkenness or swollen with pride and wilfulness, full of contention, full of envy, indiscreet, incompetent judges to determine what in the practice of life is good or evil, what lawful or unlawful. Thus furnished with judgment and for manners thus qualified, both priest and lay, they agree to choose them several kings of their own, as near as might be likest themselves—and the words of my author import as much.[2]

But when the next age, unacquainted with past evils and only sensible of their present ease and quiet, succeeded, straight followed

[1] *Ibid.* 5. 241.
[2] *Ibid.* 5. 246.

the apparent subversion of all truth and justice in the minds of most men, scarce the least footstep or impression of goodness left remaining through all ranks and degrees in the land.[1]

The year six hundred and sixty-four a synod of Scottish and English bishops, in the presence of Oswi and Alfred his son, was held at a monastery in those parts, to debate on what day Easter should be kept—a controversy which long before had disturbed the Greek and Latin churches; wherein the Scots, not agreeing with the way of Rome, nor yielding to the disputants on that side to whom the King most inclined, such as were bishops here resigned, and returned home with their disciples. Another clerical question was there also much controverted—not so superstitious in my opinion as ridiculous—about the right shaving of crowns. The same year was seen an eclipse of the sun in May, followed by a sore pestilence, beginning in the South, but spreading to the North and over all Ireland, with great mortality. In which time the East-Saxons, after Swithelm's decease, being governed by Siger the son of Sigebert the Small, and Sebbi of Seward, though both subject to the Mercians, Siger and his people, unsteady of faith, supposing that this plague was come upon them for renouncing their old religion, fell off the second time to infidelity. Which the Mercian king, Wulfer, understanding, sent Jarumannus, a faithful bishop, who, with other his fellow-laborers, by sound doctrine and gentle dealing soon recured them of their second relapse.

In Kent, Ercombert, expiring, was succeeded by his son Ecbert. In whose fourth year, by means of Theodore, a learned Greekish monk of Tarsus, whom Pope Vitalian had ordained Archbishop of Canterbury, the Greek and Latin tongue with other liberal arts—arithmetic, music, astronomy, and the like—began first to flourish among the Saxons, as did also the whole land, under potent and religious kings, more than ever before, as Bede affirms, till his own days.[2]

[1] *Prose Works* 5. 262-3.
[2] *Ibid.* 5. 287-8.

Thus they who of late were extolled as our greatest deliverers and had the people wholly at their devotion, by so discharging their trust as we see, did not only weaken and unfit themselves to be dispensers of what liberty they pretended, but unfitted also the people, now grown worse and more disordinate, to receive or to digest any liberty at all. For stories teach us that liberty sought out of season, in a corrupt and degenerate age, brought Rome itself to a farther slavery; for liberty hath a sharp and double edge, fit only to be handled by just and virtuous men; to bad and dissolute it becomes a mischief unwieldy in their own hands; neither is it completely given but by them who have the happy skill to know what is grievance, and unjust to a people, and how to remove it wisely; what good laws are wanting, and how to frame them substantially, that good men may enjoy the freedom which they merit, and the bad the curb which they need. But to do this, and to know these exquisite proportions, the heroic wisdom which is required surmounted far the principles of these narrow politicians. What wonder, then, if they sunk, as these unfortunate Britons before them, entangled and oppressed with things too hard and generous above their strain and temper?

For Britain, to speak a truth not often spoken, as it is a land fruitful enough of men stout and courageous in war, so it is naturally not over-fertile of men able to govern justly and prudently in peace, trusting only in their mother-wit; who consider not justly that civility, prudence, love of the public good more than of money or vain honor, are to this soil in a manner outlandish; grow not here, but in minds well-implanted with solid and elaborate breeding, too impolitic else and rude, if not headstrong, and intractable to the industry and virtue either of executing or understanding true civil government; valiant indeed, and prosperous to win a field, but to know the end and reason of winning, unjudicious and unwise; in good or bad success alike unteachable. For the sun, which we want, ripens wits as well as fruits; and, as wine and oil are imported to us from abroad, so must ripe understanding, and many civil virtues, be imported into our minds from foreign writings, and examples of best ages; we shall else miscarry still, and come short in the attempts of any great enterprise.

Hence did their victories prove as fruitless as their losses dangerous, and left them, still conquering, under the same grievances that men suffer conquered; which was, indeed, unlikely to go otherwise, unless men more than vulgar, bred up as few of them were in the knowledge of ancient and illustrious deeds, invincible against many and vain titles, impartial to friendships and relations, had conducted their affairs; but then, from the chapman to the retailer, many whose ignorance was more audacious than the rest were admitted with all their sordid rudiments to bear no mean sway among them, both in Church and State.[1]

The causes of these calamities and the ruin of that kingdom, Alcuin, a learned monk living in those days, attributes, in several epistles, and well may, to the general ignorance and decay of learning, which crept in among them after the death of Bede and of Ecbert the Archbishop; their neglect of breeding up youth in the Scriptures, the spruce and gay apparel of their priests and nuns, discovering their vain and wanton minds. Examples are also read, even in Bede's days, of their wanton deeds.[2]

The Saxons were now full as wicked as the Britons were at their arrival, broken with luxury and sloth, either secular or superstitious; for, laying aside the exercise of arms and the study of all virtuous knowledge, some betook them to over-worldly, or vicious, practice, others to religious idleness and solitude, which brought forth nothing but vain and delusive visions.[3]

Then began the English to lay aside their own ancient customs, and in many things to imitate French manners—the great peers

[1] *Prose Works* 5. 239–40.
[2] *Ibid.* 5. 307.
[3] *Ibid.* 5. 309.

to speak French in their houses, in French to write their bills and letters, as a great piece of gentility, ashamed of their own—a presage of their subjection shortly to that people whose fashions and language they affected so slavishly.[1]

Thus the English, while they agreed not about the choice of their native king, were constrained to take the yoke of an outlandish conqueror. With what minds and by what course of life they had fitted themselves for this servitude, William of Malmesbury spares not to lay open. Not a few years before the Normans came, the clergy, though in Edward the Confessor's days, had lost all good literature and religion, scarce able to read and understand their Latin service; he was a miracle, to others, who knew his grammar. The monks went clad in fine stuffs, and made no difference what they eat; which, though in itself no fault, yet to their consciences was irreligious. The great men, given to gluttony and dissolute life, made a prey of the common people; . . . the meaner sort, tippling together night and day, spent all they had in drunkenness, attended with other vices which effeminate men's minds. Whence it came to pass that, carried on with fury and rashness more than any true fortitude or skill of war, they gave to William their conqueror so easy a conquest. Not but that some few of all sorts were much better among them; but such was the generality. And, as the long-suffering of God permits bad men to enjoy prosperous days with the good, so His severity oft-times exempts not good men from their share in evil times with the bad.

If these were the causes of such misery and thraldom to those our ancestors, with what better close can be concluded than here in fit season to remember this age, in the midst of her security, to fear from like vices, without amendment, the revolution of like calamities?[2]

[1] *Ibid.* 5. 375.
[2] *Ibid.* 5. 392–3.

From Milton's *Commonplace Book.*

Mores Gentium

A dangerous thing, and an ominous thing, to imitate with earnestness the fashions of neighbor nations. So the English ran madding after the French in Edward Confessor's time;. . . God turn the omen from these days.[1]

From *Paradise Lost* (1667).

'Since thy original lapse, true liberty
Is lost, which always with right reason dwells
Twinned, and from her hath no dividual being.
Reason in Man obscured, or not obeyed,
Immediately inordinate desires
And upstart passions catch the government
From reason, and to servitude reduce
Man, till then free. Therefore, since he permits
Within himself unworthy powers to reign
Over free reason, God, in judgment just,
Subjects him from without to violent lords
Who oft as undeservedly enthral
His outward freedom.'[2]

'Thus will this latter, as the former world,
Still tend from bad to worse, till God at last,
Wearied with their iniquities, withdraw
His presence from among them, and avert
His holy eyes; resolving from thenceforth
To leave them to their own polluted ways,
And one peculiar nation to select
From all the rest, of whom to be invoked.'[3]

'The race elect
Safe towards Canaan, from the shore, advance
Through the wild Desert—not the readiest way;
Lest, entering on the Canaanite alarmed,
War terrify them inexpert, and fear
Return them back to Egypt, choosing rather
Inglorious life with servitude; for life

[1] *Commonplace Book*, p. 180.
[2] *Paradise Lost* 12. 83–95.
[3] *Ibid.* 12. 105–12.

To noble and ignoble is more sweet
Untrained in arms, where rashness leads not on.
This also shall they gain by their delay
In the wide wilderness: there they shall found
Their government, and their great Senate choose
Through the twelve tribes, to rule by laws ordained.
God, from the Mount of Sinai, whose gray top
Shall tremble, He descending, will Himself
In thunder, lightning, and loud trumpet's sound,
Ordain them laws; part, such as appertain
To civil justice; part, religious rites
Of sacrifice, informing them, by types
And shadows, of that destined Seed to bruise
The Serpent, by what means He shall achieve
Mankind's deliverance. But the voice of God
To mortal ear is dreadful; they beseech
That Moses might report to them His will,
And terror cease; he grants what they besought,
Instructed that to God is no access
Without Mediator, whose high office now
Moses in figure bears, to introduce
One greater, of Whose day he shall foretell,
And all the Prophets, in their age, the times
Of great Messiah shall sing. Thus laws and rites
Established, such delight hath God in men
Obedient to His will, that He vouchsafes
Among them to set up His tabernacle—
The Holy One with mortal men to dwell.
By His prescript a sanctuary is framed
Of cedar, overlaid with gold; therein
An ark, and in the ark His testimony,
The records of His covenant; over these
A mercy-seat of gold, between the wings
Of two bright Cherubim; before Him burn
Seven lamps, as in a zodiac representing
The heavenly fires. Over the tent a cloud
Shall rest by day, a fiery gleam by night,
Save when they journey; and at length they come,
Conducted by His Angel, to the land
Promised to Abraham and his seed.'[1]

[1] *Ibid.* 12. 214–60.

12. THE KNOWLEDGE OF GOD, AND TRUE RELIGION

THE NATURE AND IMPORTANCE OF THE SUBJECT

From *Of Reformation in England* (1641).

Amidst those deep and retired thoughts, which, with every man Christianly instructed, ought to be most frequent of God and of His miraculous ways and works amongst men, and of our religion and works to be performed to Him—after the story of our Saviour Christ, suffering to the lowest bent of weakness in the flesh, and presently triumphing to the highest pitch of glory in the spirit, which drew up His body also; till we in both be united to Him in the revelation of His kingdom—I do not know of anything more worthy to take up the whole passion of pity on the one side and joy on the other than to consider, first, the foul and sudden corruption, and then, after many a tedious age, the long-deferred but much more wonderful and happy reformation, of the Church in these latter days. Sad it is to think how that doctrine of the Gospel, planted by teachers divinely inspired, and by them winnowed and sifted from the chaff of overdated ceremonies, and refined to such a spiritual height and temper of purity and knowledge of the Creator that the body, with all the circumstances of time and place, were purified by the affections of the regenerate soul, and nothing left impure but sin—faith needing not the weak and fallible office of the senses to be either the ushers or interpreters of heavenly mysteries, save where our Lord Himself in His sacraments ordained—that such a doctrine should, through the grossness and blindness of her professors, and the fraud of deceivable traditions, drag so downwards as to backslide one way into the Jewish beggary of old cast-rudiments, and stumble forward another way into the new-vomited paganism of sensual idolatry, attributing purity or impurity to things indifferent, that they might bring the inward acts of the spirit to the outward and customary eye-service of the body.[1]

But to dwell no longer in characterizing the depravities of the Church, and how they sprung, and how they took increase—when I recall to mind, at last, after so many dark ages wherein the huge overshadowing train of Error had almost swept all the stars out of the firmament of the Church, how the bright and blissful Reformation (by divine power) struck through the black and settled night of ignorance and anti-Christian tyranny, methinks a sovereign and reviving joy must needs rush into the bosom of him that reads or hears, and the sweet odor of the returning Gospel imbathe his soul with the fragrancy of Heaven. Then was the sacred Bible sought out of the dusty corners where profane falsehood and neglect had thrown it, the schools opened, divine and human learning raked out of the embers of forgotten tongues, the princes and cities trooping apace to the new-erected banner of salvation.[2]

From *The Christian Doctrine.*

If I were to say that I had devoted myself to the study of the Christian religion because nothing else can so effectually rescue the lives and minds of men from those two detestable curses, slavery and superstition, I should seem to have acted rather from a regard to my highest earthly comforts than from a religious motive. But since it is only to the individual faith of each that the Deity has opened the way of eternal salvation, and as He requires that he who would be saved should have a personal belief of his own, I resolved not to repose on the faith or judgment of others in matters relating to God; but, on the one hand, having taken the grounds of my faith from divine revelation alone, and on the other, having neglected nothing which

[1] *Prose Works* 2. 364–5.
[2] *Ibid.* 2. 366–7.

287

depended on my own industry, I thought fit to scrutinize and ascertain for myself the several points of my religious belief, by the most careful perusal and meditation of the Holy Scriptures themselves. . . .

I entered upon an assiduous course of study in my youth, beginning with the books of the Old and New Testament in their original languages, and going diligently through a few of the shorter systems of divines, in imitation of whom I was in the habit of classing under certain heads whatever passages of Scripture occurred for extraction, to be made use of hereafter as occasion might require. At length I resorted with increased confidence to some of the more copious theological treatises, and to the examination of the arguments advanced by the conflicting parties respecting certain disputed points of faith. But, to speak the truth with freedom as well as candor, I was concerned to discover in many instances adverse reasonings either evaded by wretched shifts, or attempted to be refuted, rather speciously than with solidity, by an affected display of formal sophisms, or by a constant recourse to the quibbles of the grammarians; while what was most pertinaciously espoused as the true doctrine seemed often defended, with more vehemence than strength of argument, by misconstructions of Scripture, or by the hasty deduction of erroneous inferences. Owing to these causes, the truth was sometimes as strenuously opposed as if it had been an error or a heresy —while errors and heresies were substituted for the truth, and valued rather from deference to custom and the spirit of party than from the authority of Scripture. . . .

I deemed it therefore safest and most advisable to compile for myself, by my own labor and study, some original treatise which should be always at hand, derived solely from the Word of God itself, and executed with all possible fidelity—seeing that I could have no wish to practise any imposition on myself in such a matter. . . .

It was also evident to me that, in religion as in other things, the offers of God were all directed, not to an indolent credulity, but to constant diligence and to an unwearied search after truth; and that more than I was aware of still remained which required to be more rigidly examined by the rule of Scripture and reformed after a more accurate model. I so far satisfied myself in the prosecution of this plan as at length to trust that I had discovered, with regard to religion, what was matter of belief, and what only matter of opinion. It was also a great solace to me to have compiled, by God's assistance, a precious aid for my faith—or rather to have laid up for myself a treasure which would be a provision for my future life, and would remove from my mind all grounds of hesitation, as often as it behoved me to render an account of the principles of my belief.[1]

The Christian Doctrine is that divine revelation disclosed in various ages by Christ (though He was not known under that name in the beginning) concerning the nature and worship of the Deity, for the promotion of the glory of God, and the salvation of mankind. . . .

This doctrine . . . is to be obtained, not from the schools of the philosophers, nor from the laws of man, but from the Holy Scriptures alone, under the guidance of the Holy Spirit.[2]

Christian doctrine is comprehended under two divisions—Faith, or the knowledge of God, and Love, or the worship of God. . . . These two divisions, though they are distinct in their own nature, and put asunder for the convenience of teaching, cannot be separated in practice. . . . Besides, obedience and love are always the best guides to knowledge, and often lead the way from small beginnings to a greater and more flourishing degree of proficiency. . . .

It must be observed that Faith in this division does not mean the habit of believing, but the things to be habitually believed.[3]

[1] *Prose Works* 4. 1–4.
[2] *Ibid.* 4. 10–1.
[3] *Ibid.* 4. 12–3.

THE DEITY

From *The Christian Doctrine*.

Though there be not a few who deny the existence of God,
. . . yet the Deity has imprinted upon the human mind so
many unquestionable tokens of Himself, and so many traces of
Him are apparent throughout the whole of nature, that no one in
his senses can remain ignorant of the truth. . . . There can
be no doubt but that everything in the world, by the beauty of its
order, and the evidence of a determinate and beneficial purpose
which pervades it, testifies that some supreme efficient Power
must have pre-existed, by which the whole was ordained for a
specific end.

There are some who pretend that nature or fate is this supreme
power. But the very name of 'nature' implies that it must owe its
birth to some prior agent, or, to speak properly, signifies in itself
nothing; but means either the essence of a thing, or that general
law which is the origin of everything, and under which everything acts. On the other hand, fate can be nothing but a divine
decree emanating from some almighty power.

Further, those who attribute the creation of every thing to
nature must necessarily associate chance with nature as a joint
divinity; so that they gain nothing by this theory except that, in
the place of that one God Whom they cannot tolerate, they are
obliged, however reluctantly, to substitute two sovereign rulers
of affairs who must almost always be in opposition to each other.
In short, many visible proofs, the verification of numberless
predictions, a multitude of wonderful works, have compelled all
nations to believe either that God or that some evil power whose
name was unknown presided over the affairs of the world. Now,
that evil should prevail over good, and be the true supreme power,
is as unmeet as it is incredible. Hence it follows, as a necessary
consequence, that God exists.

Again, the existence of God is further proved by that feeling,
whether we term it conscience or right reason, which even in the
worst of characters is not altogether extinguished. If there were

no God, there would be no distinction between right and wrong; the estimate of virtue and vice would entirely depend on the blind opinion of men. None would follow virtue, none would be restrained from vice, by any sense of shame or fear of the laws, unless conscience or right reason did from time to time convince every one, however unwilling, of the existence of God, the Lord and Ruler of all things, to Whom, sooner or later, each must give an account of his own actions, whether good or bad. . . .

No one, however, can have right thoughts of God, with nature or reason alone as his guide, independent of the Word, or message of God.[1]

From *Paradise Lost* (1667).

> 'Fair Angel, thy desire, which tends to know
> The works of God, thereby to glorify
> The great Work-master, leads to no excess
> That reaches blame, but rather merits praise
> The more it seems excess, that led thee hither
> From thy empyreal mansion thus alone,
> To witness with thine eyes what some perhaps,
> Contented with report, hear only in Heaven;
> For wonderful indeed are all His works,
> Pleasant to know, and worthiest to be all
> Had in remembrance always with delight!
> But what created mind can comprehend
> Their number, or the wisdom infinite
> That brought them forth, but hid their causes deep?'[2]

> 'These are Thy glorious works, Parent of good,
> Almighty! Thine this universal frame,
> Thus wondrous fair: Thyself how wondrous then!
> Unspeakable! Who sitt'st above these heavens,
> To us invisible, or dimly seen
> In these Thy lowest works; yet these declare
> Thy goodness beyond thought, and power divine.'[3]

From *The Christian Doctrine.*

When we speak of knowing God, it must be understood with reference to the imperfect comprehension of man; for to know

[1] *Prose Works* 4. 13–6.
[2] *Paradise Lost* 3. 694–707. [3] *Ibid.* 5. 153–9.

God as He really is, far transcends the powers of man's thoughts, much more of his perception. . . . Our safest way is to form in our minds such a conception of God as shall correspond with His own delineation and representation of Himself in the sacred writings. For, granting that, both in the literal and figurative descriptions of God, He is exhibited not as He really is, but in such a manner as may be within the scope of our comprehensions; yet we ought to entertain such a conception of Him as He, in condescending to accommodate Himself to our capacities, has shown that He desires we should conceive. For it is on this very account that He has lowered Himself to our level—lest, in our flights above the reach of human understanding, and beyond the written word of Scripture, we should be tempted to indulge in vague cogitations and subtleties.[1]

From *Paradise Lost* (1667).

> Others apart sat on a hill retired,
> In thoughts more elevate, and reasoned high
> Of providence, foreknowledge, will, and fate,
> Fixed fate, free will, foreknowledge absolute,
> And found no end, in wandering mazes lost.
> Of good and evil much they argued then,
> Of happiness and final misery,
> Passion and apathy, and glory and shame,
> Vain wisdom all, and false philosophy!
> Yet with a pleasing sorcery could charm
> Pain for a while or anguish, and excite
> Fallacious hope, or arm the obdured breast
> With stubborn patience as with triple steel.[2]

From *The Christian Doctrine*.

This is the whole that is revealed concerning the generation of the Son of God. Whoever wishes to be wiser than this becomes foiled in his pursuit after wisdom, entangled in the deceitfulness

[1] *Prose Works* 4. 16–7.
[2] *Paradise Lost* 2. 557–69.

of vain philosophy, or rather of sophistry, and involved in darkness. . . . Let us, then, discard reason in sacred matters, and follow the doctrine of Holy Scripture exclusively.[1]

The name of Spirit is . . . frequently applied to God and angels, and to the human mind.[2]

Who this Holy Spirit is, and whence He comes, and what are His offices, no one has taught us more explicitly than the Son of God Himself. . . . If it be the divine will that a doctrine which is to be understood and believed as one of the primary articles of our faith should be delivered without obscurity or confusion, and explained, as is fitting, in clear and precise terms—if it be certain that particular care ought to be taken in everything connected with religion, lest the objection urged by Christ against the Samaritans should be applicable to us—'Ye worship ye know not what' (John 4.22)—if our Lord's saying should be held sacred wherever points of faith are in question—'We know what we worship'—the particulars which have been stated seem to contain all that we are capable of knowing, or are required to know, respecting the Holy Spirit, inasmuch as revelation has declared nothing else expressly on the subject.[3]

IDEAL HUMANITY
From *The Christian Doctrine.*

Man having been created after this manner, it is said, as a consequence, that *man became a living soul*; whence it may be inferred (unless we had rather take the heathen writers for our teachers respecting the nature of the soul) that man is a living being, intrinsically and properly one, and individual, not compound or separable, not, according to the common opinion, made up and framed of two distinct and different natures, as of soul and body—but that the whole man is soul, and the soul man, that is to say a body, or substance individual, animated, sensitive, and rational; and that the breath of life was neither a part of the

[1] *Prose Works* 4. 86–7.
[2] *Ibid.* 4. 151.   [3] *Ibid.* 4. 156–8.

divine essence, nor the soul itself, but as it were an inspiration of
some divine virtue fitted for the exercise of life and reason, and
infused into the organic body; for man himself, the whole man,
when finally created, is called in express terms *a living soul*.[1]

From *Paradise Lost* (1667).

> Two of far nobler shape, erect and tall,
> God-like erect, with native honor clad
> In naked majesty, seemed lords of all,
> And worthy seemed; for in their looks divine
> The image of their glorious Maker shone,
> Truth, wisdom, sanctitude severe and pure—
> Severe, but in true filial freedom placed;
> Whence true authority in men; though both
> Not equal, as their sex not equal seemed;
> For contemplation he and valor formed,
> For softness she, and sweet attractive grace.
> He for God only, she for God in him.[2]
>   Them thus employed beheld
> With pity Heaven's high King, and to Him called
> Raphael, the sociable Spirit, that deigned
> To travel with Tobias, and secured
> His marriage with the seven-times-wedded maid.
> 'Raphael,' said He, 'thou hear'st what stir on Earth
> Satan, from Hell 'scaped through the darksome gulf,
> Hath raised in Paradise, and how disturbed
> This night the human pair; how he designs
> In them at once to ruin all mankind.
> Go, therefore, half this day, as friend with friend,
> Converse with Adam, in what bower or shade
> Thou find'st him from the heat of noon retired
> To respite his day-labor with repast
> Or with repose; and such discourse bring on
> As may advise him of his happy state—
> Happiness in his power left free to will
> Left to his own free will, his will though free
> Yet mutable; whence warn him to beware
> He swerve not, too secure. Tell him withal

[1] *Prose Works* 4. 188.
[2] *Paradise Lost* 4. 288–99.

His danger, and from whom; what enemy,
Late fallen himself from Heaven, is plotting now
The fall of others from like state of bliss.
By violence? no, for that shall be withstood;
But by deceit and lies. This let him know,
Lest, wilfully transgressing, he pretend
Surprisal, unadmonished, unforewarned.'[1]

Thus when with meats and drinks they had sufficed,
Not burdened, nature, sudden mind arose
In Adam not to let the occasion pass,
Given him by this great conference, to know
Of things above his world, and of their being
Who dwell in Heaven, whose excellence he saw
Transcend his own so far, whose radiant forms—
Divine effulgence—whose high power, so far
Exceeded human; and his wary speech
Thus to the empyreal minister he framed:
   'Inhabitant with God, now know I well
Thy favor, in this honor done to Man,
Under whose lowly roof thou hast vouchsafed
To enter, and these earthly fruits to taste,
Food not of Angels, yet accepted so
As that more willingly thou couldst not seem
At Heaven's high feasts to have fed: yet what compare?'
To whom the winged Hierarch replied:
   'O Adam, One Almighty is, from Whom
All things proceed, and up to Him return,
If not depraved from good, created all
Such to perfection, one first matter all,
Endued with various forms, various degrees
Of substance, and in things that live, of life;
But more refined, more spiritous and pure,
As nearer to Him placed or nearer tending,
Each in their several active spheres assigned,
Till body up to spirit work, in bounds
Proportioned to each kind. So from the root
Springs lighter the green stalk, from thence the leaves
More aery, last the bright consummate flower
Spirits odorous breathes: flowers and their fruit,
Man's nourishment, by gradual scale sublimed,

---

[1] *Ibid.* 5. 219-45.

To vital spirits aspire, to animal,
To intellectual; give both life and sense,
Fancy, and understanding; whence the soul
Reason receives, and reason is her being,
Discursive, or intuitive: discourse
Is oftest yours, the latter most is ours,
Differing but in degree, of kind the same.
Wonder not, then, what God for you saw good
If I refuse not, but convert, as you,
To proper substance. Time may come when men
With angels may participate, and find
No inconvenient diet, nor too light fare;
And from these corporal nutriments, perhaps,
Your bodies may at last turn all to spirit,
Improved by tract of time, and winged ascend
Ethereal, as we; or may at choice
Here or in heavenly paradises dwell,
If ye be found obedient, and retain
Unalterably firm His love entire
Whose progeny you are. Meanwhile enjoy
Your fill what happiness this happy state
Can comprehend, incapable of more.'
    To whom the Patriarch of Mankind replied:
'O favorable Spirit, propitious guest,
Well hast thou taught the way that might direct
Our knowledge, and the scale of Nature set
From centre to circumference, whereon,
In contemplation of created things,
By steps we may ascend to God.'[1]

                    And now [Adam,]
Led on, yet sinless, with desire to know
What nearer might concern him—how this World
Of heaven and earth conspicuous first began;
When, and whereof, created; for what cause;
What within Eden, or without, was done
Before his memory—as one whose drought,
Yet scarce allayed, still eyes the current stream,
Whose liquid murmur heard new thirst excites—
Proceeded thus to ask his heavenly guest:
'Great things, and full of wonder in our ears,

---

[1] *Paradise Lost* 5. 451–512.

Far differing from this World, thou hast revealed,
Divine interpreter! by favor sent
Down from the empyrean to forewarn
Us timely of what might else have been our loss,
Unknown, which human knowledge could not reach;
For which to the infinitely Good we owe
Immortal thanks, and His admonishment
Receive with solemn purpose to observe
Immutably His sovran will, the end
Of what we are. But, since thou hast vouchsafed
Gently, for our instruction, to impart
Things above earthly thought, which yet concerned
Our knowing, as to highest Wisdom seemed,
Deign to descend now lower, and relate
What may no less perhaps avail us known—
How first began this Heaven which we behold
Distant so high, with moving fires adorned
Innumerable; and this which yields or fills
All space, the ambient air, wide interfused,
Embracing round this florid Earth; what cause
Moved the Creator, in His holy rest
Through all eternity, so late to build
In Chaos; and the work begun, how soon
Absolved; if unforbid thou may'st unfold
What we not to explore the secrets ask
Of His eternal empire, but the more
To magnify His works the more we know.'[1]

Thus Adam his illustrious guest besought;
And thus the godlike Angel answered mild:
'This also thy request, with caution asked,
Obtain; though to recount almighty works
What words or tongue of Seraph can suffice,
Or heart of man suffice to comprehend?
Yet what thou canst attain, which best may serve
To glorify the Maker, and infer
Thee also happier, shall not be withheld
Thy hearing. Such commission from above
I have received, to answer thy desire
Of knowledge within bounds; beyond abstain
To ask, nor let thine own inventions hope

[1] *Ibid.* 7. 60–97.

Things not revealed, which the invisible King,
Only omniscient, hath suppressed in night,
To none communicable in Earth or Heaven:
Enough is left besides, to search and know.
But knowledge is as food, and needs no less
Her temperance over appetite, to know
In measure what the mind may well contain;
Oppresses else with surfeit, and soon turns
Wisdom to folly, as nourishment to wind.'[1]

'Now Heaven in all her glory shone, and rolled
Her motions, as the great First Mover's hand
First wheeled their course; Earth, in her rich attire
Consummate, lovely smiled; air, water, earth,
By fowl, fish, beast, was flown, was swum, was walked,
Frequent; and of the sixth day yet remained.
There wanted yet the master-work, the end
Of all yet done—a creature who, not prone
And brute as other creatures, but endued
With sanctity of reason, might erect
His stature, and upright with front serene
Govern the rest, self-knowing, and from thence
Magnanimous to correspond with Heaven,
But grateful to acknowledge whence his good
Descends; thither with heart, and voice, and eyes
Directed in devotion, to adore
And worship God supreme, Who made him chief
Of all His works. Therefore the omnipotent
Eternal Father (for where is not He
Present?) thus to His Son audibly spake:
"Let Us make now Man in Our image, Man
In Our similitude, and let them rule
Over the fish and fowl of sea and air,
Beast of the field, and over all the earth,
And every creeping thing that creeps the ground!"
This said, He formed thee, Adam, thee, O Man,
Dust of the ground, and in thy nostrils breathed
The breath of life; in His own image He
Created thee, in the image of God
Express, and thou becam'st a living soul.'[2]

[1] *Paradise Lost* 7. 109-30.
[2] *Ibid.* 7. 499-528.

'And thy request think now fulfilled, that asked
How first this world and face of things began,
And what before thy memory was done
From the beginning, that posterity,
Informed by thee, might know. If else thou seek'st
Aught, not surpassing human measure, say.'[1]

The Angel ended, and in Adam's ear
So charming left his voice that he a while
Thought him still speaking, still stood fixed to hear;
Then, as new-waked, thus gratefully replied:
'What thanks sufficient, or what recompense
Equal, have I to render thee, divine
Historian, who thus largely hast allayed
The thirst I had of knowledge, and vouchsafed
This friendly condescension to relate
Things else by me unsearcheable—now heard
With wonder, but delight, and, as is due,
With glory attributed to the high
Creator? Something yet of doubt remains
Which only thy solution can resolve.'[2]

And Raphael now to Adam's doubt proposed
Benevolent and facile thus replied:
'To ask or search I blame thee not; for Heaven
Is as the Book of God before thee set,
Wherein to read His wondrous works, and learn
His seasons, hours, or days, or months, or years.
This to attain, whether Heaven move or Earth
Imports not, if thou reckon right; the rest
From Man or Angel the great Architect
Did wisely to conceal, and not divulge
His secrets, to be scanned by them who ought
Rather admire. Or, if they list to try
Conjecture, He His fabric of the Heavens
Hath left to their disputes, perhaps to move
His laughter at their quaint opinions wide
Hereafter, when they come to model Heaven,
And calculate the stars; how they will wield
The mighty frame; how build, unbuild, contrive,

---

[1] *Ibid.* 7. 635-40.
[2] *Ibid.* 8. 1-14.

To save appearances; how gird the sphere
With centric and eccentric scribbled o'er,
Cycle and epicycle, orb in orb.
Already by thy reasoning this I guess,
Who art to lead thy offspring, and supposest
That bodies bright and greater should not serve
The less not bright, nor Heaven such journeys run,
Earth sitting still, when she alone receives
The benefit.'[1]

'And, for the Heaven's wide circuit, let it speak
The Maker's high magnificence, Who built
So spacious, and His line stretched out so far,
That Man may know he dwells not in his own—
An edifice too large for him to fill,
Lodged in a small partition, and the rest
Ordained for uses to his Lord best known.
The swiftness of those circles attribute,
Though numberless, to His omnipotence,
That to corporeal substances could add
Speed almost spiritual.'[2]

          'But this I urge,
Admitting motion in the Heavens, to show
Invalid that which thee to doubt it moved;
Not that I so affirm, though so it seem
To thee who hast thy dwelling here on Earth.
God, to remove His ways from human sense,
Placed Heaven from Earth so far, that earthly sight,
If it presume, might err in things too high,
And no advantage gain.'[3]

    'But whether thus these things, or whether not—
Whether the Sun, predominant in Heaven,
Rise on the Earth, or Earth rise on the Sun;
He from the east his flaming road begin,
Or she from west her silent course advance
With inoffensive pace that spinning sleeps
On her soft axle, while she paces even,
And bears thee soft with the smooth air along—
Solicit not thy thoughts with matters hid:

[1] *Paradise Lost* 8. 64–90.
[2] *Ibid.* 8. 100–110.
[3] *Ibid.* 8. 114–22.

Leave them to God above; Him serve and fear.
Of other creatures as Him pleases best,
Wherever placed, let Him dispose; joy thou
In what He gives to thee, this Paradise
And thy fair Eve; Heaven is for thee too high
To know what passes there. Be lowly wise;
Think only what concerns thee and thy being;
Dream not of other worlds, what creatures there
Live, in what state, condition, or degree—
Contented that thus far hath been revealed
Not of Earth only, but of highest Heaven.'
    To whom thus Adam, cleared of doubt, replied:
'How fully hast thou satisfied me, pure
Intelligence of Heaven, Angel serene,
And, freed from intricacies, taught to live
The easiest way, nor with perplexing thoughts
To interrupt the sweet of life, from which
God hath bid dwell far off all anxious cares,
And not molest us, unless we ourselves
Seek them with wandering thoughts, and notions vain!
But apt the mind or fancy is to rove
Unchecked, and of her roving is no end;
Till warned, or by experience taught, she learn
That not to know at large of things remote
From use, obscure and subtle, but to know
That which before us lies in daily life,
Is the prime wisdom: what is more is fume,
Or emptiness, or fond impertinence,
And renders us in things that most concern
Unpractised, unprepared, and still to seek.
Therefore from this high pitch let us descend
A lower flight, and speak of things at hand
Useful; whence, haply, mention may arise
Of something not unseasonable to ask,
By sufferance, and thy wonted favor, deigned.
Thee I have heard relating what was done
Ere my remembrance; now hear me relate
My story, which perhaps thou hast not heard.
And day is yet not spent; till then thou seest
How subtly to detain thee I devise,
Inviting thee to hear while I relate—

Fond, were it not in hope of thy reply.
For, while I sit with thee, I seem in Heaven;
And sweeter thy discourse is to my ear
Than fruits of palm-tree, pleasantest to thirst
And hunger both, from labor, at the hour
Of sweet repast. They satiate, and soon fill,
Though pleasant; but thy words, with grace divine
Imbued, bring to their sweetness no satiety.'
   To whom thus Raphael answered, heavenly meek:
'Nor are thy lips ungraceful, Sire of Men,
Nor tongue ineloquent; for God on thee
Abundantly His gifts hath also poured,
Inward and outward both, His image fair:
Speaking, or mute, all comeliness and grace
Attends thee, and each word, each motion, forms.
Nor less think we in Heaven of thee on Earth
Than of our fellow-servant, and inquire
Gladly into the ways of God with Man.'[1]

   So spake the godlike Power, and thus our Sire:
'For Man to tell how human life began
Is hard; for who himself beginning knew?
Desire with thee still longer to converse
Induced me. As new-waked from soundest sleep,
Soft on the flowery herb I found me laid,
In balmy sweat, which with his beams the sun
Soon dried, and on the reeking moisture fed,
Straight toward Heaven my wondering eyes I turned,
And gazed a while the ample sky, till, raised
By quick instinctive motion, up I sprung,
As thitherward endeavoring, and upright
Stood on my feet. About me round I saw
Hill, dale, and shady woods, and sunny plains,
And liquid lapse of murmuring streams; by these,
Creatures that lived and moved, and walked or flew,
Birds on the branches warbling; all things smiled;
With fragrance and with joy my heart o'erflowed.
Myself I then perused, and limb by limb
Surveyed, and sometimes went, and sometimes ran
With supple joints, as lively vigor led;

[1] *Paradise Lost* 8. 159–226.

But who I was, or where, or from what cause,
Knew not. To speak I tried, and forthwith spake;
My tongue obeyed and readily could name
Whate'er I saw. "Thou Sun," said I, "fair light,
And thou enlightened Earth, so fresh and gay,
Ye hills and dales, ye rivers, woods, and plains,
And ye that live and move, fair creatures, tell,
Tell, if ye saw, how came I thus, how here?
Not of myself; by some great Maker then,
In goodness and in power pre-eminent.
Tell me, how may I know Him, how adore,
From Whom I have that thus I move and live,
And feel that I am happier than I know!" [1]

'When suddenly stood at my head a dream,
Whose inward apparition gently moved
My fancy to believe I yet had being,
And lived. One came, methought, of shape divine,
And said: "Thy mansion wants thee, Adam; rise,
First Man, of men innumerable ordained
First father! called by thee, I come thy guide
To the Garden of bliss, thy seat prepared." [2]

                    'Here had new begun
My wandering, had not He, Who was my guide
Up hither from among the trees appeared,
Presence Divine. Rejoicing, but with awe,
In adoration at His feet I fell
Submiss. He reared me, and, "Whom thou sought'st I am,"
Said mildly, "Author of all this thou seest
Above, or round about thee, or beneath." [3]

'He ceased. I lowly answered: "To attain
The highth and depth of Thy eternal ways
All human thoughts come short, Supreme of Things!
Thou in Thyself art perfect, and in Thee
Is no deficience found." [4]

' "Thus far to try thee, Adam, I was pleased,
And find thee knowing not of beasts alone,

[1] *Ibid*. 8. 249-82.
[2] *Ibid*. 8. 292-9.
[3] *Ibid*. 8. 311-8.
[4] *Ibid*. 8. 412-6.

Which thou hast rightly named, but of thyself—
Expressing well the spirit within thee free,
My image, not imparted to the brute." '[1]
            'Love refines
The thoughts, and heart enlarges—hath his seat
In Reason, and is judicious, is the scale
By which to Heavenly love thou may'st ascend.'[2]
            'Love . . .
Leads up to Heaven, is both the way and guide.'[3]

From *The Christian Doctrine.*

Seeing, however, that man was made in the image of God,
and had the whole law of nature so implanted and innate in him
that he needed no precept to enforce its observance, it follows
that, if he received any additional commands, . . . these
commands formed no part of the law of nature, which is sufficient
of itself to teach whatever is agreeable to right reason—that
is to say, whatever is intrinsically good.[4]

FALLEN HUMANITY

From *The Christian Doctrine.*

After sin came death, as the calamity or punishment consequent
upon it. . . .

The second degree of death is called spiritual death; by which is
meant the loss of divine grace, and of that innate righteousness
wherein man in the beginning lived unto God. . . . They who
are delivered from it are said to be *regenerated*, to be *born again*,
and to be *created afresh;* which is the work of God alone, as will
be shown in the chapter on Regeneration.

This death consists, first, in the loss, or at least in the obscura-
tion to a great extent, of that right reason which enabled man to
discern the chief good, and in which consisted as it were the life
of the understanding. . . . It consists, secondly, in that deprivation of righteousness and liberty to do good and in that

[1] *Paradise Lost* 8. 437–41.
[2] *Ibid.* 8. 589–92.
[3] *Ibid.* 8. 612–3.
[4] *Prose Works* 4. 222.

slavish subjection to sin and the devil which constitutes, as it were, the death of the will.   .   .   .Lastly, sin is its own punishment, and produces, in its natural consequences, the death of the spiritual life—more especially, gross and habitual sin.[1]

From *Paradise Lost* (1667).

> Satiate at length,
> And heightened as with wine, jocund and boon,
> Thus to herself she pleasingly began:
> 'O sovran, virtuous, precious of all trees
> In Paradise! of operation blest
> To sapience, hitherto obscured, infamed,
> And thy fair fruit let hang, as to no end
> Created! but henceforth my early care,
> Not without song, each morning, and due praise,
> Shall tend thee, and the fertile burden ease
> Of thy full branches, offered free to all;
> Till, dieted by thee, I grow mature
> In knowledge, as the Gods who all things know;
> Though others envy what they cannot give—
> For, had the gift been theirs, it had not here
> Thus grown! Experience, next to thee I owe,
> Best guide: not following thee, I had remained
> In ignorance; thou open'st Wisdom's way,
> And giv'st access, though secret she retire.'[2]

> 'O Eve, in evil hour thou didst give ear
> To that false Worm, of whomsoever taught
> To counterfeit Man's voice—true in our fall,
> False in our promised rising; since our eyes
> Opened we find indeed, and find we know
> Both good and evil, good lost and evil got:
> Bad fruit of knowledge, if this be to know,
> Which leaves us naked thus, of honor void,
> Of innocence, of faith, of purity.'[3]

> Thus fenced, and, as they thought, their shame in part
> Covered, but not at rest or ease of mind,
> They sat them down to weep. Nor only tears
> Rained at their eyes, but high winds worse within

[1] *Ibid.* 4. 263–5.
[2] *Paradise Lost* 9. 792–810.
[3] *Ibid.* 9. 1067–75.

Began to rise, high passions—anger, hate,
Mistrust, suspicion, discord—and shook sore
Their inward state of mind, calm region once
And full of peace, now tossed and turbulent:
For Understanding ruled not, and the Will
Heard not her lore, both in subjection now
To sensual Appetite, who, from beneath
Usurping over sovran Reason, claimed
Superior sway.[1]

From *The Christian Doctrine*.

It cannot be denied, however, that some remnants of the divine image still exist in us, not wholly extinguished by this spiritual death. This is evident, not only from the wisdom and holiness of many of the heathen, manifested both in words and deeds, but also from what is said (Genesis 9.2): 'The dread of you shall be upon every beast of the earth.' . . . These vestiges of original excellence are visible, first, in the understanding (Psalm 19.1): 'The heavens declare the glory of God'—which could not be if man were incapable of hearing their voice.[2]

REGENERATION—THE TRUE OBJECT OF LEARNING

From *The Christian Doctrine*.

The calling of man is that natural mode of renovation whereby God the Father, according to His purpose in Christ, invites fallen man to a knowledge of the way in which He is to be propitiated and worshiped.[3]

The change which takes place in man, by reason of his calling, is that whereby the natural mind and will of man, being partially renewed by a divine impulse, are led to seek the knowledge of God, and, for the time, at least, undergo an alteration for the better.[4]

The intent of Supernatural Renovation is not only to restore man more completely than before to the use of his natural facul-

[1] *Paradise Lost* 9. 1119–31.
[2] *Prose Works* 4. 266.
[3] *Ibid.* 4. 319.
[4] *Ibid.* 4. 323.

ties as regards his power to form right judgment, and to exercise free will; but to create afresh, as it were, the inward man, and infuse from above new and supernatural faculties into the minds of the renovated. . . .

Regeneration is that change operated by the Word and the Spirit, whereby, the old man being destroyed, the inward man is regenerated by God after His own image, in all the faculties of his mind, insomuch that he becomes as it were a new creature, and the whole man is sanctified both in body and soul, for the service of God and the performance of good works.[1]

The primary functions of the new life are comprehension of spiritual things, and love of holiness. And, as the power of exercising these functions was weakened, and in a manner destroyed, by the spiritual death, so is the understanding restored in great part to its primitive clearness, and the will to its primitive liberty, by the new spiritual life in Christ.

The comprehension of spiritual things is a habit or condition of mind produced by God, whereby the natural ignorance of those who believe and are ingrafted in Christ is removed, and their understandings enlightened for the perception of heavenly things, so that, by the teaching of God, they know all that is necessary for eternal salvation and the true happiness of life. . . . In the present life, however, we can only attain to an imperfect comprehension of spiritual things.[2]

From *Paradise Lost* (1667).

> 'Haste thee, and from the Paradise of God
> Without remorse drive out the sinful pair,
> From hallowed ground the unholy, and denounce
> To them, and to their progeny, from thence
> Perpetual banishment. Yet, lest they faint
> At the sad sentence rigorously urged
> (For I behold them softened, and with tears
> Bewailing their excess), all terror hide.

[1] *Ibid.* 4. 327–8.
[2] *Ibid.* 4. 343–4.

If patiently thy bidding they obey,
Dismiss them not disconsolate; reveal
To Adam what shall come in future days,
As I shall thee enlighten; intermix
My covenant in the Woman's seed renewed.
So send them forth, though sorrowing, yet in peace.'[1]

'Yet doubt not but in valley and in plain
God is, as here, and will be found alike
Present, and of His presence many a sign
Still following thee, still compassing thee round
With goodness and paternal love, His face
Express, and of His steps the track divine.
Which that thou may'st believe, and be confirmed
Ere thou from hence depart, know I am sent
To show thee what shall come in future days
To thee, and to thy offspring. Good with bad
Expect to hear, supernal grace contending
With sinfulness of men; thereby to learn
True patience, and to temper joy with fear
And pious sorrow, equally inured
By moderation either state to bear,
Prosperous or adverse: so shalt thou lead
Safest thy life, and best prepared endure
Thy mortal passage when it comes. Ascend
This hill; let Eve (for I have drenched her eyes)
Here sleep below while thou to foresight wak'st,
As once thou slept'st, while she to life was formed.'
To whom thus Adam gratefully replied:
'Ascend; I follow thee, safe guide, the path
Thou lead'st me, and to the hand of Heaven submit,
However chastening; to the evil turn
My obvious breast, arming to overcome
By suffering, and earn rest from labor won,
If so I may attain.' So both ascend
In the visions of God. It was a hill,
Of Paradise the highest, from whose top
The hemisphere of Earth in clearest ken
Stretched out to the amplest reach of prospect lay.
Not higher that hill, nor wider looking round,

[1] *Paradise Lost* ii. 104–17.

Whereon for different cause the Tempter set
Our second Adam, in the wilderness,
To show Him all Earth's kingdoms and their glory.[1]

    'Judge not what is best
By pleasure, though to Nature seeming meet,
Created, as thou art, to nobler end,
Holy and pure, conformity divine.
Those tents thou saw'st so pleasant were the tents
Of wickedness, wherein shall dwell his race
Who slew his brother: studious they appear
Of arts that polish life, inventors rare;
Unmindful of their Maker, though His Spirit
Taught them; but they His gifts acknowledged none.'[2]

    Here Adam interposed: 'O sent from Heaven,
Enlightener of my darkness, gracious things
Thou hast revealed, those chiefly which concern
Just Abraham and his seed. Now first I find
Mine eyes true opening, and my heart much eased,
Erewhile perplexed with thoughts what would become
Of me and all mankind; but now I see
His day, in whom all nations shall be blest—
Favor unmerited by me, who sought
Forbidden knowledge by forbidden means.'[3]

    'He to His own a Comforter will send,
The promise of the Father, Who shall dwell,
His Spirit, within them, and the law of faith
Working through love upon their hearts shall write,
To guide them in all truth, and also arm
With spiritual armor, able to resist
Satan's assaults, and quench his fiery darts—
What man can do against them, not afraid,
Though to the death; against such cruelties
With inward consolations recompensed,
And oft supported so as shall amaze
Their proudest persecutors. For the Spirit,
Poured first on His Apostles, whom He sends
To evangelize the nations, then on all
Baptized, shall them with wondrous gifts endue

[1] *Ibid.* 11. 349–84.
[2] *Ibid.* 11. 603–12.
[3] *Ibid.* 12. 270–9.

To speak all tongues, and do all miracles,
As did their Lord before them. Thus they win
Great numbers of each nation to receive
With joy the tidings brought from Heaven: at length,
Their ministry performed, and race well run,
Their doctrine and their story written left,
They die; but in their room, as they forewarn,
Wolves shall succeed for teachers, grievous wolves,
Who all the sacred mysteries of Heaven
To their own vile advantages shall turn
Of lucre and ambition, and the truth
With superstitions and traditions taint,
Left only in those written records pure,
Though not but by the Spirit understood.'[1]

From *Of True Religion* (1673).

True religion is the true worship and service of God, learned and believed from the Word of God only. No man or angel can know how God would be worshiped and served unless God reveal it; He hath revealed and taught it us in the Holy Scriptures by inspired ministers, and in the Gospel by His own Son and His apostles, with strictest command to reject all other traditions or additions whatsoever.[2]

From *The Christian Doctrine.*

The Mosaic law was a written code consisting of many precepts, intended for the Israelites alone, with a promise of life to such as should keep them, and a curse on such as should be disobedient; to the end that they, being led thereby to an acknowledgment of the depravity of mankind, and consequently of their own, might have recourse to the righteousness of the promised Saviour; and that they, and in process of time all other nations, might be led under the Gospel from the weak and servile rudiments of this elementary institution to the full strength of the new creature, and a manly liberty worthy the sons of God.[3]

[1] *Paradise Lost* 12. 486-514.
[2] *Prose Works* 2. 509.
[3] *Ibid.* 4. 379.

310

The Gospel is the new dispensation of the covenant of grace, far more excellent and perfect than the law; announced first obscurely by Moses and the prophets, afterwards in the clearest terms by Christ Himself and His apostles and evangelists, written since by the Holy Spirit in the hearts of believers, and ordained to continue even to the end of the world; containing a promise of eternal life to all in every nation who shall believe in Christ when revealed to them, and a threat of eternal death to such as shall not believe. [1]

The writings of the prophets, apostles, and evangelists, composed under divine inspiration, are called *The Holy Scriptures*. [2]

From all these passages it is evident that the use of the Scriptures is prohibited to no one; but that, on the contrary, they are adapted for the daily hearing or reading of all classes and orders of men. [3]

The Scriptures therefore, partly by reason of their own simplicity, and partly through the divine illumination, are plain and perspicuous in all things necessary to salvation, and adapted to the instruction even of the most unlearned, through the medium of diligent and constant reading. [4]

If, then, the Scriptures be in themselves so perspicuous, and sufficient of themselves 'to make men wise unto salvation through faith,' that 'the man of God may be perfect, thoroughly furnished unto all good works,' through what infatuation is it that even Protestant divines persist in darkening the most momentous truths of religion by intricate metaphysical comments, on the plea that such explanation is necessary; stringing together all the useless technicalities and empty distinctions of scholastic barbarism, for the purpose of elucidating those Scriptures which they are continually extolling as models of plainness? As if

[1] *Ibid.* 4. 382–3.
[2] *Ibid.* 4. 437.
[3] *Ibid.* 4. 439.
[4] *Ibid.* 4. 440.

Scripture, which possesses in itself the clearest light, and is sufficient for its own explanation, especially in matters of faith and holiness, required to have the simplicity of its divine truths more fully developed, and placed in a more distinct view, by illustrations drawn from the abstrusest of human sciences—falsely so-called. . . .

No passage of Scripture is to be interpreted in more than one sense; in the Old Testament, however, this sense is sometimes a compound of the historical and [the] typical. . . .

The requisites for the public interpretation of Scripture have been laid down by divines with much attention to usefulness, although they have not been observed with equal fidelity. They consist in knowledge of languages; inspection of the originals; examination of the context; care in distinguishing between literal and figurative expressions; consideration of cause and circumstance, of antecedents and consequents; mutual comparison of texts; and regard to the analogy of faith. Attention must also be paid to the frequent anomalies of syntax. . . . Lastly, no inferences from the text are to be admitted but such as follow necessarily and plainly from the words themselves, lest we should be constrained to receive what is not written for what is written, the shadow for the substance, the fallacies of human reasoning for the doctrines of God; for it is by the declarations of Scripture, and not by the conclusions of the schools, that our consciences are bound. . . .

Every believer has a right to interpret the Scriptures for himself, inasmuch as he has the Spirit for his guide, and the mind of Christ is in him. Nay, the expositions of the public interpreter can be of no use to him, except so far as they are confirmed by his own conscience. . . . The right of public interpretation for the benefit of others is possessed by all whom God has appointed apostles, or prophets, or evangelists, or pastors, or teachers . . . that is, by all who are endowed with the gift of teaching.[1]

---

[1] *Prose Works* 4. 441–4.

THE KNOWLEDGE OF GOD, AND TRUE RELIGION

From *The Doctrine and Discipline of Divorce* (1643).

If it be affirmed that God, as being Lord, may do what He will, yet we must know that God hath not two wills but one will, much less two contrary. If He once willed adultery should be sinful, and to be punished with death, all His omnipotence will not allow Him to will the allowance that His holiest people might, as it were by His own antinomy, or counter-statute, live unreproved in the same fact as He Himself esteemed it, according to our common explainers. The hidden ways of His providence we adore and search not; but the law is His revealed will, His complete, His evident and certain will; herein He appears to us as it were in human shape, enters into covenant with us, swears to keep it, binds Himself like a just lawgiver to His own prescriptions, gives Himself to be understood by men, judges and is judged, measures, and is commensurate to right reason, cannot require less of us in one cantle of His law than in another. His legal justice cannot be so fickle and so variable—sometimes like a devouring fire, and by and by connivant in the embers, or, if I may so say, oscitant and supine. The vigor of His law could no more remit than the hallowed fire upon His altar could be let go out. The lamps that burned before Him might need snuffing, but the light of His law—never.[1]

Rivetus, a diligent and learned writer, having well weighed what hath been written by those founders of dispense, and finding the small agreement among them, would fain work himself aloof these rocks and quicksands, and thinks it best to conclude that God certainly did dispense, but by some way to us unknown, and so to leave it. But to this I oppose that a Christian by no means ought to rest himself in such an ignorance, whereby so many absurdities will straight reflect both against the purity, justice, and wisdom of God, the end also both of law and Gospel, and the comparison of them both together. God indeed in some ways of His providence is high and secret past finding out; but, in the

[1] *Ibid.* 3. 222–3.

313

delivery and execution of His law, especially in the managing of a duty so daily and so familiar as this is whereof we reason, hath plain enough revealed Himself, and requires the observance thereof not otherwise than to the law of nature and equity imprinted in us seems correspondent. And He hath taught us to love and extol His laws, not only as they are His, but as they are just and good to every wise and sober understanding.[1]

We see, both by this and other places, that there is scarce any one saying in the Gospel but must be read with limitations and distinctions to be rightly understood; for Christ gives no full comments or continued discourses, but (as Demetrius the Rhetorician phrases it) speaks oft in monosyllables, like a master scattering the heavenly grain of his doctrine like pearl here and there, which requires a skilful and laborious gatherer, who must compare the words he finds with other precepts, with the end of every ordinance, and with the general analogy of evangelic doctrine; otherwise, many particular sayings would be but strange repugnant riddles.[2]

As without charity God hath given no commandment to men, so without it neither can men rightly believe any commandment given. For every act of true faith—as well that whereby we believe the law as that whereby we endeavor the law—is wrought in us by charity, according to that in the divine hymn of St. Paul (1 Corinthians 13), 'Charity believeth all things'; not as if she were so credulous (which is the exposition hitherto current), for that were a trivial praise, but to teach us that charity is the high governess of our belief, and that we cannot safely assent to any precept written in the Bible but as charity commends it to us. Which agrees with that of the same apostle to the Ephesians (4. 14-15); where he tells us that the way to get a sure undoubted knowledge of things is to hold that for truth which accords most with charity. Whose unerring guidance and conduct having

[1] *Prose Works* 3. 226-7.
[2] *Ibid*. 3. 258.

followed as a lodestar with all diligence and fidelity in this question, I trust, through the help of that illuminating Spirit which hath favored me, to have done no every-day's work in asserting after many the words of Christ, with other scriptures of great concernment, from burdensome and remorseless obscurity tangled with manifold repugnances, to their native lustre and consent between each other; hereby also dissolving tedious and Gordian difficulties, which have hitherto molested the Church of God, and are now decided, not with the sword of Alexander, but with the immaculate hands of charity, to the unspeakable good of Christendom.[1]

From *Tetrachordon* (1645).

And although it be not for the majesty of Scripture to humble herself in artificial theorems and definitions and corollaries, like a professor in the schools, but looks to be analysed and interpreted by the logical industry of her disciples and followers, and to be reduced by them, as oft as need is, into those sciential rules which are the implements of instruction; yet Moses . . . condescends in this place to such a methodical and school-like way of defining and consequencing as in no place of the whole law more.[2]

And in the fourth [chapter of Deuteronomy he says]: 'Behold, I have taught you statutes and judgments, even as the Lord my God commanded me. Keep, therefore, and do them; for this is your wisdom and your understanding in the sight of nations that shall hear all these statutes, and say: Surely this great nation is a wise and understanding people; for what nation is there so great, who hath God so nigh to them? And what nation that hath statutes and judgments so righteous as all this law which I set before you this day?'[3]

Now although Moses needed not to add other reason of this law than that one there expressed, yet to these ages, wherein

[1] *Ibid.* 3. 260.
[2] *Ibid.* 3. 346.
[3] *Ibid.* 3. 350.

canons and Scotisms and Lombard laws have dulled and almost obliterated the lively sculpture of ancient reason and humanity, it will be requisite to heap reason upon reason, and all little enough to vindicate the whiteness and the innocence of this Divine law from the calumny it finds at this day.[1]

We see the wisdom and piety of that age [of Theodosius and Valentinian], one of the purest and learnedest since Christ, conceived no hindrance in the words of our Saviour. . . . What dram of wisdom or religion (for charity is the truest religion) could there be in that knowing age, which is not virtually summed up in this most just law?[2]

Grotius, yet living, and of prime note among learned men, retires plainly from the canon to the ancient civility, yea, to the Mosaic law, 'as being most just and undeceivable.' On the 5th of Matthew he saith that 'Christ made no civil laws, but taught us how to use law'; . . . [and] proves it 'from the manner of speech, the maxims of law, the reason of charity, and common equity.'[3]

From *The Reason of Church-Government* (1642).

If, then, . . . such care was had by the wisest of the heathen, and by Moses among the Jews, . . . how much more ought the members of the Church, under the Gospel, seek to inform their understanding in the reason of that government which the Church claims to have over them! Especially for that the Church hath in her immediate cure those inner parts and affections of the mind where the seat of reason is; having power to examine our spiritual knowledge, and to demand from us, in God's behalf, a service entirely reasonable.[4]

From *Of True Religion* (1673).

It is a human frailty to err, and no man is infallible here on earth. But so long as all these profess to set the Word of God only

[1] *Prose Works* 3. 351.
[2] *Ibid*. 3. 420.
[3] *Ibid*. 3. 431.
[4] *Ibid*. 2. 440.

before them as the rule of faith and obedience, and use all diligence and sincerity of heart, by reading, by learning, by study, by prayer for illumination of the Holy Spirit, to understand the rule and obey it, they have done what man can do. God will assuredly pardon them, as he did the friends of Job, good and pious men, though much mistaken, as there it appears, in some points of doctrine. But some will say: 'With Christians it is otherwise, whom God hath promised by His Spirit to teach all things.' True, all things absolutely necessary to salvation. But the hottest disputes among Protestants, calmly and charitably inquired into, will be found less than such.[1]

The next means to hinder the growth of Popery will be to read duly and diligently the Holy Scriptures, which, as St. Paul saith to Timothy, who had known them from a child, 'are able to make wise unto salvation.' . . . The papal . . . Church permits not her laity to read the Bible in their own tongue. Our Church, on the contrary, hath proposed it to all men, and to this end translated it into English, with profitable notes on what is met with obscure, though what is most necessary to be known be still plainest; that all sorts and degrees of men, not understanding the original, may read it in their mother-tongue. Neither let the countryman, the tradesman, the lawyer, the physician, the statesman, excuse himself by his much business from the studious reading thereof. Our Saviour saith (Luke 10.41–2): 'Thou art careful and troubled about many things, but one thing is needful.' If they were asked, they would be loth to set earthly things, wealth or honor, before the wisdom of salvation. Yet most men in the course and practice of their lives are found to do so; and, through unwillingness to take the pains of understanding their religion by their own diligent study, would fain be saved by a deputy. Hence comes implicit faith, ever learning and never taught, much hearing and small proficience, till want of fundamental knowledge easily turns to superstition or Popery. . . .

[1] *Ibid.* 2. 511.

Every member of the Church, at least of any breeding or capacity, so well ought to be grounded in spiritual knowledge as, if need be, to examine their teachers themselves. . . . How should any private Christian try his teachers unless he be well-grounded himself in the rule of Scripture, by which he is taught?[1]

From *Eikonoklastes* (1649).

What greater argument of disgrace and ignominy could have been thrown with cunning upon the whole clergy than that the King, among all his priestery, and all those numberless volumes of their theological distillations, not meeting with one man or book of that coat that could befriend him with a prayer in captivity, was forced to rob Sir Philip and his captive shepherdess of their heathen orisons, to supply in any fashion his miserable indigence, not of bread, but of a single prayer to God? I say therefore not of bread, for that want may befall a good man, and yet not make him totally miserable; but he who wants a prayer to beseech God in his necessity—it is inexpressible how poor he is; far poorer within himself than all his enemies can make him.[2]

From *The Christian Doctrine.*

Magnanimity is shown when, in seeking or avoiding the acceptance or refusal of riches, advantages, or honors, we are actuated by a regard to our own dignity, rightly understood. . . . Allied to this is indignation at the unfounded praises or undeserved prosperity of the wicked. . . . Opposed to magnanimity are, first, an ambitious spirit; . . . secondly, pride, when a man values himself without merit, or more highly than his merits deserve, or is elated by some insignificant circumstance; . . . thirdly, pusillanimity.[3]

Falsehood is incurred when any one, from a dishonest motive, either perverts the truth, or utters what is false to one to whom it

---

[1] *Prose Works* 2. 516–7.
[2] *Ibid.* 1. 330.
[3] *Ibid.* 5. 94–6.

is his duty to speak the truth. . . . It follows from this definition . . . that parables, hyperboles, apologies, and ironical modes of speech are not falsehoods, inasmuch as their object is not deception but instruction.[1]

Gravity consists in a habitual self-government of speech and action, with a dignity of look and manner, befitting a man of holiness and probity. . . . Opposed to this is levity.[2]

From *Areopagitica* (1644).

Truth, indeed, came once into the world with her divine Master, and was a perfect shape, most glorious to look on; but, when He ascended, and His apostles after Him were laid asleep, then straight arose a wicked race of deceivers who (as that story goes of the Egyptian Typhon with his conspirators, how they dealt with the good Osiris) took the virgin Truth, hewed her lovely form into a thousand pieces, and scattered them to the four winds. From that time, ever since, the sad friends of Truth, such as durst appear, imitating the careful search that Isis made for the mangled body of Osiris, went up and down gathering up limb by limb still as they could find them. We have not yet found them all, Lords and Commons, nor ever shall do, till her Master's second coming; He shall bring together every joint and member, and shall mould them into an immortal feature of loveliness and perfection. . . .

We boast our light; but, if we look not wisely on the sun itself, it smites us into darkness. . . . The light which we have gained was given us, not to be ever staring on, but by it to discover onward things more remote from our knowledge. It is not the unfrocking of a priest, the unmitring of a bishop, and the removing him from off the presbyterian shoulders, that will make us a happy nation. No: if other things as great in the Church, and in the rule of life both economical and political, be

[1] *Ibid.* 5. 116.
[2] *Ibid.* 5. 123–4.

not looked into and reformed, we have looked so long upon the blaze that Zuinglius and Calvin have beaconed up to us that we are stark blind. · · ·

They are the troublers, they are the dividers of unity, who neglect, and permit not others, to unite those dissevered pieces which are yet wanting to the body of Truth. To be still searching what we know not by what we know, still closing up truth to truth as we find it (for all her body is homogeneal and proportional), this is the golden rule in theology as well as in arithmetic, and makes up the best harmony in a church.[1]

From *Paradise Regained* (1671).

> God hath now sent His living Oracle
> Into the world to teach His final will;
> And sends His Spirit of truth henceforth to dwell
> In pious hearts, an inward oracle
> To all truth requisite for men to know.[2]

From *Paradise Lost* (1667).

> He ended; and thus Adam last replied:
> 'How soon hath thy prediction, Seer blest,
> Measured this transient world, the race of time,
> Till time stand fixed! Beyond is all abyss—
> Eternity, whose end no eye can reach.
> Greatly instructed I shall hence depart,
> Greatly in peace of thought, and have my fill
> Of knowledge, what this vessel can contain;
> Beyond which was my folly to aspire.
> Henceforth I learn that to obey is best,
> And love with fear the only God, to walk
> As in His presence, ever to observe
> His providence, and on Him sole depend,
> Merciful over all His works, with good
> Still overcoming evil, and by small
> Accomplishing great things, by things deemed weak
> Subverting worldly-strong, and worldly-wise
> By simply meek; that suffering for truth's sake

1 *Prose Works* 2. 89–90.
2 *Paradise Regained* 1. 460–4.

Is fortitude to highest victory,
And, to the faithful, death the gate of life;
Taught this by His example Whom I now
Acknowledge my Redeemer ever blest.'
    To whom thus also the Angel last replied:
'This having learned, thou hast attained the sum
Of wisdom; hope no higher, though all the stars
Thou knew'st by name, and all the ethereal powers,
All secrets of the deep, all Nature's works,
Or works of God in heaven, air, earth, or sea,
And all the riches of this world enjoy'dst,
And all the rule, one empire. Only add
Deeds to thy knowledge answerable; add faith;
Add virtue, patience, temperance; add love,
By name to come called charity, the soul
Of all the rest: then wilt thou not be loth
To leave this Paradise, but shalt possess
A Paradise within thee, happier far.'[1]

EPILOGUE

There is not that thing in the world of more grave and urgent importance, throughout the whole life of man, than is Discipline. What need I instance? He that hath read with judgment of nations and commonwealths, of cities and camps, of peace and war, sea and land, will readily agree that the flourishing and decaying of all civil societies, all the moments and turnings of human occasions, are moved to and fro as upon the axle of discipline. So that whatsoever power or sway in mortal things weaker men have attributed to fortune, I durst with more confidence (the honor of Divine Providence ever saved) ascribe either to the vigor or the slackness of discipline. Nor is there any sociable perfection in this life, civil or sacred, that can be above discipline; but she is that which with her musical cords preserves and holds all the parts thereof together. . . . And certainly discipline is not only the removal of disorder, but, if

[1] *Paradise Lost* 12. 552–87.

any visible shape can be given to divine things, the very visible shape and image of virtue; whereby she is not only seen in the regular gestures and motions of her heavenly paces as she walks, but also makes the harmony of her voice audible to mortal ears.[1]

[1] *The Reason of Church-Government* 1.1; *Prose Works* 2.441-2.

NOTES ON THE TRACTATE
OF EDUCATION

NOTES ON THE TRACTATE *OF EDUCATION*

Hartlib. See Introduction, p. 3.

After the title and dedication, the second edition has the words 'written above twenty years since.' It was, in fact, published twenty-nine years after the first edition.

Page

51.3. *respect:* regard, consideration.

51.4. *the reforming:* on the reform.

51.7. *perishes:* suffers moral or spiritual ruin. Milton believed that right education is the source both of political liberty and of individual happiness.

51.7. *had not:* should not have.

51.8. *conjurements:* appeals.

51.9. *assertions:* arguments, causes.

51.11. *enlargement.* 'Diffusion, propagation;' so the *O. E. D.*, quoting this sentence. However, compare *Areopagitica, Prose Works* 2.96: 'For who knows not that truth is strong, next to the Almighty; . . . give her but room, and do not bind her when she sleeps, for then she speaks not true (as the old Proteus did, who spake oracles only when he was caught and bound).' In view of this passage one is tempted to believe that Milton used *enlargement* in the sense of *setting free, as a prisoner*—a sense that is common with Spenser; for example, *Faerie Queene* 1.8.37:

Through which he sent his voice, and loud did call
With all his power, to weet if living wight
Were housed therewithin, whom he enlargen might.

It is sometimes used by Shakespeare, as in *Henry V* 2.2.40–1:

Enlarge the man committed yesterday,
That railed against our person.

51.11. *honest:* respectable, chaste. Milton looked upon marriage as an association chiefly intellectual and spiritual, and considered the absence of sympathy and affection a sufficient reason for divorce. He believed that, if marriage could be legally dissolved for this reason, domestic unhappiness would not be so common, and transgressions of the marriage vow, therefore, not so frequent. See *Prose Works* 3. 177.

51.12. *peace:* domestic peace. 'On this subject, therefore, I published some books which were more particularly necessary at that time, when man and wife were often the most inveterate foes; when the man often staid to take care of his children at home, while the mother of the family was seen in the camp of the enemy, threatening death and destruction to her husband.' —*The Second Defence of the People of England, Prose Works* 1. 259.

51.12. *laws:* rules, obligations.

51.12. *private:* personal.

51.13. *divide. Of Education* followed *The Doctrine and Discipline of Divorce,* and preceded *The Judgment of Martin Bucer*—the first and second pamphlets, respectively, on divorce. In the *Second Defence* Milton speaks as if all the pamphlets on this subject had been completed before *Of Education* was written. See *Prose Works* 1.258–9; see also above, pp.1–2.

51.13. *transpose:* change the order of, or, perhaps, 'lay aside.' In *Areopagitica* Milton describes the assiduous care that he used in preparing a work for publication. See above, p. 255.

51.23. *either by the definite will of God,* etc. That is, you are doing the will of God, either by obeying a special decree of His for this occasion, or by following the impulse of the nature with which He has endowed you.

51.26. *forfeit:* forfeiture, loss.

51.26. *discerning ability:* ability of discernment. Milton seems rather to mean the reputation for such ability.

51.27. *over-ponderous:* literally, 'too heavy,' and hence, beyond one's power.

51.27. *argument:* theme, subject.

52.3. *so much opportunity.* The Long Parliament, now in its fourth year, was by this time virtually the supreme authority in England, and Milton's hope of a thorough reform, both civil and religious, was still high. Compare his words addressed to the Parliament in August, 1643: 'Ye have now in your hands a great and populous nation to reform.'—*The Doctrine and Discipline of Divorce, Prose Works* 3.175.

52.4. *to try what God hath determined.* Compare Romans 12.2.

52.6. *obligement:* obligation.

52.7. *voluntary:* spontaneous.

52.7. *idea:* plan or design; compare *P. L.* 7.557.

52.8. *which hath long in silence,* etc. See above, pp. 2–3.

52.15. *many modern.* As contrasted with 'old renowned' of l. 14, the words are not complimentary.

52.15. *Januas and Didactics. Janua Linguarum Reserata (The Gate of Languages Opened)* was Comenius' first published work. In it he propounded a method, for the rapid teaching of Latin and other languages, which he had himself devised, and was using with his own pupils. The book, published at Lesno, Poland, in 1631, soon attained great popularity throughout Europe, and was known in England as early as 1633—perhaps through the efforts of Hartlib.

An abstract of the *Didactica Magna,* Comenius' most important work, was published by Hartlib at London in October, 1639, as a part of *Comenii Pansophia.* See above, p. 5.

52.18. *flowered off.* '*Flower off:* to arise spontaneously in the treatment of a subject'; so the *O. E. D.,* quoting the passage. Johnson in his *Dictionary* also quotes the passage, and makes the expression signify 'to come off as cream from the surface.'

52.18. *burnishing.* 'The action of brightening or polishing'; so the *O. E. D.* 'The particles rubbed off in polishing'; so Browning, p. 27.

52.18. *studious and contemplative years.* See above, pp. 89–105, 249–60.

52.19. *religious and civil knowledge.* Compare: 'I had from my youth studied the distinctions between religious and civil rights.'—*Second Defence, Prose Works* 1. 258.

52.22. *end:* object, purpose.

52.22. *repair:* remedy, set right again. Compare: 'I can repair That detriment.'—*P. L.* 7. 152–3. Similarly: 'And yet anon repairs his drooping head.'—*Lycidas* 169.

52.22. *ruins:* ruinous condition, consequent upon the Fall of Man. By this assumption of an evil principle in human nature, Milton as an educator directly contravenes the position afterward taken by Rousseau, who assumes that man is naturally good.

52.23. *by regaining to know God aright.* Milton believed that one principal result of sin was to obscure 'right reason,' and that spiritual regeneration would restore the mind to its proper clearness and vigor. See Watson, *Vives on Education*, p. 28.

52.24. *to be like Him.* 'It is enough determined that this image of God, wherein man was created, is meant wisdom, purity, justice, and rule over all creatures.'—*Tetrachordon, Prose Works* 3.323. 'Nothing fitter for us to think on than to be like Him, united to Him, and, as He pleases to express it, to have fellowship with Him.'—*The Reason of Church-Government, ibid.* 2. 492.

52.25. *the nearest:* either 'nearest in resemblance' as a final result, or 'the most expeditiously' as to the rate of progress.

52.25. *possessing . . . of:* putting in possession of.

52.25. *which, being united to,* etc. See 2 Peter 1.5-8.

52.26. *faith:* 'a full persuasion, operated in us through the gift of God, whereby we believe.'—*Christian Doctrine, Prose Works* 4.337.

52.27. *But because our understanding,* etc. See Watson, *Vives on Education*, p. 168.

52.28. *sensible:* perceptible by the senses.

52.29. *conning:* studying.

52.30. *creature:* creation.

52.31. *so that language is but the instrument*, etc. See Watson, *Vives on Education*, pp. 90, 163. Compare Bacon: 'Here, therefore, is the first distemper of learning, when men study words and not matter.'—*Advancement of Learning*, ed. by Wright, p. 30.

53.3 *Babel*. Genesis 11. 9. Compare Milton's sentence with 1 Cor. 13. 1-2.

53.3 *If he have not studied the solid things*. See above, pp. 191, 217.

53. 6. *yeoman:* 'a man of small estate in land; a farmer.' —Johnson's *Dictionary*.

53.6. *tradesman:* a shopkeeper.

53.10. *seven or eight years*. See above, p. 145.

53.12. *one year*. 'In a year's time made them capable of interpreting a Latin author at sight.'—Aubrey's *Collections: Mr. John Milton;* Lockwood, p. xli.

53.12. *proficiency:* progress.

53.14. *vacancies:* vacations, recesses. 'Probably not the regular long vacation periods of the year, but the frequently occurring Saints' days, which were always holidays.'—Lockwood, p. 5.

53.14. *preposterous:* placing before what should come after.

53.15. *forcing the empty wits of children*, etc. The problem here touched upon is an important matter in which Milton agrees with both Quintilian and Vives. See Quintilian, *Institutio Oratoria* 1, Pr. 23-5, and 1. 10. 1-11; and Watson, *Vives on Education*, pp. 143-9, where it is evident that Vives would teach Greek by the method of reading, not composition.

Ascham, too, censured the current practice. He says: 'And in learning farther his Syntaxis, by mine advice, he shall not use the common order in common schools, for making of Latins—whereby the child commonly learneth, first, an evil choice of words (and right choice of words, saith Cæsar, is the foundation of eloquence); then, a wrong placing of words; and, lastly, an ill framing of the sentence, with a perverse judgment both of words and sentences. . . . Moreover, there is no one thing that hath more either dulled the wits or taken away the will of children from learning than the care they have to satisfy their masters in making of Latins.'—*The Scholemaster*, in *English Works*, p. 182.

As pedagogical instruments, the English 'theme,' the Latin essay, and the disputation, to which Milton objected at Cambridge (see Masson, *Life of Milton* 1. 253), are links in a chain of questionable practice that extends from our own day back to the time of the Greek sophists. Woodward says: 'The place of disputation in the mediæval school was taken in the humanist by the declamation, and later on in German and English schools by the essay.'—*Education in the Age of the Renaissance*, p. 16. And see Leach: 'The Greek rhetorician was the intellectual father of the Oxford Schoolman.'—*The Schools of Mediæval England*, p. 18.

The 'daily theme,' as a means of teaching English composition, is now rather generally discredited. An American teacher has very pertinently quoted Milton's *Tractate* in defence of the more rational way; see Cooper, *Two Views of Education*, p. 74.

53.16. *acts:* performances, accomplishments.

53.18. *elegant:* apt, well-chosen.

53.18. *maxims:* propositions ostensibly expressing general truths.

53.18. *invention:* 'the devising of a subject, idea, or method of treatment by the exercise of the intellect or imagination.' —*O. E. D.*

'After an initial division of oratory into *invention* and *expression*, [Cicero] assigns matter and arrangement to *invention*.' —Quintilian, *Institutio Oratoria* 3. 3. 7.

'The finding out of apt matter, called otherwise Invention, is a searching out of things true, or things likely, the which may reasonably set forth a matter, and make it appear probable. The places of Logic give good occasion to find out plentiful matter.'—Wilson, *Arte of Rhetorique*, p. 6.

53.21. *barbarizing:* speaking or writing like a barbarian; violating the laws of Latin or Greek grammar and syntax.

53.22. *Anglicisms:* English idioms introduced into sentences in another language.

53.24. *conversing:* becoming familiar, or conversant, with.

53.24. *pure authors:* those who observe the best usage.

53.24. *digested.* Compare Bacon: 'Some books are to be tasted, others to be swallowed, and some few to be chewed and digested.'—*Essay* 50, *Of Studies.*

53.25. *grounds:* elements, rudiments.

53.26. *certain forms:* ' "paradigms," the regular forms in which they habitually occur.'— Browning, p. 28.

53.26. *praxis:* practice; exercise.

53.27. *lessoned:* taught as a lesson.

53.29. *arts:* 'the branches of learning included in a liberal education; originally these were the "Seven Liberal Arts." ' —Lockwood, p. 6.

54.1. *an old error of universities,* etc. Compare Bacon: 'And therefore inasmuch as most of the usages and orders of the universities were derived from more obscure times, it is the more requisite they be re-examined. In this kind I will give an instance or two, for example, sake, of things that are the most obvious and familiar. The one is a matter which, though it be ancient and general, yet I hold to be an error; which is, that scholars in universities come too soon and too unripe to logic and rhetoric, arts fitter for graduates than children and novices; for these two, rightly taken, are the gravest of sciences, being the arts of arts—the one for judgment, the other for ornament; and they be the rules and directions how to set forth and dispose matter. And therefore for minds empty and unfraught with matter, and which have not gathered that which Cicero calleth *sylva* and *supellex*, stuff and variety, to begin with those arts (as if one should learn to weigh, or to measure, or to paint the wind) doth work but this effect—that the wisdom of those arts, which is great and universal, is almost made contemptible, and is degenerate into childish sophistry and ridiculous affectation.'—*Advancement of Learning*, ed. by Wright, p. 81.

54.2. *scholastic:* characteristic of the Schoolmen.

54.3. *grossness:* dulness, stupidity.

54.4. *obvious to the sense.* 'This is an anticipation of the doctrines of Pestalozzi and Froebel, who insist on the importance of beginning education with the training of the senses.'—Browning, p. 29. See above p. 44.

54.5. *unmatriculated:* not initiated, not qualified.

54.5. *novices:* beginners.

54.6. *intellective:* apprehensible by the intellect alone, not by the senses.

54.11. *controversy:* disputation.

54.14. *babblements:* 'thoughtless or unseemly chatter; babble.' —O.E.D.

54.14. *worthy and delightful knowledge.* See above, pp. 66–7.

54.15. *youthful years.* See above, p. 79.

54.16. *sway.* See above, p. 224.

54.17. *ambitious and mercenary, or ignorantly zealous.* Opposite extremes. Browning here quotes *Lycidas* 113–22.

54.18. *trade of law.* See *Sonnet 18.* 4.

54.19. *prudent and heavenly contemplation.* 'Milton here sketches the idea of what a University law-school ought to be, concerned with the theory and not with the practice of law.' —Browning, p. 29.

54.19. *justice and equity.* Compare 'the grounds of law, and legal justice,' above, p. 59.

54.23. *flattery and Court-shifts.* See above, p. 231.

54.24. *aphorisms:* axioms, principles. Compare: 'This is the masterpiece of a modern politician—how to qualify and mould the sufferance and subjection of the people to the length of that foot that is to tread on their necks.'—*Of Reformation in England, Prose Works* 2. 391.

54.25. *instilling their barren hearts*, etc.: making a virtue of passive obedience, for want of a better principle.

54.27. *delicious:* voluptuous, luxurious, dainty.

54.27. *airy:* gay, vivacious.

54.21. *which indeed is*, etc. Browning quotes *Lycidas* 67–9.

54.32. *our prime youth:* 'either our early youth or the best part of our youth.'—Browning, p. 30.

55.2. *a hill-side.* See above, pp. 139, 308.

55.6. *Orpheus:* 'the name of a mystic singer of lyrics to whom was assigned a body of poetry, including the story of the Argonauts and a number of hymns.'—Osgood, *The Classical Mythology of Milton's English Poems*, p. 68. Milton elsewhere testifies to the power of Orpheus' music, which

> Drew iron tears down Pluto's cheek,
> And made Hell grant what Love did seek.
> —*Il Penseroso* 106–7.

55.6. *charming.* Compare *Comus* 476–80; see above, p. 157.

55.8. *stocks and stubs:* senseless or stupid persons. Browning compares Spenser, *Faerie Queene* 1. 9. 34.

55.10. *wits:* young men of genius.

55.10. *asinine feast:* the scholastic studies of the university.

55.11. *all the:* the only.

55.12. *docible:* teachable.

55.12. *I call therefore*, etc. 'Worthy to be memorized as one of the noblest definitions of education; observe that the purpose is to render the man more *useful* in public and in private. Plato (*Laws* 1. 643) says education is that "which makes a man eagerly pursue the ideal perfection of citizenship, and teaches him how rightly to rule and how to obey." Again (*ibid.* 1.641), "But if you ask what is the good of education in general, the answer is easy; that education makes good men, and that good men act nobly." '—Lockwood, p. 9. See above, p. 15.

55.13. *generous:* ample, copious.

55.14. *magnanimously:* with nobility of feeling and conduct. See above, p. 318.

55.15. *offices:* duties, functions, one's part.

55.17. *sophistry:* the practice of specious reasoning.

55.19. *a spacious house.* See above, p. 9.

55.20. *academy:* a school; the term is derived from Plato's school at his house in the grove of Academus, near Athens. This school was maintained by his successors until A. D. 529. The term *academy* was applied early in the Renaissance to the humanistic schools, such as that of Vittorino da Feltre at Mantua.

55.26. *peculiar:* special.

55.26. *physic:* medicine.

55.26. *where they:* for those who.

55.27. *but as for those general studies,* etc. This statement shows that Milton intended his academy to be 'liberal,' not 'vocational.' It was evidently meant, however, to take the place of the university, in all studies except the professional.

55.28. *Lily:* Lily's Latin Grammar; see above, p. 30. This text-book was several times revised, and remained in use at Eton until 1868. See Watson, *The English Grammar-Schools*, pp. 243 ff.

55.28. *commencing:* becoming, setting up as.

55.28. *Master of Art.* In the Middle Ages, certain English schools of academic rank had at times conferred the Bachelor's degree. See above, p. 25.

55.29. *absolute:* complete, independent.

55.29. *as many edifices.* See above, pp. 222-3; 273-4.

55.32. *civility:* the state of being civilized; culture.

55.33. *to the convenience of,* etc. The military character of the school is fundamental.

56.8. *the Italian.* Compare Ellwood: 'At my first sitting to read to him, observing that I used the English pronunciation, he [Milton] told me, if I would have the benefit of the Latin tongue, not only to read and understand Latin authors, but to converse with foreigners, either abroad or at home, I must learn the foreign pronunciation. To this I consenting, he instructed me how to sound the vowels; so different from the common pronunciation used by the English, who speak *Anglicè* their Latin, that—with some few other variations in sounding some consonants in particular cases . . . the Latin thus spoken seemed as different from that which was delivered as the English generally speak it, as if it were another language.' —*The History of Thomas Ellwood, Written by Himself* (*Morley's Universal Library*), pp. 134-5. See above, p. 145.

56.8 *for we Englishmen, being far northerly*, etc. Compare Swift: 'The same defect of heat, which gives a fierceness to our natures, may contribute to that roughness of our language, which bears some analogy to the harsh fruit of colder countries.'—*A Proposal for Correcting, Improving, and Ascertaining the English Tongue* (1712), *Prose Works*, ed. by T. Scott, 11. 13.

56.11. *smatter:* mispronounce.

56.12. *law-French.* Blackstone (*Commentaries*, 13th edition (1800), 3.317-9) calls law-French a 'barbarous dialect,' and declares that it differs in its grammar and orthography as much from the modern French as the diction of Chaucer and Gower does from that of Addison and Pope.

56.14. *season:* imbue with opinions.

56.16. *seize:* catch.

56.16. *book of education:* a treatise setting forth the benefits of knowledge and virtue, such as the *Pinax* of Cebes.

56.17. *read to them.* Probably in Latin translations; see the next sentence. Elyot (*Governour*, ed. by Croft, 1.55-6) proposes that Aesop's Fables be read in Greek to beginners in that language.

56.18. *Cebes:* a Greek philosopher and disciple of Socrates; also one of the interlocutors whom Plato introduces into his *Phaedo.* Of the three treatises composed by Cebes, only the *Pinax* has come down to us. It is a moral sketch or *picture* of human life, written in a pleasing and simple style. Its authenticity has been called in question, but the testimony of the ancients clearly favors Cebes as the author.

56.18. *Plutarch:* a Greek writer born about A. D. 50, and best known as the author of the *Parallel Lives.* Milton probably has in mind Plutarch's *Moralia,* some parts of which were composed in the form of the Platonic dialogue.

56.18. *Socratic discourses:* discourses carried on in the Socratic manner; dialogues.

56.19. *classic authority.* Milton would as early as possible make his students acquainted with good models of style. By way of contrast, see Comenius' original sentences, taken from the *Vestibulum,* or 'Entrance Hall' to the *Janua,* in Keatinge, *The Great Didactic,* p. 29.

56.20. *Quintilian:* the celebrated Roman teacher. In Book 1 of his *Institutio Oratoria* are set forth the general principles of instruction.

56.21. *skill and groundwork.* Perhaps intended by hendiadys for 'skilful groundwork,' that is, foundation laid with skill.

56.21. *temper:* mingle in due proportion.

56.23. *inflamed:* ardent, burning; glowing. Compare Jonson: 'It is a good thing to inflame the mind; and though ambition itself be a vice, it is often the cause of great virtue.'—*Discoveries,* ed. by Castelain, p. 84.

56.24. *study:* zeal, eagerness; Latin *studium.*

56.28. *liberal:* becoming to a gentleman.

56.28. *art:* aptitude, adroitness.

56.29. *effectual:* earnest, urgent. Compare: 'The effectual fervent prayer of a righteous man availeth much.'—James 5.16.

56.30. *intimation:* suggestion, hint.

57.2. *arithmetic . . . geometry*. Philips says: 'Besides an introduction into several arts and sciences, by reading Urstisius his *Arithmetic*, Riff's *Geometry*, Petiscus his *Trigonometry*, Joannes de Sacro Bosco *De Sphaera*.'—*Life of Milton*, in Lockwood, p. lxvi. Aubrey (*ibid*., p. xli) says that Milton's pupils acquired the elements of arithmetic and geometry in connection with their reading of the poet Manilius. See note to p. 58, l. 17.

57.2. *even playing*. Browning says: 'Next to reading and writing (in Roman education) came reckoning. The fingers were made great use of. Each joint and bend of the finger was made to signify a certain value, and the pupil was expected to follow the twinkling motion of the teacher's hands as he represented number after number. The modern Italian game of *mora* is a survival of this capacity.'—*An Introduction to the History of Educational Theories*, p. 21.

57.3. *After evening repast*. See above, p. 45.

57.6. *Cato:* Marcus Portius Cato, or Cato the Censor (234–149 B. C.), author of the *De Re Rustica*, or more properly, *De Agri Cultura*, the earliest extant work on agriculture composed in Latin. Cato's practical shrewdness of observation, and the spirit of thrift that he inculcates, make his work of permanent interest.

57.7 *Varro:* Marcus Terentius Varro (116–28 B. C.), the most voluminous of Roman authors, and highly esteemed by the ancients for his learning. Of his writings there are extant only six books of the *De Lingua Latina*, and three books *De Re Rustica*. The latter he wrote in his eightieth year; it is the best practical treatise on farm-management that has come down to us from antiquity, and is said to be the authority from which Virgil drew the rural lore of the *Georgics*.

57.7 *Columella:* Lucius Junius Moderatus Columella, a Roman writer of the first century of our era, and author of *De Re Rustica*, in twelve books. He was born at Gades (modern Cadiz) in Spain, but probably spent the most of his life in or near

Rome. Columella's Latin prose is pure and elegant. Book 10 of his work on agriculture is in hexameters, and professes to supply the treatise on gardens which Virgil in his *Georgics* says he will leave for others after him to write. See Columella, *De Re Rustica* 10, Preface; Virgil, *Georgics* 4. 116–48. Philips adds the name of Palladius to the list of writers on agriculture whom he read as a pupil of Milton.

57.7. *for the matter is most easy.* Compare p. 54, ll. 3ff.

57.9. *And here will be an occasion*, etc. Possibly a concession to Hartlib's interest in the improvement of agriculture. See above, p. 17.

57.12. *Hercules' praises.* 'The tradition is,' says Pliny, 'that King Augeas was the first in Greece to use manure, and that Hercules introduced the practice into Italy.' See Pliny, *Natural History* 17.50. '[Hercules] was said to "tame" the land, *i.e.*, to clear it from robbers, to make roads, to cultivate it. He may be regarded as symbolical of civilization.'—Morris, p. 40.

57.13. *plying:* working, practising.

57.21. *historical physiology:* natural science, largely concerned with the origin and development of various organisms.

57.22. *Aristotle.* The *Historia Animalium, De Partibus Animalium, De Generatione Animalium*, and perhaps also the *Parva Naturalia*, are probably what Milton has in mind.

57.22. *Theophrastus:* a pupil of Plato, and the pupil and successor of Aristotle in the Lycæum. Milton probably here alludes to his works *On Plants* (Περὶ φυτῶν ἱστορίας) and *On Stones* (Περὶ τῶν λίθων βίβλιον).

57.23. *under contribution:* to be used for reference, rather than read entire. Neither Philips nor Aubrey mentions these works among those that were read by Milton's pupils.

57.24. *Vitruvius:* Marcus Vitruvius Pollio, a Roman writer of the time of Augustus or Nero; author of a work on architecture, in ten books.

57.24. *Seneca's* Natural Questions. Lucius Annæus Seneca, a native of Spain, was the tutor of Nero, and a philosopher and moralist of note. His work entitled *Quæstiones Naturales*, or *Physical Inquiries*, chiefly deals with elementary problems of astronomy, meteorology, and physical geography. It is in some sense a compendium of ancient physical science, more critical than that of Pliny; it shares with the works of Pliny and Aristotle the distinction of being a chief authority on natural science during the Middle Ages.

57.24. *Mela.* Pomponius Mela, a native of Spain, composed about A. D. 40–1, three books on geography, (*De Chorographia* or *De Situ Orbis*). The work is a valuable compendium of ancient geographical knowledge.

57.24. *Celsus:* Aulus Cornelius Celsus, a Roman writer who composed an encyclopædic work (*Artes* or *Treatises*) of which only the portion on medicine (Books 6 to 13) remains. It is compiled from Greek writers, notably Hippocrates, but is popular rather than technical.

57.24. *Pliny.* Milton doubtless has in mind the *Natural History* of Pliny the elder.

57.25. *Solinus:* Caius Julius Solinus, a Roman writer of the first century of our era. His work known as *Collectanea rerum memorabilium* is in part compiled from Pliny. It has been described, according to Masson, as 'a geographical compendium, divided into fifty-seven chapters, containing a brief sketch of the world as known to the ancients, diversified by historical notices, remarks on the origin, habits, religious rites, and social condition, of various nations enumerated, together with details regarding the remarkable productions of each region, whether animal, vegetable, or mineral.' This work was edited (Paris, 1629) by Salmasius, a French scholar, and author of the *Defensio Regia* (Leyden, 1649) to which Milton replied in his *Defence of the English People.* See Masson, *Life of Milton* 4. 162–3.

57.26. *compact:* composite store.

57.27. *physics:* natural science in general.

57.27. *instrumental:* serving as a means or instrument.

57.29. *enginery:* engineering.

57.30. *history:* study.

57.32. *read to them.* Masson says: 'Text-books are not mentioned here; and, though some must have been in view for such subjects as Trigonometry, Fortification, Engineering, and Navigation, yet it is clear, from Milton's language, that he meant a good deal of the miscellaneous instruction to be by lectures and digests of books by the teacher.'—*Life of Milton* 3.246.

57.33. *the institution of physic:* the principles of medicine.

57.34. *tempers:* temperaments. 'In mediæval physiology, the combination of the four cardinal humors of the body, by the relative proportions of which the physical and mental constitution was held to be determined; also, the bodily habit attributed to this.'—*O. E. D.*

57.34. *humors:* 'the four chief fluids (*cardinal humors*) of the body (blood, phlegm, choler, and melancholy or black choler), by the relative proportions of which a person's physical and mental qualities and disposition were held to be determined.' —*O. E. D.*

'Disease, Alcmæon [of Croton, a younger contemporary of Pythagoras] regarded broadly as a disturbance of the balance of bodily qualities. . . . Health was "isonomy" or equilibrium of the bodily parts and qualities. He rationalized, as did the Hippocratic school after him, the causes of diseases, attributing them to external agencies—plethora, inanition, fatigue; or again to dyscrases [distempers] of the elemental qualities—heat, cold, moisture, dryness; health being a true blend of opposites. This doctrine of the school of Croton was then carried forward in medical tradition, to be developed by the great Hippocratic school. . . . How admirable are these views; admirable in truth of insight, and in emancipation from fantasy and convention!'—Allbutt, *Greek Medicine in Rome,* pp. 99–100.

57.34. *seasons:* 'the effect of the seasons on the health of the body.'—Browning, p. 35.

57.34. *crudity:* indigestion.

58.3. *expenseless:* inexpensive.

58.4. *and not let.* See note on p. 62, l. 20.

58.6. *proceedings:* advances, undertakings.

58.8. *helpful experiences:* expert assistance, doubtless chiefly in demonstration.

58.13. *tincture:* tinge, smack. It evidently was no part of Milton's plan to make his pupils finished practitioners in any of the arts or crafts that he mentions above; his aim was only to give them the general acquaintance with such arts that we now expect of an educated man.

58.15. *Orpheus.* See note, p. 55, l. 6.

58.16. *Hesiod:* probably the *Works and Days*, but perhaps also the *Theogony*.

58.16. *Theocritus:* the pastoral poet, born in Syracuse, but a resident of Alexandria from 285–247 B. C. Whibley (*A Companion to Greek Studies*, p. 142) says: 'His bucolic idylls, the oldest extant examples of pastoral poetry, and the patterns of nearly all later work in that kind, are inspired by a true feeling for the rural life and scenery of his native Sicily.'

58.16. *Aratus:* a native of Soli in Cilicia; he was a contemporary and possibly an acquaintance of Theocritus. His two didactic poems, *Phænomena*, on astronomy, and *Diosemeia*, on meteorology, are for the most part compilations from other works. St. Paul (Acts 17.28) in his sermon at Athens quoted from Aratus (*Phænom.* 5) 'For we are also his offspring.'

58.16. *Nicander:* of Claros, a physician (*c.* 150 B. C.). He wrote the *Theriaca*, a metrical work on venomous animals and on the treatment of the wounds which they inflict; and the *Alexipharmaca*, a similar treatise on poisons in food or drink, with the remedies for them.

58.16. *Oppian:* the reputed author (*c.* A. D. 180) of two metrical treatises, the *Halieutica*, on the natural history of fishes, and the art of fishing, and the *Cynegetica*, on hunting.

58.16. *Dionysius:* the *Periegetes* or geographical poem of Dionysius Afer (third century after Christ). See Masson, *Life of Milton* 3. 246, note.

58.17. *Lucretius*. In the fifth book of Lucretius' *De Rerum Natura* are described the evolution of the earth from Chaos, the origin of human life, and the development of society from its beginnings.

58.17. *Manilius:* Marcus Manilius, a writer who lived probably in the time of the emperors Augustus and Tiberius, and the author of a work called *Astronomica*, in five books.

58.17. *the rural part of Virgil:* the *Eclogues* and the *Georgics*.

58.18. *By this time*. Masson estimates that the pupils would enter this stage of their training about the age of sixteen.

58.19. *act:* action.

58.20. *proairesis:* deliberate choice, resolution. Compare Aristotle: 'It is necessary that the agent, at the time of performing actions in accordance with virtue, should satisfy certain conditions; *i.e.*, in the first place, that he should know what he is doing, secondly, that he should deliberately choose to do it, and to do it for its own sake, and, thirdly, that he should do it as an instance of a settled and immutable moral state. . . . Again, whereas we are angry or afraid without deliberate purpose, the virtues are in some sense deliberate purposes, or do not exist in the absence of deliberate purpose.'—*Nicomachean Ethics* 2.3. (Welldon's translation, pp. 42–4). See above, p. 242.

58.21. *Then will be required*. See above, pp. 36 and 45.

58.26. *Laertius:* Diogenes Laertius, author of *Lives and Opinions of the Eminent Philosophers*.

58.26. *Locrian remnants:* possibly a treatise entitled *On the Soul of the World*, formerly attributed to Timæus of Locri.

58.27. *reduced:* brought back.

58.28. *determinate:* definite.

58.28. *sentence:* authoritative decision.

58.29. *Evangels:* Gospels.

58.29. *Apostolic Scriptures:* the Acts, the Epistles, and Revelation.

58.31. *economics:* the science or art of managing a household. See *Reason of Church-Government, Prose Works* 2. 443.

58.32. *at any odd hour.* Compare p. 59, l. 17, 'the Hebrew tongue at a set hour.'

58.33. *antidote:* some work that would serve to correct wrong impressions of taste, principle, or conduct.

59.2. *Trachiniæ, Alcestis.* 'Both plays present the suffering and sacrifice of a faithful wife for her husband.'—Lockwood, p. 19.

59.4. *the beginning, end, and reasons.* See above, p. 191.

59.5. *dangerous fit:* crisis.

59.6. *many of our great councilors.* See above, pp. 229–30.

59.9. *grounds:* rudiments.

59.10. *Moses.* See above, pp. 270, 310.

59.11. *Lycurgus.* Reputed by tradition to be the founder of the Spartan constitution. See above, p. 251.

59.11. *Solon:* the great Athenian legislator, born about 638 B. C.

59.12. *Zaleucus:* the lawgiver of the Epizephyrian Locrians, (*c.* 660 B. C.). His code is said to have been the first collection of written laws that the Greeks possessed.

59.12. *Charondas:* the lawgiver of Catana in Sicily.

59.12. *Roman edicts and Tables.* The Twelve Tables were the statutory law of Rome, the written code of the old *jus civile.* The edicts were announcements by the prætors of the principles on which they intended to administer the law during their terms of office. The edicts later were often followed as precedents, and thus became virtually a part of the law.

59.13. *Justinian:* Emperor of Constantinople, A. D. 527–63. During his reign he caused the Roman laws to be codified into an orderly system, known as the Corpus Juris Civilis, whic h since that time has been the authoritative record of Roman law

De Burgh (*The Legacy of the Ancient World*, p. 351), says:
'The name of Justinian is ever memorable in the annals of Roman law. By his codification he shaped it into the final form, freed, in Dante's phrase, "from the excessive and the irrelevant," in which it passed to the nations of the modern world.'

And (*ibid.*, p. 194) he says: 'The code of The Twelve Tables, compiled by the decemvirs in 451 and 450, was the earliest written law of Rome. As such, it was regarded throughout the history of the republic and of the empire as the basis of the civil law. . . . Nowhere was the aptitude of the Romans for right judgment in practical affairs more conspicuously displayed than in the field of law, their most enduring contribution to world-civilization.'

59.20. *the Chaldee and the Syrian:* dialects of Aramaic, the Semitic language most closely related to Hebrew, and for more than a thousand years the vernacular of Israel. *Chaldee,* or *Chaldaic,* is the term sometimes, though inappropriately, applied to the Aramaic of the Books of Ezra and Daniel. *Syriac* is pre-eminently applied to the Aramaic dialect of Edessa—the dialect in which the earliest versions of the New Testament probably were written.

59.22. *heroic poems:* epic poems.

59.22. *regal argument.* See *At a Vacation Exercise* 47; *Il Penseroso* 97–8.

59.29. *organic:* serving as a means or instrument.

59.30. *mean:* medium.

59.31. *logic.* See pp. 73, 186, 225.

59.32. *well-couched:* precisely stated.

59.33. *contracted palm.* Compare 'closed fist' (*Academic Exercise* 2). Masson notes: 'Milton here uses a common comparison of the schools, according to which the *rhetorical* treatment of a subject was to the *logical* treatment of the same as the opened

and outspread hand is to the closed fist. Constitutionally, Milton himself preferred the opened and outspread hand.'
—*Life of Milton* 1. 280.

59.34. *rhetoric:* theory of composition.

59.34. *Plato.* Chiefly in the *Phaedrus.*

59.34. *Phalereus: De Elocutione,* by Demetrius Phalereus, an early Alexandrine scholar.

60.1. *Hermogenes:* a celebrated Greek rhetorician, who lived during the reign of Marcus Aurelius.

60.1. *Longinus.* Milton undoubtedly refers to the treatise *On the Sublime,* which was long attributed to Cassius Longinus, a Greek philosopher of the third century of our era.

60.1. *poetry.* Evidently the criticism, but perhaps also the composition of poetry.

60.7. *Castelvetro. Poetica d'Aristotele vulgarizzata et sposta.* Vienna, 1570; Basel, 1576.

60.7. *Tasso. Discorsi dell' Arte Poetica, ed in particolare sopra il Poema Eroico;* and *Discorsi del Poema Eroico.* The latter was published in 1594.

60.7. *Mazzoni. Della Difesa della Comedia di Dante.* 1587.

60.9. *decorum:* fitness, propriety. See above, pp. 152, 157–8, 159, 167, 192, 199, 205.

60.9. *masterpiece:* most important feature, chief excellence.

60.11. *our common rimers and playwriters.* Probably Milton here only seconds the judgment of earlier critics. Sidney and E. K.'' had condemned the ignorant multitude of would-be poets. (See Thompson, *Elizabethan Criticism of Poetry,* pp. 9ff.) In view of Milton's earlier admiration of Shakespeare, it is needless to suppose, with Browning, that the dramatist was here included among the 'common' sort. See above, pp. 91, 135, 156, 166–7.

60.12. *what religious,* etc. See above, pp. 157–8.

60.14. *From hence and not till now.* Compare p. 53, ll.14ff.

60.21. *any other.* That is, any other trial.

60.22. *our noble and our gentle youth.* See above, pp. 227–9.

60.24. *unless they rely more*, etc. Milton was sturdily opposed to the uncritical acceptance of tradition. See above, pp. 184–5.

61.7. *exceed:* excel.

61.8. *Plato*. See *Laws* 2.666 B. Compare Plutarch, *Life of Lycurgus*, Langhorne's translation, 1.126.

61.10. *Lycæum:* the school in Athens where Aristotle taught.

61.17. *weapon:* sword.

61.28. *unsweating:* easing or cooling after exertion.

61.31. *music*. See above, pp. 134–5, 135–6; 137, 139, 241.

61.32. *fancied:* artistically designed.

61.32. *descant:* 'an instrumental prelude, consisting of variations on a given theme.'—*O. E. D.*

61.33. *symphony:* orchestra or chorus.

61.33. *artful:* skilful.

62.3. *ditties:* songs, lays.

62.3. *wise men and prophets*. See above, p. 41.

62.5 *rustic harshness*. Compare 'peasantly rudeness,' above, p. 203.

62.5. *distempered:* immoderate, inordinate.

62.6. *after meat*. Compare the practice of Vittorino da Feltre; see Woodward, *Education during the Renaissance*, pp. 19–20.

62.7. *first concoction:* according to the old physiology, the first stage or process in digestion.

62.10. *supper*. 'Supper was usually between seven and eight o'clock.'—Lockwood, p. 26.

62.14. *exactness:* strictness, rigor.

62.16. *battering:* attacking fortifications with cannon or other engines.

62.18. *they may, as it were out of a long war, come forth*, etc. A remark that has met with some ridicule. But it probably is half-humorous; and one should remember that the discipline of our military schools has justified itself in practice.

62.20. *They would not then*, etc. Browning (p. 41) says: 'Mr. S. R. Gardiner, whom I consulted on this subject, tells me that this passage evidently refers to Essex. "The constant diminution of his army through 1643 from sickness and desertion was a constant subject of complaint, and there was information given to Parliament in the end of that year of companies with only twenty men in them near London amongst those serving under Essex."' 'In May, 1644,' says C. H. Firth (*Cromwell's Army*, p. 23) [Essex] had 10,000 men, by December less than 5,000. . . . The pay of the soldiers was continually in arrears, and the loss from desertion was excessive. "My desire is," wrote Essex in December, 1643, "that, if there be no pay like to come to me by the latter end of the week, I may know it; I not being able to stay amongst them to hear the crying necessity of the hungry soldiers." ' The King's army fared little better. Milton's strictures are perhaps not altogether just.

62.23. *unrecruitable:* unable to obtain recruits.

62.24. *to quaff out, or convey into secret hoards.* Compare Shakespeare, *I Henry IV* 4.2.14-6: 'I have misused the king's press damnably. I have got, in exchange of a hundred and fifty soldiers, three hundred and odd pounds.'

63.7. *commodities:* conveniences, advantages.

63.15. *those old admired virtues and excellencies.* See above, pp. 262-3.

63.18. *slight:* unworthy of confidence or trust.

63.19. *kickshaws:* fantastical, frivolous persons. Commonly used as a plural, although derived from the French *quelque chose*.

63.22. *such as shall deserve*, etc. See above, pp. 72, 100-1.

63.25. *And perhaps, then, other nations*, etc. See above, pp. 151, 238, 263, 267, 278.

63.34. *not beginning, as some have done, from the cradle*, etc. See Quintilian, *Institutio Oratoria* 1.1.4.

64.2. *scope:* aim, purpose. See p. 3, l.11.

64.6. *to shoot in.* The Elizabethan form of the phrase. Compare Ascham, *Toxophilus B:* 'Take your bow into the field, shoot in him, . . . look where he cometh most, provide for that place betimes, lest it pinch and so fret.'—*English Works*, p. 77.

64.7. *those which Homer gave Ulysses.* See Odyssey 21.

64.9. *assay:* trial, attempt.

64.11. *nothing but very happy*, etc. After 'but,' the words 'what is' probably should be supplied.

64.12. *and this age have*, etc. See above, pp. 91, 109, 274–6.

BIBLIOGRAPHY

BIBLIOGRAPHY

1. MILTON

MILTON, J. *Works, in Verse and Prose*, ed. by J. Mitford. 8 vols. London, 1851.

—— ——. *Poetical Works*, ed. by H. C. Beeching. Oxford, 1912.

—— ——. *Prose Works*, ed. by J. A. St. John. 5 vols. (Bohn's Library). London, 1848–64.

—— ——. *Paradise Lost*, ed. by A. W. Verity. Cambridge, 1910.

—— ——. *Paradise Regained*, ed. by C. S. Jerram. New York, 1902.

—— ——. *Poems, etc. upon Several Occasions, both English and Latin, etc. Composed at Several Times. With a small Tractate of Education to Mr. Hartlib.* London, 1673.

—— ——. *Milton's Tractate on Education.* A facsimile reprint from the edition of 1673, ed. by O. Browning. Cambridge, 1905. [Cited as Browning.]

—— ——. *Of Education, Areopagitica, The Commonwealth*, ed. by L. E. Lockwood. New York, 1911. [Cited as Lockwood.]

—— ——. *Tractate of Education*, ed. by E. E. Morris. London, 1905. [Cited as Morris.]

—— ——. *Of Education*, ed. by W. Russell. In *Library of Education* 1. 271–86. Gray and Bowen. Boston, 1830.

—— ——. *Areopagitica*, ed. by J. W. Hales. Oxford, 1917.

—— ——. *A Commonplace Book*, ed. by A. J. Harwood for the Camden Society. London, 1877.

—— ——. *Of Reformation Touching Church-Discipline in England*, ed. by W. T. Hale. New Haven, 1916.

—— ——. *Latin Poems*, ed. and trans. by W. MacKellar. Forthcoming.

BRADSHAW, J. *A Concordance to the Poetical Works of John Milton.* London, 1894.

347

BUNDY, M. W. *Milton's View of Education in Paradise Lost.* In *Journal of English and Germanic Philology* 21 (1922). 127–8.

COOPER, L. *A Concordance of the Latin, Greek, and Italian Poems of John Milton.* Halle, 1923.

GILBERT, A. H. *A Geographical Dictionary of Milton.* New Haven, 1919.

———. *Milton's Text-book of Astronomy.* In *Publications of the Modern Language Association* 38 (1923). 297.

GOOD, J. W. *Studies in the Milton Tradition.* In *University of Illinois Studies in Language and Literature* 1 (1915), Nos. 3 and 4.

HANFORD, J. H. *A Milton Handbook.* New York, 1926.

LANGDON, I. *Milton's Theory of Poetry and Fine Art.* New Haven, 1924.

LEACH, A. F. *Milton as Schoolboy and Schoolmaster.* In *Proceedings of the British Academy* 3 (1908).

LOCKWOOD, L. E. *Lexicon to the English Poetical Works of John Milton.* New York, 1907.

MASSON, D. *The Life of John Milton: Narrated in Connexion with the Political, Ecclesiastical, and Literary History of his Time.* 7 vols. Cambridge, 1859–94.

OSGOOD, C. G. *The Classical Mythology of Milton's English Poems.* New York, 1900.

POMMRICH, E. *Milton's Verhältnis zu Torquato Tasso.* Halle, 1902.

SAURAT, D. *La Pensée de Milton.* Paris, 1920.

———. *Milton: Man and Thinker.* New York, 1925.

THOMPSON, E. N. S. *Essays on Milton.* Oxford, 1914.

———. *John Milton, A Topical Bibliography.* Oxford, 1916.

———. *Milton's 'Of Education.'* In *Studies in Philology* 20 (1918). 159.

WATSON, F. *A Suggested Source of Milton's Tractate.* In *Nineteenth Century* 66 (1909). 617.

2. AUTHORS CITED OR REFERRED TO
IN THE TRACTATE

ARATUS. *Phænomena*, ed. by E. Maas. Berlin, 1893.

ARISTOTLE. *Opera*, Academia Regia Borussica. 5 vols. Berlin, 1831–70.

——. *Works, translated into English*, ed. by J. A. Smith and W. D. Ross. Oxford, 1908–21.

——. *Nicomachean Ethics*, trans. by J. E. C. Welldon. London, 1892.

——. *Poetics*, ed. and trans. by I. Bywater. Oxford, 1909.

——. *Poetics. Aristotle on the Art of Poetry; an Amplified Version, with Supplementary Illustrations, for Students of English*, by L. Cooper. New York, 1921.

——. *Rhetoric*, trans. by R. C. Jebb, ed. by J. E. Sandys. Cambridge, 1909.

CHARLTON, H. B. *Castelvetro's Theory of Poetry*. Manchester, 1913.

CATO (Varro, Columella) *Roman Farm-Management*, [trans. by F. Harrison.] New York, 1913.

CATO (Varro, Columella, Palladius) *Les Agronomes Latins*, with a French translation, ed. by Nisard. Paris, 1877.

CELSUS. *A. Cornelii Celsi quae Supersunt*, ed. by F. Marx. Leipsic, 1915.

CICERO. *De Oratore*, ed. by A. S. Wilkins. 3 vols. Oxford, 1888.

COLUMELLA. *L'Économie Rurale*, trans. by Louis DuBois. Paris, 1844.

COMENIUS, J. A. *The Great Didactic*, ed. and trans. by M. W. Keatinge. London, 1896. [Cited as Keatinge, *The Great Didactic*.]

GALE, T. [Editor.] *Opuscula Mythologica, Ethica, et Physica*. Cambridge, 1671.

HESIOD. *Carmina*, ed. by A. Rzach. Leipsic, 1913.

——. *The Epics of Hesiod*, ed. by F. A. Paley. London, 1861.

——. *The Poems and Fragments*, trans. by A.W. Mair. Oxford, 1908.

HOMER. *Opera*, ed. by D. B. Monro and T. W. Allen. Oxford, 1908.

HORACE (Vida, Boileau.) *The Art of Poetry*, ed. by A. S. Cook. Boston, 1892.

ISOCRATES. *Orations*, ed. by G. E. Benseler. 2 vols. in 1. Leipsic, 1889–95.

JUSTINIAN. *Institutes*, ed. by T. C. Sandars. First American, from the fifth London, edition, with an Introduction by W. G. Hammond. Chicago, 1876.

LAERTIUS, DIOGENES. *Diogenis Laertii de Vitiis, Dogmatis, et Apophthegmatis Clarorum Philosophorum libri decem*, ed. by H. G. Huebner. 4 vols. Leipsic, 1828.

——— ———. *The Lives and Opinions of the Eminent Philosophers*, trans. by C. D. Yonge. London, 1853.

——— ———. *Lives of Eminent Philosophers*, trans. by R. D. Hicks. 2 vols. London, 1925.

LONGINUS. *On the Sublime*, ed. and trans. by W. R. Roberts. Cambridge, 1899.

LUCRETIUS. *De Rerum Natura*, ed. by W. A. Merrill. Berkeley, California, 1917.

———. *De Rerum Natura libri sex*, ed. by H. A. J. Munro. 3 vols. London, 1900.

MANILIUS, M. *Astronomica*, ed. by J. Van Wageningen. Leipsic, 1915.

——— ———. *Astronomicon*, ed. by A. E. Housman. 4 vols. London, 1903–20.

MAZZONI, J. *Della Difesa della Comedia di Dante*. Cesena, 1587.

MELA. *Pomponii Melae Di Chorographia libri tres*, ed. by C. Frick. Leipsic, 1880.

MELA. *Geographie de Pomponius Mela,* trans. by L. Baude. Paris, 1843.

NICANDER. *Alexipharmaca*, ed. by J. G. Schneider. Halle, 1792.

———. *Theriaca*, ed. by J. G. Schneider. Leipsic, 1816.

———. *Theriaca et Alexipharmaca*, ed. by O. Schneider. Leipsic, 1856.

OPPIAN. *Oppien d'Apamée. La Chasse*, ed. by P. Boudreaux. Paris, 1908.

ORPHEUS. *Argonautica, Hymni, Libellus de Lapidibus, et Fragmenta*, ed. by J. M. Gesner. Leipsic, 1744.

PHALEREUS. *Demetrii Phalerei De Elocutione*, ed. by L. Radermacher. Leipsic, 1901.

PLATO. *Opera*, ed. by J. Burnet. 5 vols. Oxford, 1902–6.

——. *Dialogues*, trans. by B. Jowett. 5 vols. Oxford, 1892.

——. *Works*, trans. by G. Burges. 6 vols. (Bohn's Library.) London, 1854.

——. *Timaeus*, trans. and ed. by R. D. Archer-Hind. London, 1888.

PLINY. *C. Plinii Secundi Naturalis Historiae libri XXXVII*, ed. by C. Mayhoff. 5 vols. Leipsic, 1897–1906.

PLUTARCH. *Lives*, trans. by B. Perrin. 10 vols. London, 1914.

QUINTILIAN. *Institutionis Oratoriae libri XII*, ed. by E. Bonnell. Leipsic, 1882.

——. *The Institutio Oratoria*, ed. and trans. by H. E. Butler. 4 vols. (Loeb Classical Library.) London, 1921.

——. *Institutes of Oratory*, trans. by J. S. Watson. 2 vols. (Bohn's Library). London, 1875, 1876.

SENECA. *L. Annaei Senecae Naturalium Quaestionum libri VIII*, ed. by A. Gercke. Leipsic, 1907.

SOLINUS. *C. Julii Solini Collectanea Rerum Memorabilium*, ed. by T. Mommsen. Berlin, 1864.

SOPHOCLES. *The Plays and Fragments*, ed. by R. C. Jebb. Cambridge, 1892.

THEOCRITUS. *The Idylls*, ed. by R. J. Cholmeley. London, 1919.

THEOPHRASTUS. *Enquiry into Plants*, . . . with a translation by A. Hart. London, 1916.

——. Hill, Sir John. *Theophrastus's History of Stones*. London, 1774.

TIMAEUS OF LOCRI. Anton, J. R. W. *De Origine Libelli* Περὶ Ψυχᾶς Κόσμω καὶ Φύσιος. Erfurt, 1883.

VIRGIL. *Eclogues, Georgics, Aeneid, the Minor Poems*, ed. and trans. by H. R. Fairclough. 2 vols. (Loeb Classical Library.) London, 1916–8.

VITRUVIUS. *The Architecture of Marcus Vitruvius Pollio*, trans. by J. Gwilt. London, 1826.
——. *The Ten Books on Architecture*, trans. by M. H. Morgan. Cambridge, Massachusetts, 1914.
WILAMOWITZ-MOELLENDORFF, U. von [editor]. *Bucolici Graeci.* Oxford, 1905.
XENOPHON. *Opera Omnia*, ed. by E. C. Marchant. 5 vols. Oxford, 1900.
——. *Works*, trans. by H. G. Dakyns. 4 vols. London, 1890.

3. EDUCATION

APPEL, B. *Das Bildungs- und Erziehungsideal Quintilians nach der Institutio Oratoria.* Donauwörth, 1914.
ASCHAM, R. *English Works*, ed. by W. A. Wright. Cambridge, 1904.
BACON, F. *The Advancement of Learning*, ed. by W. A. Wright. Oxford, 1891.
BENNDORFF, C. *Die Englische Pädagogik im 16. Jahrhundert.* Vienna and Leipsic, 1905.
BROWNING, O. *An Introduction to the History of Educational Theories.* New York, 1915.
COOPER, L. *Louis Agassiz as a Teacher.* Ithaca, New York, 1917.
—— ——. *Two Views of Education.* New Haven, 1922.
ELYOT, T. *The Boke Named The Governour*, ed. by H. H. S. Croft. 2 vols. London, 1880.
GRAVES, F. P. *A History of Education.* New York, 1910.
HOOLE, C. *A New Discovery of the Old Art of Teaching School*, ed. by T. Mark. Syracuse, New York, 1912.
KLÄHR, T. *Leben und Werke R. Mulcasters.* Dresden, 1893.
LAURIE, S. S. *John Amos Comenius.* Sixth edition, Cambridge, 1904.
LEACH, A. F. *Educational Charters and Documents, 598 to 1909.* Cambridge, 1911.
—— ——. *The Schools of Mediæval England.* New York, 1915.
MONROE, P. *Cyclopædia of Education.* 5 vols. New York, 1911.

————. *A Text-book in the History of Education.* New York, 1905.

MULCASTER, R. *The First Part of the Elementarie,* London, 1582.

————. *Elementarie,* ed. by E. T. Campagnac. Oxford, 1925.

————. *Positions,* ed. by R. H. Quick. London, 1888.

RASHDALL, H. *The Universities of Europe in the Middle Ages.* 2 vols. in 3. Oxford, 1895.

ROGER, M. *L'Enseignement des Lettres Classiques d'Ausone à Alcuin.* Paris, 1905.

ROUSSEAU, J. J. *Émile, ou De l'Education.* Paris, n. d.

————. *Les Confessions.* Paris, 1879.

SANDYS, J. E. *A History of Classical Scholarship.* 3 vols. Cambridge, 1906.

VIVES, J. L. *Exercitatio Linguae Latinae,* trans. and ed. by F. Watson. London, 1908. [Cited as Watson, *Tudor Schoolboy Life.*]

————. *De Tradendis Disciplinis,* trans. and ed. by F. Watson. Cambridge, 1913. [Cited as Watson, *Vives on Education.*]

WATSON, F. *The Curriculum and Text-books of English Schools in the First Half of the Seventeenth Century.* In *Transactions of the Bibliographical Society* 6 (1903). 159.

————. *The English Grammar Schools to 1660.* Cambridge, 1908.

WILSON, T. *The Arte of Rhetorique,* ed. by G. H. Mair. Oxford, 1909.

WOODWARD, W. H. *Desiderius Erasmus concerning the Aim and Method of Education.* Cambridge, 1904.

————. *Studies in Education during the Age of the Renaissance, 1400–1600.* Cambridge, 1906.

————. *Universities, Schools, and Scholarship in the Sixteenth Century.* In the *Cambridge History of English Literature* 3. 487.

————. *Vittorino da Feltre and Other Humanist Educators.* Cambridge, 1897.

4. GENERAL REFERENCES

ADAMS, J. Q. *A Life of William Shakespeare.* Boston, 1923.

ALLBUTT, T. C. *Greek Medicine in Rome.* London, 1921.

BLACKSTONE, W. *Commentaries on the Laws of England.* 13th edition, ed. by E. Christian. 4 vols. London, 1800.

BOECKH, A. *Encyklopädie und Methodologie der philologischen Wissenschaften,* ed. by E. Bratuscheck. 2nd ed., Leipsic, 1886.

BROUGHTON, L. N. *The Theocritean Element in the Poems of William Wordsworth.* Halle, 1920.

COOPER, L. *An Aristotelian Theory of Comedy.* New York, 1922.

———. *The Greek Genius and its Influence.* New Haven, 1917.

———. *The Poetics of Aristotle: its Meaning and Influence.* Boston, 1923.

DE BURGH, W. G. *The Legacy of the Ancient World.* New York, 1924.

DILL, S. *Roman Society in the Last Century of the Western Empire.* New York, 1905.

DIRCKS, H. *A Memoir of Samuel Hartlib.* London, 1865.

ELLWOOD, T. *The History of Thomas Ellwood, Written by Himself,* ed. by H. Morley. London, 1886.

FIRTH, C. H. *Cromwell's Army.* London, 1902.

FLETCHER, H. *Milton's Semitic Studies.* Chicago, 1926.

GREEN, J. R. *A History of the English People.* 4 vols. London, 1878.

HAYS, H. M. *Notes on the* Works and Days *of Hesiod.* Chicago, 1918.

JOHNSON, S. *Lives of the English Poets,* ed. by G. B. Hill. 3 vols. Oxford, 1905.

JONSON, B. *Timber, or Discoveries Made upon Men and Matter,* ed. by F. E. Schelling. New York, 1892.

———. *Discoveries,* ed. by M. Castelain. Paris, n. d.

KINGSFORD, C. L. [Editor.] *The Song of Lewes.* Oxford, 1890.

KNIGHT, S. *Life of Dr. John Colet.* Oxford, 1823.

LAMB, C. *Works,* ed. by W. Macdonald. 12 vols. London, 1903–5.

MORE, T. *Utopia.* (Bohn's Library.) London, 1910.

MUIRHEAD, J. *Historical Introduction to the Private Law of Rome.* 2nd edition, ed. by H. Goudy. London, 1899.

NEWMAN, J. H. *The Idea of a University.* London, 1875.

SANDYS, J. E. *A Companion to Latin Studies.* Cambridge, 1910.

SEEBOHM, F. *The Oxford Reformers.* London, 1869.

BIBLIOGRAPHY

SMITH, G. G. [Editor.] *Elizabethan Critical Essays.* 2 vols. Oxford, 1904.

SMITH, P. *Erasmus: A Study of his Life, Ideals, and Place in History.* New York, 1923.

SPENSER, E. *Poetical Works,* ed. by J. C. Smith and E. De Selincourt. Oxford, 1912.

SPINGARN, J. E. *Literary Criticism in the Renaissance.* New York, 1908.

SWIFT, J. *Prose Works,* ed. by T. Scott. 12 vols. 1905–8.

SYMONDS, J. A. *The Renaissance in Italy.* 3 vols. New York, 1881–3.

TAYLOR, H. O. *Greek Biology and Medicine.* Boston, 1922.

THOMPSON, G. A. *Elizabethan Criticism of Poetry.* Chicago, 1914.

WHIBLEY, L. *A Companion to Greek Studies.* Cambridge, 1906.

INDEX

INDEX

CORNELL STUDIES IN ENGLISH